"Step-by-step advice and inspiration for finding your dream second (or third!) career." —**Tory Johnson,** *Good Morning America* contributor

....

"A treasure trove for anyone hitting midlife and wondering what's next. Engaging, practical...This book will inspire you to think big and take action!"

—**Gretchen Rubin,** author of *The Happiness Project*

....

"An exceptional guide for navigating the changing landscape of the job search in the second half of life. Marci Alboher is the new employment Sherpa... A must-read for anyone looking for work." —**Lester Strong,**
chief executive officer, AARP Experience Corps

....

"Provides a unique framework for introspection, discovery, and adventure. [Its] vignettes of other people's transitions serve as an inspiration to dream fearlessly!" —**Angela F. Williams,**
senior vice president and general counsel, YMCA of the USA

....

"You launched the kids, now it's time to relaunch yourself. This book offers more than nuts and bolts, it inspires courage." —**Sally Koslow,**
author of *Slouching Toward Adulthood*

....

"If you want to create a better world for future generations, you've got the right book in your hands." —**Michelle Nunn,**
chief executive officer, Points of Light, and author of *Be the Change*

....

"A terrific resource for the millions of Americans who aren't afraid to dream big and finish strong." —**Greg Baldwin,** president, VolunteerMatch

....

"With age comes the ability to take things in stride, to know what matters. This book will show you how to take this wisdom and use it as a force for good in the world." —**Laura L. Carstensen,**
director, Stanford Center on Longevity

THE

encore career

HANDBOOK

**HOW TO MAKE A LIVING
AND A DIFFERENCE
IN THE SECOND
HALF OF LIFE**

Marci Alboher

Introduction by Marc Freedman

WORKMAN PUBLISHING • NEW YORK

Library of Congress Cataloging-in-Publication Data

Alboher, Marci.
  The encore career handbook / Marci Alboher;
introduction by Marc Freedman.
      p. cm.
  ISBN 978-0-7611-6762-4 (alk. paper)
  1. Career changes. 2. Career development. 3. Baby boom
generation—Employment. 4. Middle-aged persons—Employment. I. Title.
  HF5384.A43 2012
  650.14—dc23
                        2012021985

Interior Design by Janet Vicario
Cover design by Raquel Jaramillo
Cover photo credit: Shutterstock/Arkady

Workman Publishing Company, Inc.
225 Varick Street
New York, NY 10014-4381
workman.com

WORKMAN is a registered trademark of Workman Publishing Co., Inc.

Printed in the United States of America
First printing January 2013

10 9 8 7 6 5 4 3 2 1

For my father, who never had time for an encore,
but whose life lessons live on.

For Jay, my love, who makes me "smile with my heart."

And for Marc Freedman, I hope the book carries forward
the movement in a way that makes you proud.

Contents

A New
Map of Life

Y ou've heard it all before. A gray wave of boomers is careening toward the second half of life, hitting retirement age, morphing suddenly into senior citizens, and bringing with them a new era of cross-generational conflict and economic despair.

Don't believe it. Those of us at midlife and beyond are far from the scrap heap. We are poised to invent an entirely new stage of life—the encore years—between the end of midlife and anything resembling old-fashioned retirement.

Society brands us the young-old or the working-retired. Maybe they should just call our predicament the oxymoronic years. On the one hand, we're implored to hang on to our former youth—sixty is the new forty, it's said. On the other, "senior discounts" are dispensed indiscriminately at fifty or sixty. I'm all for saving a buck, but the broader choice seems to be cling to the past or risk being sent off to some premature pasture.

But sixty is not the new forty any more than it is the old seventy or eighty. It's the new sixty. And, for that matter, fifty is the new fifty. Indeed, the whole post-midlife period is simply new territory, and those of us flooding into this phase constitute a phenomenon unique to the twenty-first century.

Inventing life stages is anything but new. A hundred years ago, there was no adolescence (until it was invented by a sixty-year-old psychologist, G. Stanley Hall, in 1904). Look further back, and childhood barely existed. Retirement as we know it is a man-made concoction of the post–World War II era.

With close to 10,000 women and men a day crossing the midlife divide, it's high time to accelerate the social invention that is the "encore years."

This new project starts with embracing life beyond fifty as a distinct period with its own integrity, even if it has yet to acquire its own language. It's an age increasingly characterized by new perspectives, new priorities, and the capacity to do something with those hard-earned insights—not just to leave a legacy, but to live one.

It also means recognizing that for most of us this period is a new stage of work, every bit as much as a new stage of life (who wants to play thirty years of golf—and who can afford it?). Indeed, a movement is afoot to fashion this next chapter into something we can genuinely look forward to.

Millions are trading in the old dream of the freedom *from* work for a new one animated by what might be called the freedom *to* work. They are embracing encore careers, forging a new hybrid between the spirit of service and the practicality of continued income, looking for productive engagement that is not only meaningful but also means something beyond themselves.

The encore career movement holds the potential to create richer lives and a better society.

Some argue that this simply amounts to making virtue out of necessity. True enough, but what's wrong with virtue, or for that matter facing reality squarely and with ingenuity?

That goes for the nation, too. We simply cannot afford to write off the most experienced segment of the population, consigning them to spend half their adult lives in a state of enforced leisure at a time when that group is set to double in size—and at a juncture when the challenges facing the country in areas like education, health, and the environment are themselves spiraling.

The encore career movement holds the potential to turn this all around, to create richer lives and a better society. And to do so on a grand scale. It promises the biggest potential human capital windfall since millions of women broke through to new productive roles in the 1960s and 1970s.

Pulling off a similar transformation in roles for those approaching the second half of life will require a string of innovations—among them better pathways for the millions who want to take their encore careers from aspiration to action. All too often, this passage has been a do-it-yourself proposition, a rocky road with little guidance and plenty of pitfalls along the way.

But now help is on the way. You are holding in your hands something that's long been missing: a trusted guidebook for all those ready to live out a new vision for the second half of adulthood, prepared to make a monument out of what so many have dismissed as the leftover years.

This is good news as the great midlife migration gathers size and momentum, and it's good news for the future. Like those pathbreaking women who rewrote the rules several decades ago, today's encore pioneers are at the vanguard of a permanent change. They are the first wave passing into this new stage where the golden years once stood, a phase soon to be occupied by all those longer-living children and grandchildren coming quickly on their heels.

By making this new period something truly significant, we are in a position to set in motion an ongoing payoff—and in the process to revamp the nature of all the preceding life stages, opening up options for younger people who can make life decisions with the expectation of more than one bite at the apple.

That's why we all have a stake in this project. It's our best chance to turn the purported paradox of longevity—good for individuals, terrible for society—into a vast payoff for all, right now and for generations to come.

—Marc Freedman
Founder and CEO,
Encore.org

CHAPTER 1

It's Time for Your Encore

"Twenty years from now, you'll be more disappointed by the things you didn't do, than by the ones you did do."

—MARK TWAIN

I n the past one hundred years, the average life span in the United States has expanded from forty-seven to seventy-eight years. By any account, longer lives should be a cause for celebration. But all this extra time can also create anxiety.

Like Betty Friedan's housewife in *The Feminine Mystique,* millions of people are grappling, alone, with a nameless problem shared by millions of others. What do we do with these additional years? How do we make use of this extra time while we are still vital and engaged? And how do we pay for all that extra time? We wonder how to leave a legacy, contribute, and make money—and, if we're lucky, find our bliss along the way.

You probably picked up this book because you're facing a similar question. You've hit a wall, lost a job, or are just wondering "Is this all there is?" Maybe your retirement plan has been shattered. Maybe the word "retirement" doesn't even resonate with you. You may be forty and thinking about planning for another thirty years of work, or fifty-five and thinking of a ten- or fifteen-year third act, or seventy and wondering how to find a part-time job that would add money and meaning to your life.

The good news is that you still have time: Time to follow, or discover, your passion. Time to do something that matters. Time to help yourself—and others, too. We *all* have more time to make the most of our lives.

Second Acts for a Better World

There's a new trend afoot. Growing numbers of baby boomers are rewriting the narrative of twenty-first-century midlife by crafting a new stage of work: an encore career for the greater good. These pioneers have realized that with midlife comes a newfound capacity to tap into their accumulated experience and wisdom to accomplish new things, often in ways they were unable to do earlier in their lives.

The desire to have a positive impact in the world seems to grow stronger with age, as if it were programmed into our midlife DNA. It's not hard to figure out why. By this time in life, people have identified plenty of things that need fixing, and they've also figured out that helping others is one of the easiest ways to get a happiness boost. And although for many it may finally be time to play the flute or open an artisanal bakery, there is also a compelling urge at midlife to make a mark in a way that leaves things a little better for future generations. (Psychologist Eric Erickson called this kind of thinking "generativity.") With age often comes the anticipation of regret (*what if I never . . .*), as well as a sense of urgency (*if not now, when?*) and a sense of responsibility (*if not me, who?*). Some hit midlife and reconnect with the idealism of youth, when everything felt possible.

> **"I grew up on a farm. Farmers don't retire; they die in tractor seats in their eighties and nineties."**
>
> –Diana Meinhold, marketer-turned-legal-fiduciary

Interestingly, this urge to make the world a better place seems to kick in for those who never thought of themselves as do-gooders as well as those who have dedicated their entire lives to so-called social purpose work. The former find ways to get started; the latter usually decide it's time to have impact in a whole new way.

What's more, there's evidence that shows we may be hardwired for big accomplishments at midlife. We all know that certain things inevitably decline with age—we can't grab the name of *that* actor in *that* movie or we can't remember if we fed the cat; and restaurants become a minefield, with those menus you can't read (in dim light) and tablemates you can't hear (amid the ambient noise). But the latest neuroscience research shows that some things improve as we pack on the years. We become more empathic, we get better at synthesizing ideas, making connections between disparate ideas, and solving complex problems. We actually grow smarter in some ways—you know, that whole wisdom thing.

These ideas have been confirmed in study after study, and in the narratives of people's lives. Mark Walton, a CNN-news-anchor-turned-leadership-coach, studied the phenomenon of later-life achievement for his book, *Boundless Potential,* and concluded that people who remain engaged and creative into their seventies, eighties, and beyond are not only common, but they may represent what later life is supposed to look like. "You may forget where you put the keys, but you may be able to settle a major labor dispute," Walton told me, adding, "What we think of as those 'senior moments' are very normal events that most likely mean we were thinking about something else." That may explain why the average age in Congress is hovering around sixty—and why world leaders continue to wield power or great artists often hit their prime well past the years typically considered to be most productive.

Discussion Prompts Throughout the book, you'll see sidebars with discussion prompts. These questions are meant to get you talking—with someone going through a similar process, with your book group, or with an encore transition group.

There is also a very practical need driving this activity: These bonus years don't come with a prepaid gift card. With the recession's impact on retirement savings and the decline of pensions, the encore career offers a new model for providing continued income in your later years.

It's this search for purpose, passion, *and* a paycheck that coalesces into an encore career—continued work that combines personal meaning with social purpose. The grandmother who embarks on law school at fifty, sparked by an injustice she sees in her community. The advertising director who retires to become an art teacher, working another fifteen years and tapping into reservoirs of creativity she remembers from her own school years. The unemployed engineer who travels abroad, sees a problem, and returns home with an idea for a solution—and starts a thriving business.

How long does a typical encore career last, and what's the right age to get started?

An encore career is a body of work lasting anywhere from a few years to twenty or more. It really depends on your aspirations, health, finances, and energy level. Some people start thinking about an encore in their mid-forties or early fifties. Those folks often plan ahead and invest in significant retraining that can take many years to complete. They can take steps toward their encore while still in the midst of their primary careers—much like you'd do if you were planning for retirement.

Others first start thinking about an encore in their late fifties, early sixties, or beyond. Although there are no hard and fast rules, the later you start on your encore, the less likely you may be to invest in lengthy retraining because the horizon of how long you'll work will be shorter. That said, I've met plenty of people going back to school or just beginning an exploration well into their seventies.

The encore crowd is diverse. It's white collar, blue collar, and no collar, with an increasing number of virtual workers who never set foot inside a physical workplace. It includes people who have never finished college and people with multiple degrees. It includes people who have little in savings and are as consumed with finding a way to earn a living as they are with wanting to do something that matters. And there are those solely motivated by altruism.

Encore careers are commonly sparked by something on the work front—a layoff, the approach of retirement, an itch to reinvent. Just as often, an encore is shaped by what's happening outside of work—an empty nest, the loss of a parent, the end of a marriage, a new romance, an illness, or a move from the suburbs to the city.

Research shows that roughly 9 million people are already in encore careers and another 31 million are keen to move in the same direction. Although they come from different places, large numbers of people in their encore years are looking for the same thing—making a living while making a difference.

Contrary to the ubiquitous magazine profile of the lawyer-turned-teacher, moving into new kinds of work is not quick or easy. Usually, the transition is a slow metamorphosis involving baby steps, detours, persistence, creativity, and a do-it-yourself spirit. Some find their encores through a subtle tweaking of what came before, but many find the need or desire for a wholesale reinvention. This is complicated at any age, and all the more so when your friends and family worry that you've lost your mind, and when the workplace seems dominated by young people not exactly warm to working alongside people who look like their parents.

As more people begin their encores and more organizations step up to provide assistance and pathways, these shifts are getting a little easier. Local programs and encore-focused career coaches are cropping up in cities across the country to help people through this transition. Community colleges are offering courses specifically designed for people retraining for encore careers in fields like health care, green jobs, social services, and teaching. Encore fellowships now offer pathways for corporate managers who want to retrain for jobs in nonprofits. And organizations like the Transition Network, ReServe, and Coming of Age are rapidly expanding into new cities as hubs for people who want a supportive and helpful community as they build their encores.

This support is important—necessary even—because reinvention can be hard. And scary. I've talked to people who haven't written a résumé in thirty years, and for whom the thought of posting a profile, let alone a photo, on LinkedIn is daunting, self-promotional, and just plain weird. Researching academic programs and looking for internships when a child or grandchild is doing the same can feel awkward, maybe even ridiculous. And what about the fear of being greeted for an interview by someone who doesn't look old enough to have a job? What's been missing (until now) is a road map to take you through all the stages of your encore journey, from your daydreams through all the challenges—and triumphs—you'll face along the way, to the first day of your new adventure.

Getting to Your Encore Moment

So how do you know if you're ready for your encore? Usually there is a combination of signs—a set of challenges, obstacles, or realizations signaling that it is time for a change.

Everyone's encore story is different, but just as other life stages are marked by rites of passage, they fall into some familiar patterns. As you read the following stories, think about whether one—or more than one—of these scenarios is familiar to you. And don't be surprised if you find yourself nodding in agreement with several or all of them. There's a lot of overlap here.

Burning Out

At fifty-three, with her children grown and launching their own careers and families, Suwon Smith finally had a chance to assess her life. She'd risen through the ranks at Citigroup in New York City, picked up a college degree at night along the way, and somehow managed it all as a single mother. Her reward? Working six days a week, twelve hours a day. Suddenly it hit her. "It was just me and I didn't have to work like that anymore." Smith left her job with no plan for what to do next. The day after her resignation, she entered a period she called being "lost in the sauce." She was used to the phone ringing all day, and suddenly she was home and everyone around her was busy in their own lives. She first had to reestablish relationships with friends and family, but in time, she was ready to focus on herself.

"After having the same conversations for ten years and getting the same answers, at some point you feel like you're just phoning it in. There's something to be said for a change that brings about new energy."

–Paul Yingling, U.S. army colonel (retired)

If you're "Burning Out," you just can't keep up with the pace of your life anymore. You need to catch your breath, step off the treadmill, get out of the rat race (choose your cliché). But you probably can't even think about what's next until you figure out a way to slow yourself down.

A Nagging Feeling

During her twenty-seven years at the National Educational Association in Washington, D.C., Nancy Kochuk had seen others stick around long past their expiration date. She'd promised herself that she would leave before that happened to her. "Most days I loved what I did and the routine was comfortable, but I had this nagging feeling that it was time to stretch myself a bit and do some other things," she said. So eighteen months after she became eligible, Kochuk retired. She gave herself what her husband calls "time to dance," along with time to do and teach more yoga, travel, and go to the theater. She had a "desire to give back" but needed time to figure out what that meant to her.

If you have a "Nagging Feeling," you may have no idea what you want to do, but you have the sense that something has to change. You may take a leap and jump into something entirely new. Or you may start by taking small steps to explore ideas and opportunities until something clicks.

A Dream Deferred

Daniel Shungu always wanted to return to the Democratic Republic of the Congo to help his native country, a place he'd last seen when he left to attend college in the United States at age nineteen. When his son, Nick, won a full scholarship to Duke University, two dreams coalesced. Nick got to attend a great school, and Shungu was freed from huge tuition payments. He realized he could afford to take early retirement from Merck, where he'd had a long career as a researcher and manager. Without a second thought, Shungu, then sixty, gave Merck two months' notice and immediately planned his trip to Congo. That visit laid the foundation for what would become his encore work—starting United Front Against Riverblindness, an organization that brings medicine to the nearly 1 million people in remote Congolese villages suffering from or at risk of contracting river blindness, a disease that causes irreversible loss of sight.

> "Every cell of my body wanted to get out in nature, into the sunshine, and away from a hundred emails a day."
>
> —Barbara Abramowitz, nonprofit leader

If you're in the "Dream Deferred" category, you've always wanted to do something—return to school, live in another country, work with young people, tap your creative side—and suddenly you've hit a time in your life where it begins to feel possible. It's a second chance.

The End of the Line

After being laid off from her job as a forklift operator in Bridgeport, Connecticut, Priscilla Santiago did something she wished she had been able to do forty-three years earlier: She got her GED. And she didn't stop there. She went on to get an associate's degree at Housatonic Community College and a bachelor's degree at Polk University, where she graduated at sixty-three. Santiago's earlier education was derailed at sixteen when she dropped out of school after she was sexually abused. Nearly fifty years later, she's hoping her degrees will help her assist other victims of abuse.

If you've gotten to "The End of the Line," you've been laid off, your business has dried up, or your field has changed so significantly that you're beginning to feel obsolete. At this point it would be just as hard to keep doing what you've always done than it would be to try something new. Between a recession that has decimated entire industries and the shift from a manufacturing to a knowledge-based economy, just about every family seems to have someone who has reached this moment.

A Loss

Sally Bingham's three grown children were on their own, as was she, after the end of a long marriage. Bingham wondered what she would do and what she was even capable of doing. In all her years of marriage, she had never even managed her own money. Finding the courage to change, Bingham returned to college in her forties, then to seminary, ultimately becoming an ordained priest at the age of fifty-five. Now seventy, Bingham heads an organization she founded to help congregations make more environmentally sound decisions. To top it off, Bingham is earning a living for the first time in her life and a pretty significant one at that.

Illness, the death of someone dear, divorce, even an empty nest—these kinds of upheavals can all be the pivotal point for an encore shift. If you've experienced "A Loss," you may find that the way to move forward is to immerse yourself in a project that channels your grief or emotional energy into purposeful work.

A Crisis of Conscience

Marcy Gray Rubin remembers the moment when she knew she would leave a successful career as a television writer. Her father was terminally ill, and she'd taken off from work to spend time with him. She'd only been gone a few days when her agent called. "Just let me know when it's a done deal," he said, "so you can fly back for the pilot season." Rubin fired her agent that day and stayed with her father until his death six weeks later. After a period of mourning, she focused on finding a new career. "I just had to get away from a world where a lousy parking space or a bad hair day are considered important," she said. After going back to school for her master's degree, Rubin is now a practicing psychologist. Her new life has its trade-offs. She makes a fraction of what she made as a television writer, but she said she feels honored to do the work. "You get to be part of people's lives in the most joyous and most tragic circumstances."

"A Crisis of Conscience" can happen over an extended period or hit you suddenly, but you know you can't continue what you've been doing any longer. You know there must be a better way to use your talents and earn a living.

"Hello, I used to be somebody. . ."

You've been a banker, human resource specialist, salesperson, electrician, lawyer, whatever, for a long time. So expect to feel strange when you leave an identity behind and no longer have an easy way to describe yourself. You may also feel like what some have started calling a PIP (previously important person).

As you shift into a new identity, there's no need to abandon what came before. You'll likely find new ways to use skills, contacts, and instincts cultivated in earlier roles. You may even find that mentioning a former title or identity can be a help to something you're trying to accomplish in your new work.

Dick Goldberg achieved renown as a playwright early in his career. Years later, he reinvented himself as a nonprofit executive director. (He runs Coming of Age, the national encore-oriented initiative based in Philadelphia.) When I asked him how he felt about moving away from his earlier identity, he put it this way: "I may not be the parent to a toddler anymore, but I'm still very much a dad. It's like that with the writing. It's not what I'm doing now, but it will always be a major part of my identity."

Sure it can be awkward to meet new people when your public-facing identity is in flux. "I'm in transition," may not feel right. So what do you say?

- "I'm rewiring, not retiring."

- "I'm taking a sabbatical."

- "I'm busy exploring options for what's next."

- "I'm training to be a ___."

- "I'm doing pro bono work to learn more about ___."

- "I've left ___ to find something more meaningful."

- "I'm searching for my encore."

Are You a Leaper or a Planner?

Once you arrive at your encore moment—regardless of how you get there—there are pretty much two ways you can go forward. You can leap. Or you can plan. If you're a leaper, an opportunity strikes and you plunge right in without much thought. After the initial leap, you may find that you dig in for a long period of time, having found your place. Equally likely, you may step back to reassess and adjust or find that the initial leap was just the first step on a longer journey.

Some Truths About Encore Careers

As you navigate the sometimes overwhelming waters of an encore transition, remember the following:

- It is common to get to your encore years and not know what's next. Many people are just finding the time to ponder the question.

- Encore paths don't look the same for everyone. Some people contemplating encore careers are empty nesters. Some are just getting around to raising kids. Some never had them. Some are getting divorced and some never married. Your life situation will shape what you can do, want to do, and need to do in these years.

- Some people plan for years. Others slide into encore careers. Some will settle into new work that may last fifteen to twenty years. Others will shake it up every few years.

- Encore work involves trade-offs. You may trade money for meaning and flexibility. You may trade power and influence for the chance to work more closely with people you can help.

- Whereas many shifts into encore careers involve a salary cut, there are plenty of encore jobs that provide competitive pay and benefits.

- Transitions will take longer than you think.

Patricia Brune was a leaper. Within seven days of retiring from a thirty-year position with the federal court system in Kansas City, Brune got a call from a friend asking if she'd consider filling in for a departing executive director at the local YMCA. Brune thought about it briefly and then jumped in. She said her learning curve was like drinking from a fire hose. "Court bureaucracies I knew," she said. "Volunteers and children's programming, not so much."

Barbara Gomperts took a more cautious approach. After a few massage sessions relieved her of chronic pain in her shoulders and knee, she was determined to do for others what her therapist had done for her. She researched massage training programs catering to midcareer people with full-time jobs. She compressed her schedule at the university where she works as an office manager from five days to four. And she and her husband made some extra cash by selling their house and moving to a less expensive townhouse. After she is certified as a therapist, she plans to launch her own massage practice and slowly move away from her office job.

If you're a planner, you do your homework and come up with an idea, then research options about how to make it happen. You may be waiting to hit a milestone—last child off to college, an eligibility age for early retirement, a round amount of savings that makes you comfortable taking a risk. You may modify the way you work so that you have some free time for an immersion experience like an internship or volunteer work. You may need some new skills or even a certification or degree. Whatever the case, if you're a planner, you're thinking about the steps to an encore before you pull the trigger.

My Early Encore Moment

Like Marcy Gray Rubin, I can identify the exact moment I knew I had to make a change in my working life. I was on vacation in Rio de Janeiro when I got a call from my boss asking if I'd consider coming home early to work on a matter that had heated up in my absence. I didn't even give it a moment's thought; I knew I wouldn't come home.

Even though I was a hard worker, I didn't care about what I was doing as an in-house lawyer for a magazine subscription company. In fact, I felt like I was using my talents in a way that didn't mesh with my values. The request to sacrifice even more of my life for a job I didn't feel good about was just the push I needed to do something about it. As soon as I got home, I gave notice and began the process of figuring out my next steps. After nearly a decade as a lawyer, I was ready to return to an earlier interest—writing.

In time I became a freelance journalist, as well as a writing teacher/coach. It wasn't easy. And it took years. I had to retrain myself and build an entirely new network in a new field. And while I had achieved some level of seniority as a lawyer, I was a beginner in journalism, competing against "kids" right out of school for assignments. Hard as it was, it was worth it. I ended up in a career that fit me a whole lot better than the one I left. And I was so profoundly affected by going through a career change that the topic of work and careers became the focus of my writing.

For the next ten years, I wrote hundreds of newspaper and magazine articles about how the workplace was changing and how people were changing to keep up and stay afloat. I wrote mostly for *The New York Times,* where I created the "Shifting Careers" column and blog. I also taught freelance journalism and coached aspiring writers. Along the way, I wrote a book, *One Person/Multiple Careers,* about the phenomenon of slashers—people who, like me (lawyer/writer/teacher), had trouble describing their working lives without the use of a slash or two.

Through my *New York Times* column, I got a chance to interview Marc Freedman, the author and social entrepreneur who helped create the Purpose Prize, which awards $100,000 to social innovators over the age of sixty who are making extraordinary contributions in their encore careers. Freedman had just published his latest book, *Encore,* about a group of people finding ways to use their experience to give back in the years formerly occupied by retirement. I read *Encore,* did an extensive interview with Freedman, and wrote a column about the way he looks at new stages of life. Unlike other stories I'd done, this one stuck with me. While so many people bemoan the wave of aging boomers as a demographic disaster, Freedman sees just the opposite—a huge population with the potential to use their later working years to contribute to the greater good in all kinds

"In my crowd, it's not cool to be retired."

–Lynda Mandlawitz, former high school guidance counselor

of ways. It made sense to me. People wanted and needed to work longer, but just as I'd felt earlier in my career, so many of us want to work in a way that matters, a way that feels different from what came before.

In the meantime, I was trying to figure out my own place in the changing landscape of journalism. Though I relished my work as a writer, it was becoming increasingly difficult to make a living as a freelancer. *The New York Times* canceled my column for financial reasons, and while I was looking for other assignments, I started to wonder if there were ways I might be able to use my background on careers and workplace issues to help people more directly. Oddly, after years of advocating the benefits of an independent working life, I was also hankering to be a part of a team.

Which is how I came to work at Encore.org, where I spend my time learning about what it takes to make encore careers a reality for more people and sharing that information through appearances and interviews in the media, public speaking, writing articles, and now this book.

People often ask if I'm in an encore career myself, and the answer is a little fuzzy. I often describe the encore period as the time in one's fifties or sixties, and even seventies. But those of us in our forties are often laying the foundation for what our encore years will look like. When I took this job and moved into the nonprofit sector, I saw it as a career shift that would prepare me for my next twenty-plus years of work. So in that sense I'm in the planning stages of my own encore.

I'll be your main guide throughout this book. But you'll also hear from others—career coaches, financial experts, encore entrepreneurs, and lots of people who are making encore careers a new reality, in the way a leisure-based retirement was for our parents' generation.

Along the way, I'll share pieces of my own transition story where it's relevant. You'll also read dozens of stories of people in their encore years—people who are struggling with uncertainty as well as some who've come out the other side with renewed vigor and enthusiasm. You'll even meet some who've given up or abandoned plans when they didn't have the drive, the time, or the money to push forward.

Transition stories can seem easy, too easy, so I intentionally included the strugglers to make it real. Going back to school, learning new technology, and getting advice from mentors young enough to be your kids can be both exciting and terrifying. I hope this book makes it easier for you.

Keep in mind that your transition is not only deeply personal but also part of a bigger story. As you find ways to use your talent and experience to do something useful in the world, you're also participating in a growing social movement that may just change what it means to hit midlife. You have the opportunity for a triple win: You can make an impact through your work. You can experience the sense of renewal that comes with doing something new and significant. And you can help change expectations—for future generations—about what success in and beyond midlife looks like. That's a big potential payoff.

How to Use This Book

Figuring out your encore—what it'll look like, when it'll start, how you'll afford it—is a highly personal process. People are finding and crafting opportunities even in a slow job market. But they are rarely doing it by applying to job postings. In almost all cases, they are finding or creating roles through networking, volunteering, and retooling for a new kind of work. A large number are skipping out on jobs altogether and going solo either as freelancers, consultants, or encore entrepreneurs. Just as there's no one destination, there's no one path to follow. Which is why this book doesn't take you through a chronological process. Rather, the chapters address particular issues that may come up for you (possibly multiple times) throughout your transition.

You might decide to go through the chapters in order, treating the book like your own Encore 101 course. But feel free to read out of order, dipping into the chapters in a way that makes the most sense given where you are

The Encore Readiness Quiz

Are you ready for your encore? Take a look at the following ten questions and answer each one *yes, no,* or *maybe.* If your answer sheet is loaded with *nos* and *maybes,* you're probably more in the planning than the launching phase of your encore. You will likely benefit from investing some time in the early chapters of the book. If you've got a lot of *yeses,* you might find yourself drawn to some of the later chapters; consider starting with Chapters 7, 8, 9, 10, and 11.

1. Are you in a place in your life where you can comfortably move forward in your encore without having to deal with another pressing aspect of your life (e.g., where you live, caring for someone else, getting through a health issue)?

2. Do you have some ideas for what you might want to do next?

3. Is there some issue you can't stop thinking about?

4. Do you have a sense of how far away you are from making a big change in your working life?

5. Do you feel financially ready to make a shift?

6. Do you have someone you can comfortably talk to about your ideas and plans?

7. Are you open to the idea of taking classes or doing some other kind of on-the-job learning to update your skills or learn something new?

8. Do you know what kind of environment you want to work in and how much time you want to work?

9. Do you know if you want to work for yourself or for an organization?

10. Can you succinctly describe where you are in your encore process or what it is you want to do?

right now. Taking the Encore Readiness Quiz on the previous page will give you a sense of where to start.

Chapter 2 explores the *whats* and *hows* of encore work. You'll want to start here if you're wondering where the best opportunities and greatest needs are—and how people set up their working lives. If you'd find it helpful to peek at some promising encore jobs, jump right to the Encore Hot List on page 255.

Chapter 3 will help you identify what your encore could look like: What are you looking for at this stage of your life? What does purpose mean for you? What about passion? What would make you eager to get to work each day? What do you want your work to include and what would you be thrilled to never do again?

Chapter 4 will help you create the time and space in your life for an encore transition.

Chapters 5, 6, and 7 deal with the nitty-gritty of encore transitions: How much money do you really need? How do you connect with new people and communities? How do you talk about yourself when you're a work in progress? How do you update a fifteen-year-old résumé? Do you still need business cards? (The answer is yes, but your email signature or online profile might be just as important.)

Chapter 8 gets you out of your head and into the world—giving you ideas for ways to go out and do the things that will help you hone your ideas and move forward.

Chapter 9 will help if you're considering going back to school—whether for a couple of courses or a certificate or degree.

Chapter 10 is for the growing number of people considering encore entrepreneurship.

You may not want to wait until the very end to read Chapter 11, which tackles some of the bigger issues people deal with once they're in their encore. I think you'll find it illuminating—and inspiring—at any point along your encore journey.

Answering Your Questions

After talking to hundreds of people who have moved into encores or are trying to get started, I'm pretty sure I've heard almost every question that

If you have questions that haven't been answered, send them to ECH@encore.org. When I see that enough people have a similar question, I'll be answering them on my blog at Encore.org and in the Encore.org newsletter.

comes up. In each chapter, I've tried to anticipate what you might be wondering as we go along. Sometimes, that will happen right in the main text. I will also include a bunch of questions clumped together at the end of each chapter. So I urge you to take a good look at the "FAQs" (frequently asked questions), as it's pretty likely there will be answers you were looking for.

FAQs

Can I really make a living doing something I love that also makes a difference in the world?

It very much depends on what you love doing. If you love playing the ukulele and are determined to both make a living and do some good in the world, you might have a harder time than if you love fund-raising for a cause you care about.

That said, most people who tell you they love what they do have found a way to craft a career by knitting together something that matters to them with some other talent or skill—and by thinking creatively. Fred Mandell, for example, was nearing the close of a long corporate career at American Express. In his mid-fifties, he had an itch to work with his hands and do something creative. He took a sculpture workshop and quickly discovered that he had a talent. When he left his job a few years later, he wanted to make time for his art but he needed to make a living. Unexpectedly, sculpture led Mandell to the work that would support him. As he studied the great art masters, it occurred to him that they had a lot they could teach us about leadership and creativity. That led to a book, *Becoming a Life Change Artist,* and a blossoming consulting practice where he takes his perspective on creativity to the corporate audiences he understands so well.

As for the ukulele playing, don't give up on that idea either. Robert Frazier, a veteran jazz musician, has created an encore that combines his lifelong passions of playing music, working with children, and public service. After a yearlong fellowship with Musician Corps, which places musicians in high-needs public schools, Frazier began leading music programs in various schools in the San Francisco Bay area.

What about age discrimination? And don't say it doesn't exist.

Age discrimination is real. Many employers just don't consider older people for some roles. Plus, many employers are concerned that older employees won't want to learn new things or will have outdated technology skills. You can counter those expectations by making sure that your skills are up to snuff, especially when it comes to technology. Having a great LinkedIn profile is one easy way to show you understand how today's job market works. You can try to emphasize parts of your background that might shake employers out of their stereotypes. But if an employer doesn't value your experience, the organization might not be an ideal fit even if you are able to change a few minds. Better to focus on places where you see evidence that older, experienced people are already part of the team. It would also be a good idea to tailor your résumé to show your strengths as an adviser and mentor. And certainly talk about mentoring in interviews, explaining how gratifying it is to pass on your experience and to learn from others. (In Chapter 7, we'll focus specifically on how to address the age issue head-on.)

Can I be in an encore career while staying in the same job?

It's common for people to discover ways to contribute to the social good in the jobs they've had all along—or because of expertise they've acquired while working in one area for a long time. If you already work in the social sector and want to shake things up, you could explore creating a role where you mentor young people just joining your organization or stretch yourself in some other, new way.

Consider Liza Donnelly. A cartoonist at *The New Yorker* for thirty years, Donnelly long ago mastered the art of creating great cartoons, and she loves doing it. But in recent years she has been using her talents and platform as a seasoned cartoonist to get involved in public conversations about politics, women's advancement, world peace, and other issues that matter to her. She has given talks at TED and the United Nations that now circulate widely on YouTube.

John Reynolds is in an encore that grew directly out of his life's work in the National Park Service. Reynolds and several other recently retired managers from the U.S. Park Service started Global Parks, an initiative that offers mentorship to current park service employees and works on conservation partnerships with other countries.

In the current economy, is it really possible to find a paying encore career?

The job market is tight, no question, but it's no harder to find work in the non-profit or public sector than it is in the private sector. In fact, the nonprofit sector has added jobs at a rate of 2.1 percent over the past decade, while for-profit jobs have decreased by an annual average of 0.6 percent in the same period.

After a period of extreme cutbacks in 2008 and 2009, there are several signs that the nonprofit sector will be hiring in the coming years. A 2011 Idealist.org survey of 3,000 nonprofits described the sector as "cautiously optimistic," and that's a good way for you to feel as well.

Saving the world is intimidating. How much can I really do on my own?

No one person is going to save the world, so let's get away from that idea right now. Instead focus on work that allows you to do something you know will matter, even if it's just to a small group of people. Teachers, social workers, health care professionals, and social entrepreneurs may not enjoy every day of their working lives, but they often report high levels of satisfaction from their work because they believe they are contributing to the greater good in some way. Barb Quaintance, who heads up AARP volunteering and civic engagement programs, told me that her mantra is: "We don't all need to be amazing to make a difference because the cumulative effect of a lot of us doing what we can adds up." That's certainly a good way to relieve the pressure.

Can I find my encore while working in a for-profit company in the private sector?

Yes. Let's say you work for a big oil company, and you create a way to supply low-income families with cheaper heat in the winter months. That would make a difference for a lot of people. You might also work in a for-profit company developing a new vaccine or a for-profit nursing home that provides quality care. You may be a teacher at a for-profit university, a writer at a for-profit textbook company, or a nurse at a for-profit hospital. There's no magic in the nonprofit sector. There are many ways to contribute to the greater good while working in a business setting.

I'd love to focus on my own next steps, but I can't figure out how to manage the caregiving responsibilities that now fill my life.

It's a difficult reality: The encore years often coincide with an escalation in caregiving responsibilities and health problems. These issues naturally limit the time you can put toward a significant new project. It's also possible that you need to hold on to a flexible work arrangement or great health benefits, and therefore can't rush into a change right away.

Suzanne Mintz, the founder of the National Family Caregivers Association, offers this advice: "Recognize that if you're playing the role of primary caregiver, you already have a full-time job." So be easy on yourself and be okay with taking it slow.

Spend some time reading and thinking about what you'll do when you're able to make a bigger move. You might also find that you can take some small steps toward an encore that will start the ball rolling at a speed that you can handle.

Feeling limited by a health concern? Check out page 247 for some guidance.

I'm interested in reinventing, but I'm not really focused on the social good. Mostly, I want to make a living and do something that matters to me.

You're not alone. Lots of people reach their encore years and feel that it's time—finally—to have a chance to do what they want to do, not what anyone else wants them to do. That's why the media is filled with stories of people reinventing and having second acts as interior designers, innkeepers, and vintners. This book doesn't focus on those kinds of careers, but it does provide a blueprint for reinventing that will be useful to anyone in midlife, regardless of career goals.

You'll notice that all the examples and advice are about finding both personal meaning and social impact. As it happens, a large percentage of work with social impact is in high-growth fields and high-need fields like education, health care, and services for the aging. So if your interests lie in those areas, you'll find the book especially helpful.

I've never been one of those people who finds meaning through my work. I've always looked at the stuff I do outside of work as the stuff that really matters.

Some people like having big boundaries between what they do for work and what they do for pleasure. Others find it natural to blend and blur, spending their free time doing things that look a lot like work to others. It's possible you'll find your encore outside of what you think of as your job. But it's also possible that you might hit a point where you'd like to do something for your work that feels more connected to the things that matter deeply to you.

I like the idea of an encore career, but the words don't feel right.

Good words that describe work in the second half of life are hard to come by. If the words "encore career" are useful to you, then embrace them. If you'd prefer to talk about your work in other terms, feel free.

CHAPTER 2

The Encore Landscape

"To find joy in work is to find the fountain of youth."

—PEARL S. BUCK

There are many ways to find ideas for an encore. You can read. You can surf (the Web or the waves). You can go back to school. You can talk to lots of people. You can work with a career or life coach. You can travel and play and think and wait for inspiration. You can do self-assessments and exercises, like the ones you'll find in the next chapter. And you can take your cues from the people in this book who crafted custom encore roles that made great use of their particular backgrounds, experiences, and skills.

But mustering up that kind of can-do spirit is a challenge when you simply have no idea *what* it is you want to pursue. What roles make sense for you at this time in your life? What organizations are just waiting to get their hands on someone with your experience? And what will the work look like on a day-to-day basis?

Discovering the *what* of your encore can be as elusive and challenging as figuring out the *how*. This book will help you answer both questions. But before you dive in, let's take a quick look at the encore landscape—how people are working in their encores and where they are finding opportunities.

What Encore Work Looks Like

It's become trite to say that the world of work has changed. But it's true. The boundary between full-time jobs and self-employment has become porous, with people easily moving between the two. And jobs themselves have changed. With the rise of the global virtual office, you may be able to work from home—or pretty much anywhere—as long as you can log onto a computer.

As you build your encore, your needs may dovetail nicely with this new world of work. But you may need to do some reframing. Instead of jobs, think about projects. Instead of what you want to do forever, think about what you want to work on for a year or two. Instead of one job, think about a series of engaging commitments with periodic gaps for a personal break, retraining, or travel in between.

And keep in mind that you are just as likely to invent your encore work as you are to find it in an existing full-time job. Many of us have no desire (and truth be told, a pretty hard time) fitting into the employee box after a certain age. Instead, you may end up creating your own role through some combination of self-employment, entrepreneurship, or even activism.

> "People in the encore stage of life have a psychic and a financial reason to stay in the game. And the country has never needed their engagement more, both for their skills and for the simple human and community connections."
>
> —John Gomperts, president and CEO, America's Promise

In some ways, all encore roles have a do-it-yourself aspect. Encore transitions are roundabout. You have a hunch or an interest and chase that idea for a while, and, as you dig in, things happen. You may find that your hunch was spot on and you stay the course, refining as you learn. You may find that when you're in a role, something doesn't feel right and you need to make some changes. Or you may find that as your own ideas or life situation evolves, you'll want to explore different directions. But everything you do along the way will likely be of some value.

Believe it or not, old-school jobs, with regular hours and benefits, still exist. Given the past few years, it's hard to imagine a welcoming job market, but labor economist Barry Bluestone argues that by 2018, assuming

Encore Profile: Embracing a Detour

After getting laid off from a marketing job in 2009, Terri Ward decided to move into work that would have an impact on future generations. She knew she had to make a living—there were six children at home. But she had some time while collecting unemployment, and she'd always wanted to finish her college degree. She enrolled in an online program for working adults at Eckerd College, the school she had gone to twenty years earlier. After taking just four courses, she proudly completed her bachelor's degree.

A month later, Ward enrolled in Shenandoah University's six-month Career Switchers program, determined to become a middle- or high-school English teacher. She started substitute teaching to get experience while applying for jobs, but soon into it, she started doubting whether teaching was what she really wanted. "I would come home with headaches. I was very stressed out," she said. At the same time, the job market was discouraging—because of budget cuts in Virginia, many schools were hiring English teachers for only one-year positions.

Ward thought about what really made her happy and what she was best at—and, surprisingly, she came back to those skills she had used in her marketing work. Ward applied for a copywriting job at Shenandoah University, the same school where she did her Career Switchers program. "I fell in love with both the job description and the people," she said. "When I got the offer, I was in the grocery story with my kids and had to try not to jump up and down in the middle of the aisle."

As for the investment in her teacher training, Ward says the experience was worth it. "I have a provisional teaching license, and when I retire, I'd just need a couple of courses to renew it," she said. "I still think of that as a possibility down the road."

the economy continues to recover, there will be more jobs than people to fill them, particularly in fields that meet social needs. Part of the reason: Younger generations are so much smaller in number than the boomer generation, but social needs will continue to grow.

In fields where there is anticipated demand, it's crucial to know where to look. For example, even as educators are being laid off around the country, there is still a great need in many locations for math, science, and special education teachers. If you're looking to find a full-time or part-time position, be sure to look at the Encore Hot List on page 255 for a rundown of thirty-five promising encore-friendly jobs.

Encore Profile: Accidental Entrepreneurship

Judi Henderson-Townsend, a former account executive in health care and travel, stumbled into a green business when she was searching for a used mannequin for an art project. She ended up buying fifty used mannequins from someone who was closing a mannequin rental business and, in the process, came up with an idea for a new business venture.

Townsend and her husband started Mannequin Madness to sell, rent, and recycle mannequins to event planners, trade-show vendors, museums, artists, and retailers. Their business keeps those mannequins out of landfills and has received a special achievement award from the Environmental Protection Agency for recycling 100,000 pounds of mannequins.

On Your Own—From Soloist to Encore Entrepreneur

Tina Brown famously wrote in a 2009 essay on *The Daily Beast,* "No one I know has jobs anymore. They all have gigs." We could talk about how disastrous this may be for the economy (and if this were a different kind of book, we'd do that), but it's hard to deny that self-employment is quickly becoming the norm.

As businesses and nonprofits shed workers in favor of contractors or freelancers, growing numbers of people are making a living as independent workers. According to the Freelancers Union, which advocates for better economic protections for the self-employed, 42 million Americans (roughly 30 percent of the workforce) fit into this category. It includes freelancers, contingent workers, part-timers, consultants, and pretty much anyone else who isn't working in traditional full-time employment.

Self-employment can fit nicely with some of the goals many people have for their encore years—less than full-time work, flexibility, plus some amount of control. You may not always work for yourself, but it's extremely useful to know how to do so from time to time should you want to or need to.

Your brand of self-employment could be a one-person operation or you could also become an encore entrepreneur: someone who opens a business or starts a nonprofit with the goal of improving the quality of life for others. According to recent Encore.org research, one in four Americans ages forty-four to seventy is interested in starting a business or nonprofit venture during the next five to ten years, and half of these people want to make a positive impact as well as a living. This research also shows that many aren't looking to start something big with enormous overhead and huge staffs. Encore entrepreneurship usually involves starting or leading an organization, but your brand of encore entrepreneurship may be a venture you run on your own or with a partner.

Adopt a "Slash" Mind-set

It's entirely possible that the elements of your encore will be a package, a portfolio, or a collection of slashes—sales director/music teacher, for example. (Full disclosure: I'm partial to the slash careers concept, since it was the subject of my last book, *One Person/Multiple Careers*.) There are several ways this can play out. If your best way to have an impact is through volunteering, you find another way to earn an income (money gig/pro bono gig). You may also divide the work part of your life into a few different kinds of activities that interest you (activist/writer/teacher). The *slash* approach is also a common way to transition. By hanging on to a prior type of work, you can support yourself while easing your way into your encore.

You may even decide to work less than full time to free yourself up for travel, eldercare, child care, or some other pursuit. Ultimately, it's about creating a life that allows you to do all the things that are important to you, while also figuring out how to earn the income you need.

Here are a few ways others have established their slash combinations:

- **Nonprofit fund-raiser/encore entrepreneur.** After five years leading the encore organization SHiFT, David Buck was ready for something different. He also needed a more stable source of income. He landed a part-time job raising money for the Benedictine Health System, which operates long-term care facilities for aging adults. The job not only covers his family's expenses and health insurance but also leaves him enough free time to work on his newest nonprofit venture, Abundant Philanthropy, which helps churches tap into the skills and talents of their congregants in ways that benefit their communities. (For more on Buck's story, see page 113.)

- **Homeless advocate/professor.** Ed Speedling, a former health care executive, followed an urge to work with the homeless and has been doing that in various ways for the past ten years. Since 2005, he has worked in different capacities for Project H.O.M.E. On the side, he teaches public health as an adjunct faculty member at Johns Hopkins University. "I like to hold on to some part of my former identity," he told me. "I like thinking that I don't have to shed who I was before, but that I can bring it along with me."

• **Consultant/children's center volunteer.** Stephen Ristau, a consultant who calls himself "the library guy," feels so strongly about the volunteer work he does in a children's center in his neighborhood that he includes it in many of his bios with this line: "As part of his own work portfolio, Ristau volunteers weekly at an inner-city early-childhood center in Portland, Oregon, where he reads to toddlers and serves as a human jungle gym."

The key is to know what you want to make room for and try to set up your life to make sure that it happens.

What If You're Already Working for the Greater Good?

Encore careers are not only for those doing social purpose work for the first time. Often experienced nonprofit workers move into encores that change the way they work or the orientation of their work. A person who has worked for a foundation or at a nonprofit in an office role, for instance, might feel the urge to do work that puts her in closer contact with the people her work is helping—a move from 10,000 feet to an on-the-ground role. It's also common to move into work with a different kind of population.

That's what happened with Susan Gilson. After nearly thirty years in various roles at a regional educational agency focused on at-risk youth, Gilson found that the more senior she became, the farther away she got from the kids being helped. She realized that it was time to do something else. Gilson said she did "everything all those good books tell you to do," from self-assessments to volunteering and working with a coach. Ultimately she landed a position as director of Elm Court Loaves and Fishes, a Portland, Oregon, program that serves hot lunches to people over sixty and coordinates Meals-On-Wheels deliveries to homebound seniors.

Encore Profile: Healing Herself, Coaching Others

Heidi Duskey can trace her midlife career trajectory to a doctor's visit when she was forty. Her cholesterol was high, she was smoking two packs of cigarettes a day, and, all of a sudden, she realized she was mortal. After meeting with a nutritionist and joining a smoking cessation program offered by the American Lung Association, Duskey kicked the habit, joined a health club, and started going to classes every day during her lunch hour. Within three months, she said she wasn't the same person.

The new Duskey slowly moved away from a business that provided typesetting services to graphic designers. She taught smoking cessation classes, got certified as an aerobics instructor, and thrived as a fitness manager and trainer.

At a conference in Florida, Duskey learned about a training program to certify people as health and wellness coaches. Two years later, she got certified and, through a program offered by the Coaches Training Institute, she became a life coach, too.

With her new credentials in place, Duskey was ready to veer away from personal training and move toward coaching. She assumed she would start by taking on a few private clients, but by chance she noticed a posting for a new position as a health coach for a local medical practice. "My jaw completely dropped," she said. "I wondered if I had read it correctly, because the description was literally right out of my résumé." She immediately applied. After multiple interviews, she got the job. She started in the position in 2008, in her mid-fifties. A full-time job with benefits, at a time in her life where she thought she'd be making a go of it as a solo worker.

Another common path is to move into a position leading, training, or mentoring others who are newer in the field.

John Fanselow, seventy-four, who began his career with the Peace Corps in Africa, has come full circle in his encore. After retiring from a tenured faculty position at Columbia University and taking on professor emeritus status, Fanselow remained active in his field—English as a Second Language (ESL). For years, he wrote and developed ESL programs and led teacher trainings at colleges and universities in New York, New Zealand, and Tokyo. He eventually became involved with two start-up ventures working to provide teachers in remote parts of the world with courses delivered online and through mobile phones, an endeavor that echoes his early teaching experiences in Africa.

Many people find their way to an encore because years of experience and perspective helped them see an unmet need. Teachers often get involved as reading coaches or in charter schools, and those who've worked in government sometimes become activists. (To read about a prison-administrator-turned-death-penalty-fighter, see page 42.)

Some people just want to shake up the way they work. They want to get out of the office or work less than full-time and trade responsibility for more freedom. For these people, finding the right structural fit is the most important factor in an encore decision.

Promising Encore Fields and Roles

Then there's the question of what kind of work you're going to do. It's possible that you already know the answer. If so, feel free to skip right past this section. But if you're still wondering where there might be a good match between your experience and paid work that makes a positive difference in the world, there are a few fields—and types of roles—that are particularly encore friendly. By encore friendly, I mean that these fields and roles anticipate high demand in the coming years, include opportunities for flexible work and self-employment, and are well suited to people with years of experience. Many encore careers involve teaching, coaching, and mentoring skills—the kinds of activities where life experience is a useful attribute. Chapters 6 and 7 go into far more detail on how to sniff out opportunities and best position yourself to do the work you want to do.

Job Opportunities
Check out the Encore Hot List on page 255 for the lowdown on jobs in these fields.

Education

A desire to fix our broken schools, help young people succeed, and pass on knowledge makes education a popular encore choice. Many people are drawn to becoming public school teachers—as evidenced by the rise of mid- and late-career transition-to-teaching programs around the country. There are also support roles and part-time positions—tutoring, substitute teaching, even coaching teachers—where you can make a significant impact outside of the teaching role.

If you're better suited to working around adults, consider teaching older students—as an adjunct or full-time professor in a community college or other environment—or nonteaching roles in education. Schools need everyone from accountants to marketers to peer advisers who work with midlifers returning to school.

"If you've been teaching for forty years, maybe it's time for something else, but not for me. What a great way to expend energy."

—Sandy Faison,
actor-turned-teacher

Social Services, Counseling, and Coaching

Many people in their encores crave the personal connections that only come through face-to-face human contact. If people come to you for a good ear, support, and counsel, you may be drawn to a role involving one-on-one interaction like counseling, coaching, or directly helping others in some way. Social services or counseling roles focused on addiction and bereavement —or even career and vocational counseling—are ideally suited to people who have been through some personal challenges of their own and are now eager to help others.

The Nonprofit Sector

As the for-profit sector bled jobs during the recession, the nonprofit sector actually experienced modest growth. And as the delayed wave of retirements starts kicking in, nonprofits will be in need of new talent.

So what kind of jobs are in high demand in the nonprofit sector? Fund-raising, for one. A lot of people stumble into fund-raising but stay in it, as nonprofit consultant Janine Vanderburg says, "because they are passionate about an issue, not because they want to go around asking for money."

Mission-focused organizations are also facing increasing pressure to professionalize their operations and take programs to scale. So people with operational, technological,

Nonprofit Job Growth
Nonprofits employed nearly 10.7 million paid workers in 2010, just over 10 percent of the U.S. private workforce, making it the third-largest among this country's industries. From 2000 to 2010, nonprofits had an annual growth rate of 2.1 percent. In the same period, the for-profit sector lost jobs at a rate of about 0.6 percent.

managerial, and financial skills are in demand, along with people who are comfortable working with data, metrics, and ways to report impact.

Health Care

Health care is one area where job growth is expected to skyrocket in coming years, and experienced workers can bring valuable life skills, empathy, and wisdom to their positions. According to the Department of Labor, ten of the twenty fastest-growing fields are in health care. And as the health care industry works to contain costs, expect to see many more ways to help people manage their health.

In addition to nurses and nurse practitioners, there will be an enormous need for home health care workers, physical therapists, and a host of roles that are just catching on, such as community health workers, chronic-illness coaches, and home-modification specialists. The health care field and the related niche of age-related services are also fertile ground for those who want to start socially minded businesses or nonprofit organizations.

> **"I knew from the time I made the decision to resign that I really wanted to do something with seniors and aging issues. I just was unsure of how that would look."**
>
> –Diana Meinhold, marketer-turned-legal-fiduciary

Don't assume that working in health care means you need to have a medical or even a scientific background. Life experience sends a lot of people into health care roles, many of which are completely nonmedical. If you're bilingual, you may find opportunities with hospitals and social-service agencies hungry for people who can bridge a language divide.

Green Jobs

Green jobs are roles focused on the environment or sustainability—anything related to cleaner or renewable energy sources, preservation of the land and other parts of nature, efforts to improve recycling, and the like.

If you care about environmental issues, the good news is that thinking about sustainability has become ingrained in many industries. Companies are increasingly paying attention to how their manufacturing practices affect the environment, which has translated into new jobs in corporate social responsibility, communications, and quality control.

And for those whose work touches on construction, engineering, and architecture, there are ways to acquire green skills—like getting LEED (Leadership in Energy and Environmental Design) certification training. Explore trade associations and community colleges for webinars, courses, and continuing education programs focused on energy-efficient construction, weatherizing homes, and other green skills. You can get an idea of pending demand by analyzing what kinds of programs are being offered.

There's been a lot of hype about green jobs, leading some to conclude that the number of new jobs hasn't lived up to expectations. To some extent that's true. Many so-called green roles, like jobs in the solar industry and other clean technologies, rely on government subsidies. In regions where

Encore Profile: From Volunteer to Employee

Judy Wolfe is the kind of volunteer who was so legendary that she literally got a plaque in her name. Hers is nailed to a bench in a prominent spot at New York City's Central Park Zoo, where she has given her time for more than twenty years.

Wolfe started volunteering on Fridays to get herself out of her art studio and spend time with other people. Then a forty-five-year-old artist and printmaker, Wolfe had heard that a new zoo opened in Central Park and was looking for volunteers. Wolfe was assigned to be a liaison between the zoo administration and the public, responding to questions from visitors.

Though she has always loved animals, Wolfe's motives at the time were somewhat selfish, she admitted. She wanted to make friends. It wasn't until years into the work that she became a serious conservationist. "The people you meet are there because they are passionate about animals or conservation, so right away you have a common interest with a potential new friend," she explained.

About eleven years into her volunteering, Wolfe retired from printmaking and painting and immersed herself in digital photography. Over time, she brought that interest to the zoo, taking photos of the animals, which she shared first on holiday cards, then in an email newsletter, and later on a blog where she also posted her art, movie reviews, and political thoughts.

After about two decades of volunteering, the zoo's assistant director asked Wolfe if she would consider taking a paying job at the zoo, as its photo documentarian. He said he approached her because she had been there longer than anyone else and had become the zoo's "institutional memory."

She accepted.

incentives have been strong—such as New Jersey, California, and parts of New England—there has been a flurry of hiring in a wide range of job functions, from installers and project managers to salespeople, engineers, and executives. In other parts of the country, there's been no action at all around clean energy, and therefore no hiring.

Government

With about 2 million employees, the federal government is the largest employer in the United States. Contrary to popular wisdom, the vast majority of federal employees—85 percent—don't live in Washington, D.C.

Between now and 2018, experts say there may be as many as 1.7 million jobs available at all levels—local, state, and federal—of government. According to Max Stier, president and CEO at the Partnership for Public Service, "Even with prospects of significant budget cuts and reductions in the federal workforce, record numbers of baby boomers will be retiring in the coming years, while our government's need for highly skilled employees in such fields as science, engineering, public health, cybersecurity, finance, and legal affairs is continuing to grow."

If you're itching to be outdoors, there are even part-time jobs in national parks and the Forest Service.

Brainstorm Possibilities

One of the trickiest things about finding fulfilling work is knowing what roles exist. If the Encore Hot List on page 255 doesn't spark anything, try tapping the brains of friends and other encore seekers. Here's an exercise you can try.

1. Gather a few people together who want to brainstorm ideas. (If you don't have a group, post on the Encore.org Facebook page or LinkedIn group to see if others will join you. Find two or three people to do this with online, via email, or in person.)

2. Think about a skill you want to use; the environment you want to work in; or an issue, group of people, or cause you want to focus on. Then pose it as an "if" statement that others can help you answer. Feel free to string together a few of your "if" statements. Here are some examples:

- If I want to mentor
- If I want to counsel
- If I want to get out of an office
- If I want to use my creative talents
- If I want to be around kids, but not in a classroom
- If I want to work with elders
- If I'm tired of managing people

3. Ask the others to come up with all the roles they can think of that meet the criteria you posed. As the group comes up with ideas, think about how you can learn more and weigh the pros and cons of each one. Examples of additional information you'll need:

- How's the pay?
- What level of training or education is required?
- Is it conducive to a part-time or flexible schedule?

Here's an example for this challenge:

If statement—If you want to get out of an office, have a part-time or flexible schedule, and work around kids . . .

Suggestion #1—Spend some time at a local zoo, garden, or state or national park and see if they have any children's programming. If so, check it out. If not, consider starting something. Do the same with art or science museums and community centers in your area.

Pros and Cons—If there's a program up and running, test it out and see if the program appeals to you. If there isn't something in your area and you see a need, what about starting small? (For some entrepreneurial types, that's a pro; for others, maybe that's a con.)

Suggestion #2—Consider working as a crossing guard.

Pros and Cons—It's an ideal position if you want to be around kids, work outside, and have a part-time schedule. That said, the hours are odd—an hour in the morning, at lunch, and again at 3 p.m. This may be great if schools are hiring near where you live, but not if the commute doesn't make sense.

Figuring Out What Jobs Pay

One of the easiest ways to get information on salary ranges is to search job listing aggregators such as Indeed.com. Just plug in the job title and the city under the salary tab, and the site will bring up average salaries for jobs that fit the criteria.

Make sure to include as many helpful words as possible in your search. For example, if you want to know about communications roles in nonprofits or government agencies use "director of communications government" or "director of communications nonprofit."

The Department of Labor's CareerOneStop.org has a tool for researching salaries by region. Under the Salary + Benefits link, you can put in a job title and the zip code or state, and it will provide you with median, high, and low salaries, as well as how your area compares with the national numbers. Though the ranges tend to be big, it will get you in the ballpark.

A number of sources provide free salary information based on anonymous details provided by users of the site. It's usually a give-get scenario, so you may have to become a member (usually free for basic services) or input anonymous information about your pay and other details (other kinds of compensation, city, title, number of people managed, and so on). On Payscale.com, after you've provided details on your situation (you can use your most recent job if you're not currently working), you can then play with what-if scenarios that will help you find salary information for a career change.

The salary section on Glassdoor.com lets members search for salaries by job function, company, or organization. Salary.com is another site that is very handy for getting free general salary information by job title or geographic area.

If you are researching salaries at a particular nonprofit, you can also review the organization's federal tax forms (Form 990) on Guidestar.com, which will show the salaries of the top five people in the organization—it might not tell you very much about salaries below the executive or management level, but at small organizations, it could tell you quite a bit.

You can also look at the total payroll versus the number of employees; and it's good to compare one year to a prior one. Nonprofit salaries can be subject to big swings related to cash flow and state and federal budgets. FoundationCenter.org can also be a helpful resource.

Government pay is probably the easiest to determine because salaries are transparent. Jobs are listed along with a pay range. In fact, in some city and local government offices, the names and salaries of all public employees are posted on websites.

What Happens Next?

As you move from identifying what you want to do to figuring out how you're going to do it, the questions start to change. As career coach Carol McClelland explained, "At some point, you make a commitment and point your navigation system toward something. That's when you go from preparing, researching, and learning to the actual search for the right opportunity."

You'll identify people who are active in the work you want to do, the hubs of relevant activity, and how to plug yourself in. You'll begin to ask questions about which organizations hire people like you to do the kinds of work you want to do. Or what would it take for you to start something on your own. And what's already going on in the community where you want to live or work.

The deeper you get into your exploration, the more you will learn. Don't be surprised if your vision for what you want to do shifts as you learn more about what certain occupations are like and what kinds of needs exist where you live. You can read about the national nursing shortage in the newspaper, but if you live in a place where the market is flooded with nurses, you may decide that path doesn't make sense for you. In the end, you'll arrive somewhere that blends the dream with the practical.

FAQs

Say I like gardening, cooking, or building things. How would I match my skills and interests with a way to make a difference in the world?

Start exploring ways to take your interests and apply them to an underserved community or population. Nancy Kochuk, a retired communications professional, is working on ways to bring yoga to senior centers in her area. Barbara Allen, an experienced arts administrator, created the nonprofit Fresh Artists (freshartists.org) to bring children's art to corporate offices. In turn, the companies make donations to underresourced schools for art supplies.

Look at volunteer and nonprofit job listings to see how others are using talents or interests like yours. A cursory online search of nonprofit jobs turned up postings for a video producer for a youth organization, a cook and

Encore Profile: From Housekeeper to Activist

Working as a housekeeper in Oakland, California, Margaret Gordon, then fifty, got an unlikely education. When cleaning the home of Michael Herz, the founder of Baykeeper, a nonprofit group that monitors the air quality in the Bay Area, Gordon began flipping through the Herz's collection of environmental magazines, digging deeper into stories on air pollution.

Gordon began to connect the dots between the pollution in her Oakland neighborhood and the fact that so many people in her community—including herself and her grandchildren—were suffering from asthma. That's when she started going to meetings and asking hard questions about cancer, asthma, exhaust from trucks on the freeway, trains, and air quality.

Gordon began to educate herself. When regulators wanted input from community members, she was there to provide it. She organized with neighbors to protest a freeway construction project that exposed workers to toxic substances. Eventually, she cofounded the West Oakland Environmental Indicators Project, which conducts studies on air quality and advocates for reform—and pays her a salary.

Gordon's advocacy has been so effective that the mayor of Oakland named her a deputy commissioner of the Port of Oakland. Looking back, Gordon said she never thought any of this activism would result in her earning a living. "I just did the work," she said. "There was no plan."

Gordon's advice on becoming an activist: "You can get the technical skills from college and read about all the theories. But when it gets down to the realities of day-to-day lives, no one can teach you that. It's total experience. You have to get out there, listening and asking questions. And you have to be willing to be uncomfortable."

kitchen manager for an adventure-based educational program, and an event planner for a fund-raising effort. All these are positions that could easily tap into some talent or skill set you may want to use.

Should I bother with job boards, and if so, which ones?

Job sites can be very useful, as long as they are a part of your search process, not your only method. For nonprofit jobs, make sure to keep an eye on Idealist.org, OpportunityKnocks.org, nonProfit-Jobs.org, CommongoodCareers.org, Philanthropy Careers (philanthropy.com/jobs), Council on Foundations (jobs.cof.org), and Encore.org. For government

positions, check USAJobs.org and Government jobs.com. And don't forget
to look at the general job sites like Yahoo!'s Hot Jobs (hotjobs.com), Monster
.com, Indeed.com, CareerBuilder.com, AOL Jobs (jobs.aol.com), and
SimplyHired.com. Your local paper and Craigslist.org may also have relevant
postings.

If you do apply for a job through an online posting, don't just rely on that
submission. Try to use your network to find out more about the job and try to
enhance your application by finding someone connected to the organization
who can put in a good word for you. (See Chapter 6 for more on tapping your
network.)

You may very well learn about an opening from seeing a posting on
Idealist.org or some other site, but think of scanning job sites as one of many
ways you can stay on top of the market and notice trends. Paying attention to
positions and fields in high demand, as well as the kinds of skills that various
positions require, will be useful information no matter what.

Can my encore be something completely unrelated to my work?

Sure. Throughout this book you'll see several examples of people whose
encore work was completely unrelated to what they do for a living. In fact,
many social entrepreneurs create their organizations while still working in
a day job of some kind. There are also people whose encore work consists of
high-commitment volunteering or pro bono activities.

I'd like to find something that isn't too physically demanding. Any ideas?

If you're looking for work that won't be at all physically taxing, consider roles
that are primarily knowledge based (meaning the main criteria for the work
is thinking, problem solving, research, or other creative output) or involve
one-on-one work with people. Nonprofits, government agencies, and social
ventures employ people in just about every functional area you can think
of—legal, financial, technology, communications, marketing—as well as
in jobs particular to the sector, like development professionals, program
managers, and case managers. Many counseling roles may be emotionally
difficult from time to time, but they don't usually require physical strength.

Plenty of health care roles that are in high demand also fit the bill. Medical office assistant, dental hygienist or assistant, phlebotomist (someone who collects blood and other fluid samples), hearing-aid specialist, MRI technologist, pharmacy assistant, and other various roles in medical offices don't require any particular physical strength, though some do require you to be on your feet for part of the day.

What are the best ways to break into government jobs?

If you're interested in federal jobs, spend some time on the site of the Partnership for Public Service (ourpublicservice.org), a nonprofit organization focused on reinvigorating the federal government. The website and its "Where the Jobs Are" and "Best Places to Work in the Federal Government" reports (both available on the site) do a great job in laying out the top areas for federal government hiring. You can search by field and get a breakdown for each specialty of the number of projected hires in that area. Federal job listings are posted at USAJobs.gov. For state and local job postings, visit Statelocalgov.net.

Start by thinking about what issues you care about and start to get acquainted with the various agencies and departments that cover those issues. Also think about the roles you want to play.

As with searching in the private or nonprofit sector, don't underestimate the value of your network. And don't just rely on websites. One of the trickiest things about government jobs is that if you don't know your way around, figuring out what people do in various roles can be daunting. Knowing some people on the inside who can help to demystify things for you can be immensely helpful.

As for the application process, be prepared for something way more time-consuming than you're used to and don't let it discourage you. When Sharon Ridings, a lifelong corporate dweller, applied for federal government jobs at the suggestion of her husband, a long-term government worker, she was astounded by the process. "I'd never seen anything like that before. I tried to cut it down to its simplest components," she says. "I answered questions exactly how they were asked." She eventually snagged a great position with the Environmental Protection Agency.

With school districts laying off teachers and hospitals laying off nurses, is it really possible to find work in those fields these days?

It's true that both teaching and nursing have been areas where even experienced people have lost jobs in recent years. The key is knowing where there are needs before you go for additional training or education. For example, there is high demand for teachers of special education, math, and science, and those who can teach those subjects will find jobs even as schools are shedding teachers of other subjects. Nursing is an area where needs vary considerably by geography. So before you do any retraining, it's very important to understand the opportunities and needs in the community where you want to work.

Is it possible to succeed working with a population that is very different from me?

It is possible. And those who have done it usually find something within themselves that allows them to forge a connection with the community they serve. Mark Goldsmith was a retired cosmetics executive when he started a program to work with mostly young men in prison. He said that from the start he saw his younger self in these men and immediately knew what they needed. Others make a point of involving people in the community to build trust and learn to respect how a culture operates.

CHAPTER 3

What Do You Want?

"It's a helluva start, being able to recognize

what makes you happy."

—LUCILLE BALL

You may know exactly what you want to do with this stage of your life. Or you may have no idea at all. It's possible that this is the first time in your life that you're asking what it is you *want* to do. Not what you *can* do. Not what you *should* do. Not what *someone else* wants or expects you to do.

If you're a blank slate, you'll be thinking a lot about the *what*. If you have some ideas already, you'll be thinking about the *how*. Do you want to work for yourself or for an organization? What kind of environment do you want to work in? How many hours do you want to work? How much money do you need to earn? Will your encore work be your primary focus or something you do outside of your so-called day job?

Career transitions have two essential parts. The first part is internal, where you reflect and do self-assessments. The second part is where you test things out in the real world. "It's a twisted, braided kind of thing," said Michael Melcher, a lawyer-turned-career-coach. Most people have a preference for one or the other, but in an ideal scenario you'd do both.

The exercises in this chapter will take you through self-assessment and reflection in a way that sets you up for an experiential phase. I recommend you go through them in order, doing all of them even if you think you don't need to; you may be surprised at the connections you make. (Because you may revisit this process at another time, you may want to photocopy or scan the pages before writing in them.)

Patterns of Reinvention

As you think about your own transition, you may find it helpful to see a few of the common ways that people discover and move into their encore work.

CIRCLING BACK

Ten years into his retirement from a career in food services, Don Tarbutton knew he had to return to work to bolster his battered retirement account.

A mailing about a training program for hospice chaplains came at just the right time. While in college at Cornell, Tarbutton was a chaplain in his fraternity and on track to continue his education in divinity school. He was accepted into a graduate program at Rochester, but abandoned the idea before he could start. Now he was ready to reconnect with his earlier passion.

Tarbutton went through the training program and took a job as an on-call chaplain at a hospice. "The work is perfect for me," he said. "It is invaluable training as we age, witness death around us, and think about our own mortality."

ELEVATING A HOBBY

Rob Laymon was surviving as a freelance writer, but knew he could not sustain a life of being holed up in his house forty hours a week, barely getting outside except to walk his dog. Around the same time, he bought a sailboat. He was so consumed with sailing that he wondered how he might turn sailing into something more than an expensive hobby.

One day he went into a marine supply store near his Philadelphia home and started talking to the manager. "I wish I could find a job that would pay me to sail," he said. It turns out the manager was the former director of a sailing program on the Chesapeake Bay for the Boy Scouts of America. Within three months of that conversation, Laymon was in command of a thirty-four-foot boat with eight Boy Scouts aboard.

CHANGING ORIENTATION

Jeanne Woodford rose from being the first female prison warden at San Quentin State Penitentiary to the top job in the California Department of Corrections.

Throughout her career, she championed programs that emphasized rehabilitation rather than purely punitive approaches, but during her tenure she oversaw four executions, which reinforced her opposition to the death penalty.

Woodford found it increasingly difficult to work in a system that she saw as resistant to reform. So she resigned from her position and got involved in several organizations working

As you complete the following exercises, you'll pull together clues to help you figure out what you're looking for. Don't expect instant clarity. These exercises won't reveal your encore like a crystal ball, but they will help you discover or confirm the things that interest you and the elements

on criminal justice reform, extending the work she had done earlier in her career.

She is now executive director of the nonprofit Death Penalty Focus, an anti-death penalty advocacy organization.

FOLLOWING A NEW INTEREST

For years, Diana Meinhold served as legal fiduciary to a close friend suffering from Alzheimer's. It was a huge and fulfilling task, and it convinced Meinhold that when it came time for a reinvention, she would do something related to aging.

When Meinhold decided to leave her job as an executive with the Automobile Club of Southern California, she volunteered for the Alzheimer's Association, which led to some consulting work with senior centers—all while researching certification and licensing to become a fiduciary.

Meinhold now runs a private practice as a fiduciary case manager, becoming "a thinker and doer for people who can no longer think and do." She likes the work so much that most days she wishes she could do more. As she told me: "I can provide dignity to those who cannot advocate for themselves. I can try to right some wrongs. And I can provide tenderness and humanity where there is only process and detachment."

ADDING SOMETHING NEW

Katherine Klein is a professor of management at the Wharton School of the University of Pennsylvania. She was diagnosed with breast cancer in 2011 and took an eight-month leave from work to undergo treatment.

That experience gave her time to reflect. When her older brother proposed a trip to East Africa to see the animals—his expertise and passion—Klein said yes. But given her passion for people—not animals—she put out the word to colleagues and friends that she was traveling to Rwanda and put together a packed day of meetings in Kigali, Rwanda, before her brother and the rest of the group arrived for the safari.

What she saw in Rwanda on that first trip moved her and left her eager to return. She traveled to Rwanda three more times within the space of a year, each time learning more about the country.

After returning to teaching, she did something with her new passion. She organized a minicourse called "Conflict, Leadership, and Change: Lessons From Rwanda" for a group of twenty-seven Wharton MBA students. Her Rwanda experience also primed her for a new role as vice dean for social impact at Wharton.

you'd like to be present as you move into your encore work.

What interested you thirty or even five years ago may not be what interests you today. We all evolve over time, and we do it against a backdrop of a world that's constantly evolving, too. Take the time to check in with yourself on where you are now, where all the years have taken you. You may have fallen into your work for reasons of happenstance; pressure from parents, partners, or others with influence; the desire for a certain kind of security. New factors are probably influencing what you want this time around. Listen to them.

As you think about your ideal situation, put aside reality for a little while. Later you can be more practical, but if you keep an open mind and expand your sense of what's possible, you might identify desires you wouldn't otherwise notice.

Don't assume that there is *one* answer for what your encore should be. And don't try to draw big conclusions until you complete all the exercises. One exercise might spark more ideas than the others. There are probably multiple things that you could find fulfilling at this stage of your life. Ideally, you'll come up with several ideas. Later you can decide which ones you want to explore.

If you're stuck on a particular question or an entire exercise doesn't bring you any insight, don't worry. Just move on. It's possible that question isn't hitting on something that is particularly important to you. The questions you leave blank can teach you a lot about your priorities.

When you get to the summary section, you'll take a look at your results from all the exercises and decide on the next steps. In the meantime, be creative and have some fun.

Discussion Prompts

Do you already know what you're interested in pursuing as an encore or will you be trying to figure that out? • Are you drawn to self-assessments and other exercises to learn about yourself or are you more the type who learns by jumping in? • Have you ever done exercises like the ones in this chapter? • If so, what do you remember about that experience?

Exercise 1

Clearing the Decks

Write down any encore ideas already on your mind. They may be as specific as "teacher" or as vague as "community service." That's fine. By jotting down the ideas you've already been considering, you clear the way for new ideas to come in. If you don't have any ideas, just jump ahead and revisit this page if something comes to mind in the later exercises.

"People don't get stuck because they are too dreamy. They get stuck by being too cautious or safe."

—Michael Melcher, career coach

Ideas You've Already Been Thinking About

1. _____

_____

2. _____

_____

3. _____

_____

4. _____

_____

5. _____

_____

6. _____

_____

As you work through the following exercises, you may find confirmation for some of these ideas or you may discover new directions you haven't considered before. Either way, it should be interesting to revisit this list after you've gone through all the exercises and see if the ideas you jotted down are still contenders. For now, put these ideas on the back burner.

Exercise 2

What's Your Attraction Signal?

We all have an internal guidance system that alerts us when we're attracted to something. If you've lost your connection with this feeling, you probably don't have much confidence in what you like and what you don't like. Without this method for making choices, you may be tempted to rely on the voices of others—spouses, media, children, peers, siblings—to determine what is best for you. To get a sense of your internal guidance system, choose an environment—it could be your yard, a local park, or a room in your home—and scan the area until you notice one thing that attracts you. It's not so important *what* you are drawn to—a flower, a fountain, a bird, a vase, a painting, an empty can of diet soda. Instead focus your attention on *how you know* you are drawn to that thing. It may be a feeling, a sense, a thought, or an internal shift. Each person has a different signal. Others have described their signal as:

> Warmth . . .Tingles . . . Goose bumps . . . Excitement . . .
> Sense of alignment . . . Feeling empowered . . . Happiness . . .
> Clarity . . . A pull . . . A knowing . . .

What words would you use to describe the feeling or signal you experience when you know you are drawn to something? Do your best to articulate what you experience. It doesn't have to be perfect. Only you need to be able to understand.

Words That Describe Your Signal

_____

_____

_____

Now that you have this clue, continue using it as you make simple decisions in your daily routine—what are you drawn to wear, order for dinner, watch at the movies, or read? The more you access this internal signal, the more you'll trust it to uncover clues about your encore career.

Exercise 3

Work/Life Snapshot

Describe your work/life situation now without mention of what it is that you work on. Instead, describe qualities and details of your day-to-day activities.

For example: What time do you get up and go to sleep? Do you commute to a workspace? Do you have a regular schedule? Do you travel as part of your job? Do you have any daily rituals? With whom do you share meals? Whom do you see or work with on a regular basis? Do you play any caregiving roles? Do you have time for community activities/hobbies? When and how do you exercise? What do your weekends and vacations look like?

"At Chevron, we did these personality tests to help us understand our communication styles. People ended up being classified as four animals. I was an owl (analytical) and a dolphin (social-worker type). I think I worked my owl side for all those years and now I'm getting to tap into my dolphin!"

—Ken Wong, Chevron-retiree-turned-health-coach

Exercise 4

Examine Your Motivations

Mark the following statements that explain what you're looking for in your next career.

I want an encore career to . . .

☐ *earn income*

☐ *be engaged*

☐ *feel fulfilled*

☐ *have fun*

☐ *socialize with people who share my interests and values*

☐ *give structure to my day/week*

☐ *stimulate my mind*

☐ *feel satisfied*

☐ *use my innate skills and talents in a new way*

☐ *have meaning in my life*

☐ *be inspired*

☐ *have a flexible schedule*

☐ *get health insurance and other benefits*

☐ *feel productive*

☐ *work on an issue or social problem that matters to me*

☐ *contribute what I know*

☐ *stay challenged*

☐ *be my own boss*

☐ *do the work I've always wanted to do*

☐ *solve problems*

☐ *be part of a team*

☐ *feel needed*

☐ *lead others*

☐ *mentor others*

☐ *get a change of scenery*

☐ *develop new skills*

☐ *be creative*

☐ *leave a legacy*

☐ *remain active and healthy*

☐ *help others*

☐ *do something interesting*

☐ *continue to learn*

☐ *make unique contributions to society*

☐ *make a full-time salary*

☐ *supplement my retirement income*

Review your selections and take a moment to identify up to five motivations that are *most* important to you.

I want an encore career to . . .

1. _____

2. _____

3. _____

4. _____

5. _____

Exercise 5

What Issues Pull You In?

Now you're going to turn your attention to the substance of the work you want to focus on. How would you describe the issues you're drawn to or the kinds of people you might want to help or serve?

If you've volunteered in the past or followed a particular issue with a strong interest, it's likely that you already have some inkling of the issues you care about. But it's possible that you've never thought of yourself as especially motivated by any social issues—or even if you have been, you may never have given any thought to what it would be like to focus your work on something you care about rather than thinking of work solely as a means of generating income.

If you're having trouble coming up with anything, think about what you're drawn to when you read the newspaper, watch the news, or flip through magazines. Are there any societal problems you wish you could help solve? If you've volunteered, what kinds of issues and causes have attracted you? If you had to commit to volunteering, what kind of program would interest you? What kinds of charities do you contribute to when you donate? What do you find yourself doing when you have free time and absolutely nothing you have to do?

> **"I didn't even know the world I work in existed until I started digging."**
> —Rob Laymon, freelance-writer-turned-sailing-captain

Still stumped? Spend some time on Change.org (the "Top Causes" section) or Dowser.org, two websites focusing on social change issues.

Write down four areas that interest you. For each area, start with a vague category and see if you can narrow it down a bit. (Broad: working with young people. Narrowed down: helping children of immigrants get ready for college.) To help focus, try asking questions that use the words *what, where,* or *how.* Helping women in what way? What kind of students? What kind of teaching? What kind of mentoring? What kind of mediating? How can I help older people? Where can I learn about community needs? How can I serve the animals of my community?

1. **Broad:** _____

_____

Narrow: _____

_____

2. **Broad:** _____

_____

Narrow: _____

_____

3. **Broad:** _____

_____

Narrow: _____

_____

4. **Broad:** _____

_____

Narrow: _____

_____

Exercise 6

What Roles Appeal to You?

As you consider your encore options, it's helpful to think about the kind of role you'd like to play. You may be drawn to contribute in a way that leverages your past experience or you may want to stretch. Even if you don't know what you want, you may have a good idea of what you *don't* want to do.

Which of the following appeals to you right now? (Mark all that apply.)

☐ **Direct service**—*Working directly with those in need—individuals, groups, or communities.*

☐ **Advocacy**—*Speaking out for those in need. This work may be focused on a specific cause, community, group, or individual.*

☐ **Teaching/Coaching/ Mentoring**—*Working in an educational/coaching role to help people learn, gain new skills, and grow.*

☐ **Policy**—*Shaping the laws, treaties, regulations, and policies that impact key issues and communities.*

☐ **Fund-raising**—*Raising the money that allows others to provide direct service, advocate, and develop policies for specific causes and populations.*

☐ **Leading/Directing**—*Creating an organization or helping a cause or existing organization have more social impact. This could be at a strategic level, management, or day-to-day operations.*

☐ **Program Design/Management**—*Developing and implementing programs to provide services to an organization's clients.*

☐ **Communications/Marketing**—*Getting the word out about an organization and its work to create social change.*

☐ **Research/Evaluation**—*Conducting research on best practices and program results to ensure an organization's efforts are as effective as possible.*

Roles That Appeal to You Do you want to continue the same kind of role you've had in the past? Or would you like to transition to a different role?

_____

_____

_____

_____

_____

Roles You Want to Avoid Do you have a been-there-done-that feeling about a particular role? Do you feel you aren't qualified or interested in taking on a particular role?

_____

_____

_____

_____

_____

Roles You Would Like to Grow Into Are there any roles that intrigue you, but may feel a bit out of reach right now?

"Everyone thinks career discovery should be revelatory, arriving with a lightning bolt on Mount Sinai. More often, it's exploratory."

—Belinda Plutz, career coach

Exercise 7

What Are Your Skills and Interests?

Think about the various jobs and roles you've had throughout your working life—everything from being a camp counselor when you were sixteen to working as a cashier in a convenience store to your longer stints and bigger gigs in recent years. In the chart on pages 54–55, list jobs that stand out in your memory in the first column. In the second column, write down some of the things you remember doing in those jobs using words that end in *-ing,* such as planning, talking, building, designing, coaching, cooking, communicating, writing, giving feedback, and so on. In the third column, write down the focus of the job or what the work was about, such as banking, youth activities, health care, law, construction, wildlife conservation, insurance, or technology.

   As an example, here's what I'd put for my two longest career stints, as well as some random short-lived jobs—even internships—I had when I was younger.

Jobs	-ing Words	Focus/Topics
Nonprofit professional	Writing, speaking, advocating	Encore careers, baby boomers, social entrepreneurship
Lawyer	Counseling, advising, researching, billing hours	Advertising, publishing, business
Journalist/writer	Researching, interviewing, writing, speaking	Careers, work, publishing, nonprofits
Teacher	Lecturing, mentoring, reading	Education, writing
Legal intern, prosecutor's office	Researching, observing, filing, reading, reviewing documents	Criminal justice
Law clerk	Filing, taking notes, doing research, reading, editing	Business, real estate, contracts
Motel desk clerk	Talking, helping customers, answering the phone, giving travel advice, managing conflicts	Travel/tourism

After you've done that for most of the jobs that come to mind, do the same thing for parts of your life outside of work. Look at what stands out as activities where you've spent a lot of your nonwork time—volunteer work, education, clubs, associations, family time.

Here are a few examples I'd add to the nonwork part of my chart:

Nonwork Activities	-ing Words	Focus/Topics
Advisory board member, The OpEd Project	Connecting people, coaching and mentoring, advising, writing	Diversity, communications, training, education, writing, women's advancement
Executive committee member, New York Writers Workshop	Teaching, organizing, and promoting community events, coaching and mentoring writers	Writing, community events, publishing
Playing poker	Organizing the game, talking, socializing, analyzing people, honing my card skills	Games, play
Long walks or hikes	Exploring the outdoors, walking, talking, socializing	Nature, environment

Now it's your turn. Fill in as many rows as come to mind, being as comprehensive or brief as you like.

Jobs	-ing Words	Focus/Topics

Jobs	-ing Words	Focus/Topics

Nonwork Activities	-ing Words	Focus/Topics

After you've got the chart nicely filled out, cross out anything in the second or third columns that you know you don't want to carry forward into your next phase of work. Of the remaining items, circle the *-ing* words and the focus/topic words that are most interesting to you at this point in your life.

Use this chart to create a list of your favorites.

YOUR LIST OF FAVORITES	
Favorite -ing Words	Favorite Focus/Topics
1.	1.
2.	2.
3.	3.
4.	4.
5.	5.
6.	6.
7.	7.
8.	8.
9.	9.
10.	10.

Exercise 8

What Do You Want from Work?

In this exercise, you'll build on the work you did in Exercise 3 about your current work/life situation.

Now imagine your ideal work setting—the kind of place you would create if you could design a workplace and workspace that met all your needs. Don't worry if your answers seem unrealistic; what you write might help you figure out what matters to you and what you're craving. If it's hard to believe you might be able to get all these things in a work setting, add the words "in an ideal world" to each of your answers.

"Like a lot of people, I started with what I didn't want to do. It's like paying attention to your dreams. You sometimes get flashes of images that are really appealing. Pay attention to those little flashes."

—Ruth Wooden, former nonprofit executive director

If a question doesn't mean much to you, move on to the next one. If you want something that's not included in the prompts, add it to your list. On your first pass, record your initial thoughts. Then put the worksheet away for a few days. When you review it again, you'll have more insights to add. (Your answers may go over the lines provided, so have some scrap paper handy.)

Location/Work Environment Where do you want to work? How far away is it? What's the commute like? Do you drive, walk, bike, or take public transportation? Do you work indoors or outdoors? What kind of building is it? Is it even in a building? What amenities are nearby? How much time do you spend working from home or some other nonoffice location (e.g., a café or coworking space)?

What does your workspace look like? What does your desk look like? Do you even have a desk? Do you have a defined office or are you mobile? Is it important for you to leave work at work?

_____

_____

People Whom do you want to work with (coworkers/colleagues, employees, clients)? What size group do you envision? Less than ten people/more than a hundred? Do you want to provide services directly to clients or customers? What do you know about the kinds of people you enjoy working with? Any preferences for ages/diversity/other characteristics?

_____

_____

_____

Culture How do you want to feel at work—cooperative, informal/formal, innovative, traditional, service-oriented, creative, helpful, friendly (add your own words)? What do you want to wear to work? Is your ideal organization a start-up or more established? Do you care whether you work for a small or large organization? Do you have a preference for a specific kind of organization (e.g., nonprofit, social venture, government agency, hospital, self-employment)?

_____

_____

_____

Schedule What would your typical workday look like? Do you want to work full time, part time, set hours, or more flexible ones? How much vacation time or other time off are you looking for?

_____

_____

Benefits What benefits do you need? Are there any benefits that matter more to you than income (e.g., flexibility to meet caregiving obligations, a certain amount or kind of time off)? Which benefits can you provide yourself?

_____

_____

Income How much income do you require from your encore work? (Answer if you know. And if you don't, take a look at the budgeting exercise in Chapter 5.) Do you have a preference for working on salary or by project, by the hour, or on commission?

_____

_____

_____

Self-Employment/Job/Portfolio Do you imagine working for yourself in some way or working for an organization? If for yourself, are you thinking of freelancing, consulting, or starting a business or nonprofit? Do you imagine having one primary work role, or do you think you'll have a portfolio or slash career (e.g., teacher/consultant)?

_____

_____

_____

Take a Step Back

Look at all of your answers. What are you learning about your ideal work setting? Do your preferences feel stronger in some areas than others? For example, if flexibility is more important to you than any other aspect of your work setting, your answers will probably reflect that.

_____

_____

Adding It All Up

Now it's time to pull together the various clues from all of the exercises so far. Look for repeated themes and inconsistencies. Don't be surprised or disappointed if some aspects are clear and others are still muddy (or everything is still muddy!). The picture will become clearer in time.

Before you started the exercises, I advised you to be as dreamy as possible. Now that you've allowed yourself to dream, it's good to rein yourself in a bit and see how you might translate some of that pie-in-the-sky thinking into some real-life career possibilities.

As you review your answers, think about patterns and themes. What are the most pressing motivations for you at this stage? For example, the clues you're pulling together may tell you whether you are primarily motivated by an issue (Exercise 5), by values (things like "helping others" or "being part of a team" from Exercise 4), or by something relating to work environment or lifestyle choices (Exercises 7 and 8).

Career coach Phyllis Mufson likens the process to building a pyramid. At this stage, you are laying the foundation. In her experience, the first step is establishing what you want and need to have, along with your priorities and passions, which could be hinted at through those favorite skills and interests. After you have these things in place, you can start building up the pyramid. That's when you'll start doing research, learning more about fields that interest you, building your network and, ultimately, finding or creating the work that's right for you.

Go back to the very first exercise, "Clearing the Decks," where you wrote down ideas for your encore. Think about whether these exercises confirmed or refined your initial hunches or whether they took you in some new directions. If you didn't write anything I hope you have a couple of ideas at this point.

Based on all that you've learned with these exercises, now you're going to revisit—or visit for the first time—the question of your top three ideas for an encore. It's possible that you won't know much more than you knew at the beginning, but it's likely that at least some things will be clearer.

Describe your ideas in as much detail as you can, including elements such as where you'd work, what your commute might be like, whether you think you'd need to get some training or education to do the work.

If you can't come up with anything, take a look at the Encore Hot List on page 255, and visit Encore.org to read a few profiles. It's also fine to leave this blank. Mark the page and continue reading.

Top Three Contenders

1. _____

_____

_____

_____

_____

2. _____

_____

_____

_____

3. _____

_____

_____

_____

When you've completed this exercise, take a break. Put all of your papers away for a day or two (and skip ahead to the next chapter if you want). When you return, review your conclusions and the top three ideas you listed. Tweak your list based on any new thoughts.

Making Sense of It All

I f your assessment results are all over the map, don't despair. First, realize that you could probably do several different things and be fulfilled, and that you may end up doing more than one of them, either concurrently or consecutively. Try to use this process to think about what makes sense for you right now or what direction you want to explore first.

If you find yourself faced with some inconsistencies and gaps at this stage, take a look at the following strategies for ideas on how to reconcile your findings. Your goal is to identify just a few things to explore further.

- Listen to your attraction signal. Are you drawn to one of your clues more than the others?

- Is it a matter of timing? Could one clue give you new insights about a near-term project and another clue point you toward the ultimate direction you want to take?

- Are the conflicting clues telling you what works in different settings and circumstances? For example, do you have positive memories of times you spent performing or doing arts and crafts projects? Do you want to find a place for those activities in your life? If yes, do you need them or want them in the work part of your life?

- Brainstorm ways to combine seemingly inconsistent factors into a viable path. Perhaps you want to travel and you want a meaningful role in a nonprofit. One possibility is to get involved with an organization doing work internationally. You could use some of your travel time to reach out and build alliances, discover best practices, and establish partnerships. Or you might decide to keep your travel separate from your work, and if so, it might be important to negotiate a schedule that allows you to have as much time for travel as you want. Or something altogether different. The key is to keep an open mind and think creatively.

The Passion Problem

Even in the do-good world, many consider their families, their hobbies, and what they do in their free time as their passions and their work as work, meaningful as it is. So go easy on yourself. Try to focus on the kind of work that helps you feel like you're making a contribution on a regular basis. That mind-set will go a long way when you realize that even the most fulfilling work will still come with occasional dreadful days, difficult colleagues, and the usual workplace challenges.

Career coach Phyllis Mufson avoids using the word passion because it can lead to a lot of confusion. She said that often it isn't a direct translation such as, "I love flowers, so I'll open a flower shop." More often, it is about figuring out what is underlying that love of flowers and then incorporating that into your work.

Sometimes you can find a direct link between your passion and a way to earn a living and do good. Remember Rob Laymon (page 42), the freelance writer who turned his passion for sailing into a viable career that both puts him on a sailboat and manages to help kids. "I get a paycheck and get to work with kids," he said.

It's even possible that ideas that seem distinct can be bundled together. Career coach Carol McClelland, who advised on the exercises for this chapter, put it this way: "Say someone wants to be a writer, a speaker, and a facilitator. That's not necessarily a choice. They could do all of that on the same subject or topic."

This is where your research and checking in with your attraction signal will help you hone your ideas. "It's a three-dimensional puzzle," McClelland told me. "You really have to jiggle and massage all the pieces until they fit together. That's why the more clues you have, the more likely you are to discover that an element that seemed important is actually something you can live without."

Given the right opportunity, you may decide that it's okay to drive an extra ten miles to work or go back to school. It's a lot like having a checklist for dating. When you click with someone, it's pretty common to chuck the checklist and go with your instincts.

Go for a Test Drive

As you develop your encore work, you will continue to refine the ideas you've sketched out here. You will abandon some and replace them with others, each time using a similar process. "After you've got a few candidates for ideas, you're not going to go out and get a Ph.D. in it," said McClelland. "What you're looking for is a little bit of clarity."

If you'd like to learn more about what a particular job entails, do your homework. Start with MyNextMove.org (see box on pages 66–67), a great resource for getting the basics on a job, its average salary (by zip code), and even whether there are likely to be good job prospects in the future. You can also find out what education is needed for a particular job and whether there are any licensing or certificate requirements. If you're looking for something specific, you may have to try several different words.

Identify people in your network or friends of friends who would be willing to talk to you about what it's like to work in a certain field or particular job and where they see the best opportunities for someone like you. Assign yourself a certain number of interviews per week or month. As you talk to people, tap into the work you did in the attraction signal exercise and document how you felt after hearing a person's story. Could you imagine doing what the person you interviewed did? Would you feel comfortable in the working environment she described? (See the detailed section on informational interviews beginning on page 122.)

As you start meeting people in a field you're exploring, ask what they read and start keeping up with the trade publications, blogs, and newsletters that cover the sector. If you see notices for webinars or teleseminars about current topics in the field, check those out. Also consider going to lectures, panel discussions, and conferences so that you're learning about current trends and meeting people at the same time. As you do these things, remember that attraction signal. What are you feeling as you start learning more?

One of the best ways to figure out whether you'll really like a type of work or whether you just like the sound of it is to find a way to get a closer look. Because it's hard to go down multiple paths at once, choose one of your ideas and come up with a way that you can test it out in a relatively short period of time. Doing a series of experiments is a good way to hone your ideas and decide which you want to pursue and which may not be right for some reason. If you're still trying to get a sense of what the work looks like, see if you can find someone who would let you shadow them for a day, a half-day, or even a series of meetings. Say you want to know how you'd feel about working overseas. Consider doing a service-oriented trip abroad. If you think you'd like to be a teacher, try a few days of substitute teaching and see if you like it. Chapter 8 goes into more detail about ways to craft experiments and immersion experiences.

You may go down several paths before you determine what you want to do. And going down a path—as you'll see from the stories in this book—can be a detour that lasts months or even years. But don't equate a detour with a waste of time. Although the phrase may be overused, you are on a journey. If you learn that a certain kind of work isn't what you want, that's progress. When you're on the journey, expect some discoveries that take you in an entirely unexpected direction. That's progress, too.

FAQs
I'm determined not to do anything that involves learning new technology—or, for that matter, using much of it. Will that limit my options?

As someone who spends way too much time on a computer, I fantasize about spending a lot less screen time in my own encore. Whenever I think about it, I imagine roles that involve one-on-one work with people or something that would get me outside more—as far as possible from my desk! Needless to say, wanting to avoid technology is a legitimate desire but, yes, it will limit your options.

For most people, there is no escape from email and at least basic cell phone technology. There are some fields in which avoiding technology is unrealistic. IT, fund-raising, and communications come to mind. At the most senior levels, you can probably delegate some amount of tech work to others, but not all of it.

Many other social-sector roles involve a lot of time on the computer, but how much and in what way will vary greatly depending on what you're doing

Want More Self-Assessments?

While researching this book, I revisited the Myers-Briggs personality assessment, something I'd done quickly and without much impact years ago. This time the experience was powerful. My score identified me very clearly as an ENFJ, a type sometimes called the "ideal seeker," someone always focusing on visions and possibilities—and tending to live in the future more than the present.

That explained so much for me. I always knew I was an extrovert and understood that my energy came from interacting with people, but seeing the kinds of careers other ENFJs tend to choose gave me clarity on why law was such a bad fit (too much emphasis on facts, details, analysis—too little on feelings) and why writing, speaking, and advocating around issues come so naturally to me.

MYERS-BRIGGS—Based on the work of psychiatrist Carl Jung, the Myers-Briggs Type Indicator (referred to as MBTI) is a time-tested tool for determining psychological preferences and how people make decisions in the world. Knowing your MBTI type won't necessarily tell you what kind of work you should be doing, but it can give you lots of information about why you behave in certain ways and what kinds of people you may have an easier time working with. You can take the assessment in a paper version included in several books (search online book sites for MBTI and several choices come up). The official site of the MBTI Foundation (myersbriggs.org) offers the assessment online for about $150 with the opportunity to have one-on-one feedback with a certified MBTI practitioner. Because the Myers-Briggs test is so widely used, you can readily find information about people who scored like you did and read about what careers they chose and why.

PERSONALITYTYPE.COM ASSESSMENT—This assessment was created by Paul Tieger,

and where. Even within fields and roles, technology usage will vary based on the environment you're working in and how tech-oriented it is in its approach.

If you're working in some teaching jobs and direct service—in an organization that works with children, with nature, with the homeless, or with people with disabilities, for example—you may find that you can spend a lot of your day without touching any kind of technology at all, but that you have to get online occasionally to check email, use certain kinds of software, or file reports.

This is another area where the best answers will come from people doing the work that interests you. Ask them how technology-intensive their work author of the book *Do What You Are*. Also derived from Jungian personality type, this test uses personality type as a starting point for determining career choices. Basically, this is a shortcut of the MBTI, using four questions that could be completed in five to ten minutes to get to a result you might get from taking the full MBTI. For $14.95, Tieger offers a customized report on your personality type, along with suggested career roles. Available at PersonalityType.com.

STRENGTHSFINDER—Marcus Buckingham and the late Don Clifton have been recognized for the theory that people do best in situations that play to their strengths rather than in situations where they work to overcome their weaknesses. The Strengthsfinder, available in the book *Now, Discover Your Strengths*, is a process to help you determine your five top strengths from a list of thirty-four possible talents.

MYNEXTMOVE.ORG—This one isn't a personality assessment, but it's a very well-designed tool for playing around with career ideas. Sponsored by the Department of Labor, this site is loaded with useful information about career direction—all of it free. The interactive tool "Tell us what you like to do" is an easy way to see what kinds of work match up with your various interests and preferences.

Keep in mind all of these assessments are tools, not tests, meaning there are no right or wrong results. The idea is to use what you learn to better understand what kind of work might feel good or satisfying to you. As career coach Michael Melcher told me, "Don't expect any of these tools to rescue you." The key is to think of them as a way to provoke or spur your thinking. "You're the master and the assessment is a tool, not the other way around."

is, and what kinds of roles exist in their field that require the least amount of technology.

I feel strongly about not wanting to work full time or in an office. Will those things end up being deal-breakers?

They could be, but they don't have to be. And oddly, in some situations an employer might be thrilled to hear that you don't require a full-time salary and/or office space because they may not have the budget to cover another full-time staffer or the place to put one. There are many roles that aren't, by definition, full time or office-bound—everything from an occupational therapist to substitute teacher to solar-panel installer.

What if my biggest need in any new job is flexibility?

You're not alone. A slew of roles—massage therapists, yoga instructors, grant writers, even nursing and EMT positions—appeal to encore seekers because they can be done flexibly on an hourly or part-time schedule, or in shift work. Think about roles in fitness, wellness, and coaching—all of which lend themselves to hourly and part-time scheduling. Some nonprofit management roles can be done on a project or part-time basis—IT work, marketing, communications, grant writing, even interim executive roles. Many roles in health care—nursing, EMTs, and home health aides—are often conducive to shift work or part-time schedules. (Several roles in the Encore Hot List on page 255 are in this category.)

Get Some Feedback

After you identify a few encore possibilities, you may find it helpful to get feedback from others. If you feel like you'd benefit from other opinions, this would be a good time to share both your general insights and your ideas with a few people you trust to get some reactions. Think of colleagues, family members, and friends who know you well and whom you trust to give you solid, constructive feedback. You might want to focus on people who understand your values.

Keep in mind that getting feedback can be tricky. I spoke to several coaches who warned me about the minefields of getting too many opinions. "If you're in a time of transition, you're probably getting lots of unsolicited feedback," said Phyllis Mufson, "so hearing from others can be overwhelming or discouraging."

It's best to be specific about the kind of help you're looking for and even pose questions that will lead to the kinds of answers you're looking for. Michael Melcher tells his clients to use open-ended questions in addition to any yes/no ones. Questions such as: "Does this sound like something you could see me doing? If so, why? If not, why not?"

Mufson has a great way of thinking about this. She tells her clients to think of themselves as one of those newly planted trees with a protective fence around it. "Decide who you're letting inside the fence, and for anyone else, develop some Teflon answers. For example, 'I'm looking into a few different things, mostly having to do with education and youth.' This kind of response will make a friend feel heard and valued, but doesn't expose feelings you don't want to share, like, 'I have no idea what I'm doing right now.'"

CHAPTER 4

Prepare for What's Next

"... every transition is an ending that prepares the ground for new growth and activities."

—William Bridges, *Transitions: Making Sense of Life's Changes*

Arlene Carter's encore moment came as a shock—she was laid off.

Thanks to a severance package and an employed husband, she had a bit of time to regroup. Carter began taking early morning beach walks during which she "asked the universe for guidance" and thought about her future. She spent time thinking about what she liked best about jobs she'd had in the past and what she might like to have more of going forward. "Someone told me a long time ago that work is the most fulfilling if you have three components—make a difference, make money, and have fun," she said. Carter looked at her past jobs—in real estate, a dot-com start-up, and even a period of self-employment—and realized that she had been missing the make-a-difference part. She resolved to try to include it in her next job.

Carter then began to take small, practical steps. She went to a seminar promoted on a flier posted at a local coffee shop. That session, with six other people and a coach, helped her get her résumé and job-seeking skills refreshed. She also joined a group at her church for people who were unemployed, underemployed, or unhappily employed. "That group was helpful in keeping my faith strong, my spirits up, and keeping me focused on the positive and exciting part of changing jobs and looking for new opportunities," Carter said.

About two months after her layoff, a friend she knew from volunteering called about a fund-raising job opening at a nearby senior housing facility. Though Carter hadn't been drawn to fund-raising initially, she was impressed by the facility. She had some past public relations experience that would serve her well in the role—and she had exhibited some talent for raising money through her volunteer work with the American Lung Association. So when an offer came, she decided that this was the make-a-difference job she was looking for.

Discussion Prompts

What do you know about how you move through transitions and figure things out? • Are you the walk-alone-on-the-beach type or do you benefit from brainstorming with others? • Is your life set up to give you some time and space to work on your transition? • If not, are there any small changes you can make to free up some room? • How would you feel about working with a partner, coach, or group?

Though most encore transitions will take considerably longer than two months, Carter's experience touches on many of the different ways you can open up your life to change: She gave herself space and time to reflect. She met with a coach and joined a group for people trying to make a career move. She let people in her network know that she was looking for a new position and that it had to involve helping people. Ultimately, she trusted her instincts.

No two encores are the same—but nearly every one begins with a period of exploration. Your exploration is a time to get used to a new version of yourself—one that is still evolving, one that doesn't know what's next. It's about going public with your desire to make a change.

It's about opening your eyes and ears to new possibilities. It's about asking questions, asking for help.

All career transitions include a mix of things you can control and things you can't. You may not have much say in the timing or the outcome. But you can initiate the process of self-discovery. You can work to be open to change. And you can control the decisions you make when options present themselves.

Get Comfortable with Uncertainty

For most people, transitions are intensely unsettling. So it's important to get comfortable with feelings of uncertainty—and to develop techniques to get you through any rough patches.

Like Carter, you might have a free block of time to jump feetfirst into a transition. That's great. But if you're working full time in a job you're not planning or able to leave for a while, exploring something new can occur alongside the familiar.

Either way, you will no doubt hit a time when you are neither fully invested in what you have been doing nor fully involved in what you hope will be a new kind of work. When you're in that in-between nowhere space, expect to feel uneasy or even anxious. Reactions of others may rile you. How will you introduce yourself when you meet someone new? How long can you hang onto your former title as a way of explaining who you are? What do you do with your time—when only so much of it can be consumed by reinvention?

> "I have learned over the years that panicking when things aren't looking great isn't really very helpful."
>
> –Arlene Carter, on being laid off from her job

After twenty-seven years, Betsy Werley left a corporate career in banking without a plan for what would come next. "There was a period when there was nothing going on and I didn't know where I was going, and I remember walking down the street and looking at all these other people and feeling so envious because they all seemed like they had somewhere to go," she said. Werley survived her transition and is now the executive director of the Transition Network, a national nonprofit that helps women over fifty face a wide variety of transitions together. Hard to miss the irony there!

In his classic book, *Transitions*, William Bridges defines the stages of transition that accompany all sorts of big life shifts—marriage, divorce, a job change, a birth of a child, a loss of someone you love, or even an inner change like a spiritual awakening or adjustment in self-image. In each instance, Bridges identifies a process that needs to happen. "First there is an ending, then a beginning, and an important empty or fallow time in between," he writes.

Herminia Iberra writes of a similar phenomenon in her book, *Working Identity*:

Most people experience the transition to a new working life as a time of confusion, loss, insecurity and uncertainty. And this uncertain period lasts much longer than anyone imagines at the outset. An Ivy League Rolodex doesn't help; even ample financial resources and great family support do not make the emotions any easier to bear. Much more than transitioning to a similar job in a new company or industry or moving laterally into a different work function with a field we already know well, a true change of direction is always terrifying.

That "empty or fallow" time is an important part of the process, and many agree that it's often necessary to pass through it, not just skip around it, to get to the other side of a transition. (Bridges might say that people who don't go through the necessary stages end up with unfinished business, but no need to focus here on what might send you to a shrink down the road!)

Suzanne Braun Levine calls this in-between time "the fertile void." In her book, *50 Is the New Fifty,* she likens the stage to adolescence, a time of losing one's way, not knowing, doubt, and confusion. Difficult as this sounds, nearly everyone eventually emerges from the fertile void, even if they don't end up where they thought they would. Though Levine was writing specifically about women hitting midlife, men struggling to try on new identities will find similar hurdles. Whatever you choose to call it, don't be surprised if you have a period where you aren't quite sure who you are anymore or where you want to be going.

Ways to Cope

In Zen Buddhism there is a concept called "beginner's mind," a place in which you revel in the thrill and novelty of learning or trying something for the first time. As Zen teacher and author Shunryu Suzuki writes in his book, *Zen Mind, Beginner's Mind*: "In the beginner's mind there are many possibilities, in the expert's mind there are few." This explains why so many of the people I interviewed for this book sounded almost euphoric when they told me about adventures like returning to college or graduate school at the same time as their grown children.

You are part of a huge club. In the domain of work, nearly all of us—whether we work for ourselves or for organizations—now feel a nearly constant sense of transition and uncertainty. If you're going to remain in the workplace, it's a given that you'll be tweaking your career again and again as you and the circumstances around you continue to evolve. And as part of the first generation with both the time and ability to craft a meaningful encore, you have plenty of compatriots.

If there's someone in your life you turn to for guidance or spiritual support, this is a good time to check in. When young people graduate college, they are part of a big community of peers trying to break into the job market. As someone trying to reinvent at midlife, you may feel like you're alone. That's why it's imperative to surround yourself with others in the same place. (For more on the benefits of joining a group, see page 81.)

Practice introducing yourself in ways that highlight your interests and what you've been doing with your time, rather than by your job title. Not only will you deflect attention from the fact that you're in transition, but you'll also improve your chances of making connections with people who share your interests. Take a look at the sample scripts in Chapter 6 for ideas on how to do this.

If you talk openly about your transition, understand that if others appear unsettled, it could be that they, too, are at a moment when they would like to be making a change, but aren't yet able for some reason. Be prepared for your transition to cause some difficult feelings for those closest to you, such as a partner or grown children. Work on ways to communicate about your transition that acknowledge these feelings.

Make Time to Transition

Whether you are still at your job or dedicating yourself full time to moving into your encore, you'll want to set aside some time for thinking, planning, and reflecting. It can be part of a weekend, an evening, a long walk, or a coffee date. It can even be a full-on vacation or sabbatical. You might be the type who benefits from taking a workshop to move this process along. Or maybe you'll find a friend going through her own encore transition and plan to meet or speak weekly to check in on each other's progress and cheer each other on.

Arlene Carter carved out time during her early morning walks. Others give themselves permission to figure things out over a defined period of time, say, a few months or a year.

💡 Find Small Ways to Measure Your Progress

When I made my first career transition, from lawyer to writer, I had a visual barometer of my progress. I would look at the messages in my email inbox each day and count how many related to my emerging life as a writer—correspondence with new mentors, attempts to get my first assignments, conversations with members of my writing group. Initially, the inbox was still loaded with evidence of my former identity, but little by little I noticed a shift. Tracking it that way gave me comfort that I was making progress, even if it was only in the form of small interactions with people in the new world I so wanted to join.

Like so many people, Celeste Miller gave herself a year to test things out. After a twenty-seven-year career in financial technology sales, recruiting, and management consulting, her business took a big hit after 9/11 and never really recovered. At the same time, Miller was "waking up too many mornings with a feeling of 'what am I doing with my life?'" The combination of financial hard times and an opportunity to discover something new propelled her to make a change. A change to what? She didn't know.

She took a variety of part-time jobs including a stint at a jewelry store in her neighborhood and a job as a receptionist at Weight Watchers (which helped her to lose forty pounds) while she thought it through.

One evening shortly into her exploration year, her aunt called. "If you didn't have to worry about money, what would you do?" she asked. Miller's first thought: teaching. This came as a surprise. Her early career goals involved making money and traveling for business, anything that would take her away from the traditional women's zones like education and social work. But that night, spurred on by the conversation with her aunt, Miller searched online and discovered the New York City Teaching Fellows, a program geared to midcareer sector switchers. Ambivalent but intrigued, she applied. A few months later, she was accepted.

Like Carter, Miller wasn't certain that teaching was exactly what she wanted. But she decided to give it the summer. At the end of the summer, she stayed on, still uncertain but willing to give it a chance.

Turns out it was the right move. Miller got her first teaching job at fifty-four. Now sixty-three, she is the director of tutoring programs at the Professional Performing Arts School, a public high school in New York that requires students to audition for admission.

Find a Sounding Board

The idea of a personal board of directors gets a lot of play these days as shorthand for the collection of people you rely on for counsel at pivotal junctures in your life. Unlike a literal board of directors, the idea isn't to assemble these folks in one room for a serious meeting, though you should try to meet in person or by phone with each of them on a regular basis. By this time of your life, you probably know who is on your board—a friend whose opinions you always trust, a mentor or colleague who has a great sense of your potential, even a spiritual leader you turn to in times of confusion. Your partner or other members of your family are also likely to be on your list, but it's good to have some people who can give you objective advice (something that can be hard to come by in families).

Sometimes you need to consult with a person who has some kind of specialized knowledge or a background relevant to something you're exploring. These people may be worth meeting or inviting to join your board for a period of time. You may also hire a professional—a life or career coach, social worker, therapist, or other kind of counselor—to help you think through the tougher questions.

Engaging others can help you develop a plan or stay on track. Arlene Carter found support in a church group and through a small group facilitated by a job coach. Marcy Gray Rubin (the screenwriter-turned-therapist from Chapter 1) came to the realization that she wanted to be a therapist in the midst of her own therapy session. Celeste Miller began to consider becoming a teacher after a provocative conversation with an aunt she respected.

Cathy Abbott, a senior executive at an energy company who had become disenchanted with her job, started meeting with a colleague who was also thinking about making a change. "We were both complaining about work and decided it would be helpful to have a safe place to go to whine and blow off steam," she told me. "But I thought maybe we should also be doing something constructive." So she proposed that they become "accountability partners." The plan was to meet regularly to go out for a meal or drinks, and each time they'd prod each other into action. They would end the meeting with a statement of what they would do before the

Give Yourself a Break

You may hear the word *sabbatical* and think, "Never gonna happen in my life," but sabbaticals aren't just for academics anymore. They are becoming increasingly common for others—both those taking breaks from work to recharge or accomplish a goal and those needing a period of reflection or retooling before launching an encore career.

If you're thinking about any kind of structured break, get yourself a copy of the book *Reboot Your Life: Energize Your Career & Life by Taking a Break,* which covers everything from how to make the case to your employer and family members to creative ways to fund time off from work.

I've known Rita Foley, one of the book's coauthors, for a long time—well before she ever took the reboot break that helped her move from a hard-charging corporate executive to what she calls her "current portfolio." Today she runs a consulting firm and is active on several nonprofit boards. We worked together on an outline for how to use a reboot break to jump-start an encore transition.

- **Try to give yourself a minimum of three months.** According to Foley, the first two weeks are decompressing, the last two are worrying about what you're going back to, so the time does get whittled down. (That said, a minisabbatical of even two weeks could be useful in recalibrating.)

- **Think into the future.** If you know you want to take a substantial time away from your regular life or work, plan as far ahead as you can. With significant time to organize yourself, you can save money, develop a plan for work and other responsibilities,

next meeting to explore what's next. After a few meetings her colleague decided that he wasn't into accountability, but he agreed to still meet with Abbott while she reported in.

Around the same time, Abbott and her husband planned a weekend retreat. They booked a babysitter and went to a bed-and-breakfast where they talked extensively about what each of them wanted for the next stage of life. While there, they completed a list of questions (much like the exercises in Chapter 3) given to her by "a fellow sufferer at work." Questions like "Where do you find meaning?" and "How do you want to be remembered?" They even reviewed their finances. It still took Abbott nearly two years to be ready for a big reinvention, but those steps were crucial to her process. Abbott ultimately got a master's in Divinity and is now a minister at the Arlington Temple United Methodist Church in Virginia.

and prepare the various people whom your time off will affect—from colleagues and managers to family members.

- Be creative about funding your time off. These breaks don't have to break the bank. Start saving money over time and consider starting a reboot fund by asking friends and family to donate to that instead of giving birthday or holiday gifts. If your plan involves travel, look into home swaps or rent out your place. Taking time off from work doesn't have to mean that you're not earning money— think about whether there's something you can do to bring in some income while also flexing some new muscles. (Chapter 5 gives you ideas for ways to bring in extra cash.)

- Create a project plan. Plot out the nitty-gritty—how you'll finance your break, how you'll separate from work and reenter, where you'll travel or live—but leave time for dreaming and spontaneity. The ideal reboot break is a combination of preparation and responding to serendipity.

- Take a reboot break even if you're still working. Set aside a chunk of time on your calendar and treat it as if it is an unmovable meeting. Use that time each week to make calls, read and research, and have informational interviews and other meetings related to your transition.

- Communicate. Although you may see no downside to taking time to recharge your batteries, keep in mind that your partner, your children, or others who are invested in your life might not see it that way at first. Make sure to consider the issues your exploration might raise for others and address them head-on.

Call in a Professional

When I changed careers nearly fifteen years ago, hiring a coach gave me the jump-start I needed. Although I had plenty of people to turn to for advice, I didn't want to overburden supportive family and friends with my constant need to talk about my reinvention. I knew that career transitions could be long and emotional. And I was impatient. I wanted to get things going quickly so I sought advice from an outside professional who had plenty of experience guiding others through similar processes.

I met with my coach once every two weeks for a few months. When we were finished, I had a sense of what I wanted and how I was going to try to get there. When our formal process ended, I still called her from time to time for a strategy session, but that initial immersion was just the push I needed.

If you think you could benefit from working one-on-one with a coach, you'll have plenty of choices as the coaching field has exploded in recent years. There are now even coaches who focus on encore careers, and over time you should expect to see more. Because there are no uniform guidelines on what kind of training a person has to have to call herself a coach, it's wise to go with someone who comes personally recommended or through a reputable referral source.

I found my coach the same way I'd find a hairdresser or doctor—asking everyone I knew if they'd heard of anyone great. One name came up twice, and that was enough to sell me. If you search online, you will find many directories—usually affiliated with coaching certification programs—that offer listings of coaches by geographical region.

Professional help doesn't come cheap. According to a recent survey by the International Coach Federation (ICF), the average hourly rate for

Consider a Career Coach

After you identify a coach (or two), identify the parts of your process where you want help. Unlike therapy, which can be used for open-ended self-discovery, coaching is usually a short-term relationship designed to achieve a certain goal. Are you stuck trying to figure out what it is you want to do? If so, you'll probably work with someone on a series of assessments like the ones in the previous chapter. You might want help developing a strategy for networking and interviewing. Or maybe you're feeling stuck in some other area, like figuring out whether it pays to go back to school for a particular career path.

Don't expect a coach to find you a job. A coach can help you develop a strategy or find ways to overcome obstacles. But a coach won't do the work for you. And whereas some coaches do make introductions on behalf of clients, it isn't typical.

Ask for a free consultation or sample session so that you can "try before you buy." Some questions to ask:

• What is their background and what kind of approach do they use with clients?

• Are they available by email for questions between sessions?

• Is one-on-one the only option or do they offer groups as well?

• What is the price for sessions and what are the policies around cancellation or missed sessions?

• Is coaching by phone an option when you can't meet in person?

coaching in North America is more than $200. That said, rates vary widely across the country, and many coaches just starting out work in the $80–$90/hour range. Some coaches offer a certain amount of their time on a sliding scale or pro bono; ask when you interview them. The ICF (coachfederation.org) also has a good coach referral directory. The Life Planning Network (lifeplanningnetwork.org) and 2Young2Retire.com are smaller directories focused specifically on coaches who work with people at midlife and beyond. Also check out PivotPlanet.com to book a session with a mentor. ←——

"At fifty-three, I left without a plan. All I know is that I had to stop moving to figure it out."
—Suwon Smith, on leaving Citigroup after twenty-three years

Many coaches have websites and blogs; reading them is a good way to get a taste of someone's background or philosophy and to find coaches in your area or with a specific kind of focus (e.g., encore careers, retiring federal workers, working while chronically ill, nonprofit jobs). Start by searching with the word "coach" and whatever other criteria you're looking for. To find coaches who are blogging, search on directories such as Alltop.com for blogs or WeFollow for Twitter (search under #coach to find the Twittering coaches on WeFollow). You might even be able to get some preliminary advice on Twitter by striking up a chat with a coach whose posts appeal to you.

Join a Group, Take a Class

Through the 1970s and '80s, Jim Betzold worked in the field of alternative energy, something he has been passionate about for as long as he can remember. (He devised a solar powering system for his own home in 1985, long before solar panels on rooftops became trendy.) But when government regulation made it increasingly difficult to make a living, he found his way to the mortgage industry. As he put it, it wasn't a calling, but it was a living. For a time. When the recession decimated the real estate market in 2011, it became harder to close deals. Betzold knew he had to make a change.

Betzold heard about a program offered through a local community college, which focused on civic leadership for people over fifty. The eight-week

Coaching on a Budget

Free job or career coaching isn't easy to find, but here are a few places to look:

- Call up one of the coaching certification programs and see if it offers pro bono coaching by coaches in training.

- Check CareerOneStop.org, a program run by the Department of Labor, to see if there are any offerings in your area.

- The International Association of Jewish Vocational Services (iajvs.org) is an excellent resource for job search assistance in most metropolitan centers.

- Keep an eye out for programs at libraries, faith-based organizations and community centers, community colleges, and alumni offices of any schools you attended. They may not offer one-on-one counseling, but they could offer coaching in a group setting.

- If you're unemployed, ask your contact at your local unemployment office about any free services in your area. Those will mostly be job training or educational options, but if coaches are offering free sessions in your area, your unemployment office is likely to know about it.

program required taking a day off each month. It was a big commitment, but Betzold thought it might jump-start his job search. He signed up, got a scholarship for half of the $750 tuition, and didn't miss a single session. For the class, he had to create a project that related to a passion. The instructor provided a blueprint for developing the project—how to assess its validity, create a road map, and establish a timeline.

Betzold knew immediately that his project would relate to alternative energy, specifically an independent online resource to help people reduce their energy costs.

By the time he finished his project, Betzold knew every alternative energy company in the region. And when he heard that several of these companies would be presenting at a "Going Green" expo, he went. At the expo, he found one company especially interesting and talked with the man staffing the booth for half an hour. By the end of that conversation, Betzold had an invitation to come in for further discussions the next week. Within days, he met the company president, who offered him a job.

Betzold attributes his new job to the leadership course. "There's no way I would have done all that research," he said. "The class made me accountable, and when you have to do something—like a project—it gets done."

Transitions can feel extremely isolating. "Getting into a group setting can normalize the entire change process," said Carol Vecchio, the founder of the Centerpoint Institute for life and career renewal in Seattle. Vecchio, who has led groups on transition and self-discovery for more than thirty years, says that just knowing that there are other "bright, self-aware people going through similar kinds of transitions" can be incredibly helpful.

Bill Thomson unretired twice, first from the U.S. Air Force and then from a three-year post-retirement stint with the defense contracting firm BAE. When he moved from New Hampshire to Arizona in his early sixties everyone around him had ideas for what he should do with his time. Become an usher at the baseball stadium. Work as a chairlift operator at a ski resort to get free ski passes. Shuttle kids and grandkids to the mall in between golf games. None of that felt right. Then he heard about Experience Matters, a hub for all kinds of encore-related activity in the Phoenix area, and joined a four-week Coming of Age "Explore Your Future" program. By the end of the four weeks, Thomson had a plan for what he wanted to do. It was so clear he created a PowerPoint slide to explain the plan to himself and others. His vision is to divide his time three ways—working at a nonprofit, substitute teaching, and learning Spanish—over a ten- to fifteen-year period.

Ken Wong took the same program through Coming of Age in San Francisco after retiring from Chevron at sixty-nine. It helped him decide to continue or amp up his community work as a volunteer health care workshop leader for Kaiser Permanente's Healthier Living program. Shortly after taking the course, he parlayed that volunteer gig into a part-time job helping to expand the reach of the workshops. Wong said he appreciated seeing that others were in the same situation and that they were so comfortable sharing. "When you see others thinking about next steps—and all the variety and diversity of ideas—you realize that everything is okay."

The number of organizations focused on helping people through encore transitions is

"What I've learned in this business of transitions is that you don't know exactly where you're going to go . . . but you can have a sense of a direction. It's like tacking with a sailboat. You go in one direction, find something, then angle it a little differently."

—David Buck, real-estate-professional-turned-nonprofit-leader

Start Your Own Group

When I made my transition from law to journalism, I formed a writing group that was integral to my process. I had a great connection with two women I met in a writing class and when the class ended, we wanted to find a way to keep up our momentum. So we started a career-goals group we called the "goils." For five years, we met religiously for a weekly lunch during which we worked on the nitty-gritty of becoming freelance journalists and generally kept each other on track with our goals. I credit that group with turning all of us into professional writers.

growing. Some of them, like Coming of Age and the Transition Network (for women over fifty, in more than a dozen cities and growing), are becoming national in scope. Others, such as Experience Matters in Maricopa County, Arizona; Discovering What's Next in Boston; Life by Design, in Portland, Oregon; and SHiFT, in Minneapolis, are local. Check out the map at Encore.org/connect/local for a current listing of local organizations in your neck of the woods.

If your area doesn't have any encore activity, consider joining a transition group that isn't specifically encore-focused. Community colleges, community centers, faith organizations, Rotary clubs and other service organizations, women's or men's groups, alumni associations, and libraries are all good places to look. If you can't find an existing group, consider starting one of your own. It might be easier to relate to people who are going through a transition similar to your own, because you're either in the same life stage or at the same point in your exploration process.

FAQs

All this sounds great, but I can't possibly focus on my transition until I leave my job. What should I do?

You have a few options. If all you have time to do is read this book and do some thinking, then that's all you'll do. Underline things that spark ideas and take some notes. Another possibility is to do some creative multitasking. Do you exercise? If so, think about listening to relevant audiobooks while walking or on the treadmill (see the "Further Reading and Resources" section beginning on page 293 for some recommendations). Do you take time out for lunch? Find someone willing to meet you over sandwiches to brainstorm about how you can support each other. Some people find that hanging on to a job where they can coast on autopilot is the best situation for working on a transition; they figure out the minimum they have to do to get by and use their extra energy for strategizing about their next move.

Why connect with others going through this same stage of life? So we can all be lost together?

It's common to feel isolated without the routine and social connections of a daily job. "Even if you can maintain your old networks, they may not be in sync with what your new life design will be," Carol Greenfield, founder and president of Discovering What's Next, an encore-focused organization in Boston, told me. Meeting with others who are going through the same thing can be incredibly helpful, she said, especially if you're feeling a sense that people you have been around for a long time "just don't get you anymore."

"If you're new to a community, you can be whoever you *want* to be rather than who you *are*," said Steven Joiner, coauthor of *Idealist's Guide to Nonprofit Careers for Sector Switchers*. "Some people take this to an extreme and move to a new city where they can start the next chapter of their life," Joiner said. But you don't have to move to redefine yourself. It helps, Joiner said, to "forge new friendships and alliances with other reinventors."

How are encore transitions different for men and women?

It's always dangerous to generalize, but here are a few facts about men, women, and encore careers. According to a recent survey, 60 percent of people between the ages of forty-four and seventy who say they are in an encore career are women; 40 percent are men. Of those interested in pursuing encore careers, 58 percent are women and 42 percent are men. So it seems that more women than men are attracted to the idea of moving into meaningful work with social impact—or at least using that language to talk about it. Experts speculate on how women and men differ when going through transitions, and a common observation is that women are more likely than men to join transition groups and create ways to share their process with others. It's also typical for people who are the primary breadwinners of a household—male or female—to have a much harder time with any career change than those who are not supporting families.

CHAPTER 5

Find Your
Encore Number

"You save not to have freedom from work,

but to have freedom to do the work you want to do."

—Marc Freedman

Money is a lot like sex. Everyone wants to know what everyone else is doing, but few people want to share what's happening in their own lives. That said, I've now talked to a lot of people, and there are a few things I can say with certainty.

First, one of the biggest challenges of an encore transition—perhaps even bigger than the emotional side of things—is figuring out how to manage the financial side. Second, although people at every income level find ways to move into an encore career, people who manage well financially have one critical thing in common: They have a good handle on what kind of lifestyle they want and how much money they need to support it.

So let's cut right to the heart of the issue. What will moving into an encore career mean for your finances and your lifestyle?

Let me start with one caveat: This chapter isn't exactly about financial planning—there are lots of good books on that, and you'll find a bunch in the resources section on page 293. This is about how to plan your next phase of work in a way that reflects your values while also taking care of your financial future. And that's as much a matter for your mind as it is for your wallet.

Making Trade-offs

Just as people seeking to retire think about retirement planning, moving into an encore should involve a similar kind of process. There is one significant difference. Retirement planning is all about figuring out how to live off your savings and passive income like Social Security, investments, or pensions and retirement accounts. With an encore you'll likely be able to count on some amount of added income even if it's less than what you earned earlier in your career.

Occasionally, moving into an encore can mean higher earnings and a more secure future. That's how it was for Sally Bingham (see page 8), the stay-at-home mom whose passions for her religious faith and the environment merged in her encore as an ordained priest with an environmental ministry. Now seventy and divorced, Bingham continues to earn a competitive salary as the environmental minister at Grace Episcopal Cathedral and the president of the Regeneration Project. Thanks to her new career, Bingham has been able to stay in the house where she raised her children.

Discussion Prompts
Do you feel like you're financially ready to make an encore transition? • Or do you have a lot of planning to do? • Are you where you want to be in terms of retirement savings? • Do you have a sense of how much income you need in order to be happy and comfortable?

Still, having a life with impact often means more psychic rewards than financial ones. In a word, trade-offs. If you love what you're doing and feel like you're making a difference, can you live a bit lighter and cut unnecessary overhead?

Most people would say that depends. How much lighter? And what's unnecessary? What size trade-off makes sense for you?

Your encore shift may not involve any income shift at all, especially if you continue to work full time. But many people moving into encore careers experience a modest reduction in earnings, either because they're moving from the for-profit sector to a nonprofit or government position, or because they're moving from a full-time job with benefits to a part-time, more flexible arrangement. (People tend to assume that nonprofits pay considerably less than for-profits, but that's not always the case. Large or well-funded nonprofits often pay more than small businesses or other for-profit employers. So don't equate nonprofit

What's Your "Number"?

In his 2006 book, *The Number*, Lee Eisenberg posited that in order to figure out the rest of your life, you need to know how much money you need to sock away to have the security you want and the freedom to do whatever it is that you want to do. Figuring out your "encore number" puts a bit of a twist on that concept. In the new world order—where most of us will be working longer than imagined and few will have the kind of savings that will support us into old age—continuing to make an income will likely be critical. Your encore number is the amount of income you'd like to bring in through your encore work. (This chapter will help you think about how best to calculate it.)

with low-paying.) If you're making this kind of shift, you may find the trade-offs are right for you. You'll save less, do without cable television, bring your lunch, and check your books out of the library. You may even be willing to downsize to a smaller home or move to another city, if that works for you.

I do hear, from time to time, about people who are willing to make bigger sacrifices or throw themselves into dramatically new lifestyles if their encore goals require it. Some are willing (and able) to dip into their savings and work for almost nothing for a cause they care about. For many entrepreneurs I've talked with, the pull to start their own ventures was so strong they were willing to take big financial risks, like going without health insurance or taking on debt. (More on encore entrepreneurs in Chapter 10.)

I'd put myself in the middle category—willing to make medium-sized changes. I left a high-paying legal career to become a journalist and later a nonprofit staffer. I soon realized that I'd likely never return to the earnings level I'd hit by the time I was thirty. Plus, I got divorced from a man with a much higher income and remarried one who, like me, was pursuing a career where money wasn't the main priority. We also both plan to continue working as long as we are physically able—and at forty-six and fifty-two that means at least another two decades.

> **"I went to Afghanistan three times on my own penny. I was nervous about it financially because I have three kids, but each time I made that money back in some way or another."**
>
> —Masha Hamilton, journalist/author/nonprofit founder

The trade-offs are worth it to me. Although I still clock long hours, there's a different feel to it. I value that I get paid to think and question. And my work puts me in constant contact with committed, smart people dedicated to doing work that matters. I like the flexibility and ease of working at home, just a ten-minute walk from my husband's business. No commute for either of us. As they say in the credit card ad, "priceless."

In the end, it's really about knowing what kind of life you want and what kind of trade-offs you're willing to make.

Set Priorities

What kind of trade-offs would you be willing to make in order to move into work that meets your criteria for an ideal encore career? Think about items in your personal budget that you could change. The biggest lifestyle change for most people would be to downsize a home or move to a less expensive city. It's possible that some things that provide you with a lot of satisfaction aren't high ticket at all—like living near friends and family or having a beloved pet. The classic cuts are things such as a latte habit, hair coloring at a salon, or updates to a wardrobe.

What do you need to have, what would you like to have, and what would you be willing to give up if it meant that you could have the kind of work arrangement you want to have?

Three must-haves:

1. _____

2. _____

3. _____

Three like-to-haves:

1. _____

2. _____

3. _____

Three can-give-ups (try to include one big-ticket item that represents a big chunk of your monthly or annual overhead):

1. _____

2. _____

3. _____

Next, think about the different forms of compensation that can come from working. One, of course, is money. Another is a sense of purpose or gratification. Others might be community involvement, a great work environment, a nice social life, flexibility, or stability. As you weigh various encore options, try thinking about money as just one form of compensation. And as you compare your options, look back at prior jobs to see how they stacked up in terms of nonmonetary compensation. A job may have paid well, but how did it score on the other factors? Did you learn a lot? Did you enjoy the lifestyle? Did you feel good about the work you were doing?

As you try to identify these factors, return to Exercise 8 on page 57 and write down the top five things you identified as being important to you in your next stage of work.

1. _____

_____

2. _____

_____

3. _____

_____

4. _____

_____

5. _____

_____

Now tie it all together. Would you be comfortable giving up the three things in your can-give-up list to have one or more of those things on your list of what you want from work? Which one(s)?

_____

_____

Would you go further for anything on that list—meaning, would you give up anything from your like-to-have list to have any of the elements on your what-you-want-from-work list? Which one(s)?

_____

_____

Can You Embrace the New Frugality?

Instead of the twentieth-century model of save-save-save-for-thirty-years-of-retirement, a more sustainable course involves continued earnings and lower costs over a longer period of time. Many of us will live into our eighties and beyond in good health; we should plan on being able to lead full lives, with meaningful work.

Chris Farrell, chief economics correspondent for Minnesota Public Radio, builds a case for this kind of living in his book, _The New Frugality: How to Consume Less, Save More, and Live Better_. Farrell believes the spending spree that got our country into its recent economic mess has caused a backlash, and that more and more people will embrace simpler values and cut consumption. Frugal will become chic—not cheap.

According to Farrell, _frugal_ is downsizing to a home in a college town with an encore-friendly job market, great cultural offerings, and reliable public transportation. _Cheap_ is living in a tiny apartment in a city with an exorbitant cost of living. _Frugal_ is buying fewer but higher-quality possessions, shopping in thrift stores, and organizing swaps with friends. _Cheap_ is buying inexpensive clothes that fall apart after a month.

How can you embrace the new frugality in your own day-to-day life? Can you move to a place that's cheaper to live? Buy a home or car that is more energy efficient? Rent out part of your home? Can you give up any splurges and negotiate better rates on insurance, cell service, Internet, or cable? Can you get by without a car? Can you sell things you don't need on eBay, repair rather than buy new?

For now this all may be completely hypothetical. But going through this exercise could help you clarify what matters to you most as you mull over what's next. So fill this out now, put it aside and, as you get closer to some real possibilities, consider doing the exercise again when the choices before you are real ones.

Make Ends Meet

Thinking about finances is a little like the old saw in weight loss: There are only two ways to move the scale—consume less or move more. Similarly, if you're trying to free up money to help your encore transition, there are only two ways: cut expenses or bring in more income. And just as there are some habits and tricks that make the scale happy, there are some financial habits and tricks that can ease your way into an encore.

Housing provides many options for reducing expenses. Barbara Gomperts (see page 10) and her husband downsized from a single-family home to a smaller condominium and used the proceeds to cover her training as a massage therapist.

Co-living is an option that doesn't necessarily involve downsizing. That's when people choose to move into shared living spaces. It can be as posh as two friends consolidating into a city apartment and a beach house nearby or as budget-oriented as a group of people living roommate-style in an old house in a college town.

Masha Hamilton and David Orr, two journalists, created the financial security they needed for Hamilton to pursue her work as a novelist and nonprofit executive director by turning their Brooklyn brownstone into a bed-and-breakfast. The whole family pitches in to help. On the day I visited, her son and daughter were hustling to get rooms ready for arriving guests.

Friends share responsibilities for dogs and other pets to have the love without the full burden. Artists and others have long mastered the art of paying through bartering. Do you have some skill or possession you're willing to barter in exchange for something you need—say, providing editing assistance, a home-cooked meal, or a basket of vegetables from your garden in exchange for some computer tutoring? You can do this informally with people in your immediate network or with strangers on sites like Craigslist, which has an active bartering section.

Plan, Train, and Save

If you're the planning type, you may want to stay put in your midlife career as long as possible while using your free time to get the training you will need to make a shift down the road, pay off big expenses, and invest in all available benefits programs. If you choose this route, be prepared for a difficult juggle—and a loss of some leisure time, at least for a while.

It's no surprise that fifty-three-year-old Dennis Duquette, a long-time executive for Fidelity Investments, has carefully planned out his financial future. About three years ago, he enrolled in an online master's program at Northwestern University to adapt his experience in communications, marketing, and the nonprofit sector and pave the way for a potential encore in government or public policy down the road. He finished his degree—an M.A. in public policy and administration—in December of 2011 but he's in no rush. He enjoys his work at Fidelity and is taking on other projects as he continues to plan for his next phase of life in "retirement."

Take Time Out, If You Can

Do a cost-benefit analysis. Can you afford to invest in a year or two of school, if the job at the end of the line provides security and solid benefits that will more than refill your savings account or pay off any debt you accrue? If yes, you may just want to be a full-time student.

Celeste Miller (see page 74) is making a lot less money than she used to as a recruiter and consultant, but she loves being an educator. Her job is secure now that she's got tenure, something with no equivalent in the business world. She's even got summers off for long stints of travel. And her finances are stable and well managed. During the two years it took Miller to become certified, she worked with a financial planner and now she's doing a better job of managing her money than she did when she was earning far more.

Before and After

Don't just think about your encore income needs—be sure to plan for your transition, too.

Research by Encore.org and pollsters at Penn Schoen Berland show that 67 percent of those already in encore careers experienced gaps in their personal income during their encore transitions. Of those, nearly 70 percent say they experienced a gap of six months or more; more than 36 percent say their income gap lasted more than two years.

Found money can be a blessing. Terry Ramey, an autoworker in Detroit, paid for his nursing education by using an educational credit he received as part of a buyout from Ford. At forty, he saw it as a chance to reinvent himself for a career that would serve him for the long haul. When Barbara Abramowitz left a thirty-six-year career in nonprofit management, she was able to fund the transition to part-time work from a combination of long-term savings and inheritances that she and her husband received. Today, she divides her time among coaching, psychotherapy, writing, and speaking. When Fred Mandell left a long corporate career at American Express, rather than accept an exit package that included the standard outplacement services, he negotiated to have some funding put aside to pay for a year's worth of sculpting workshops.

> "I didn't expect to be earning a living at this point in my life, let alone a substantial one. I didn't manage my own money until I was fifty-six."
>
> —Sally Bingham, stay-at-home-mother-turned-Episcopal-priest

Generate Income

If you're between jobs and searching for your encore, consider finding a stopgap job that will generate income, even if it doesn't jive with your long-term goals. Some people find work doing something that best uses their marketable skills in order to maximize earnings. Others prefer to do something that leaves them with enough energy to focus on reinventing, even if it means less income. The right job will allow you to support yourself during a transition and sock away some money in case the work you really want to be doing pays less.

Don't be surprised if a stopgap job ends up helping or fueling your transition in some way. Dave Hughes was trying to make a move to the nonprofit world, but after months of searching without success, he took a three-month position at a new Walmart that needed people to help with setup. It was menial work, paying just about minimum wage. When that work ended and he still hadn't found the encore he was looking for, he took another position as a receiving manager, checking on deliveries of time-sensitive food items. Eventually, he landed a job as executive director at Agape House, a Christian mission that provides food, clothing, and shelter for those in need. His two-year detour through Walmart proved useful in his new role. "That job was a

Finding a Stopgap Job

If you're looking for a money gig to help you bridge the transition, first consider work where you have some solid experience, a strong network, and a good reputation.

Another option: look at what you're good at and what people might pay you to do. I brainstormed with Kerry Hannon, AARP's career columnist and the author of *What's Next: Follow Your Passion and Find Your Dream Job*, and came up with a bunch of quick ideas for very small businesses: Are you good with pets? Animal care has all kinds of possibilities. Good with academics? Consider tutoring. If you're a great cook, consider informal catering. I know a personal trainer who has a thriving side business doing stereo installations on cars, something that grew out of a hobby. Hannon knows someone who built a small business out of night driving for seniors who were no longer able to drive in the dark. These kinds of activities require a little entrepreneurial instinct and creativity, but they could set you up with an extra stream of income that you'll always be able to fall back on when you need it.

Another approach is to look at trends and from there think about opportunities. Though I'm not a big fan of relying exclusively on job sites, they are an excellent way to see what fields have opportunities. We all know that health care is a growth industry, but if you want to know where the jobs are in health care, checking out sites like VCN.org, Monster.com, Indeed.com, and CareerBuilder .com will help you figure that out.

There is a new breed of firms that specialize in part-time and flexible work

godsend," he told me. "I learned so much about warehouse management, and I met all these food distributors that can now be helpful to Agape House."

At the very least, you want to find something that brings in some income while leaving you energy and time to develop your encore.

Work Your Slashes

Working two jobs (chef/tutor) is a common encore model, particularly when one is for the money and the other is to fulfill your desire to give back. This can be a long-term or transitional arrangement. The most common slash model is to continue doing work that you are established in and that leaves you with the energy and time to focus on something new.

Molly McDonald, a mother of five, was inspired to start the Pink Fund, a nonprofit that helps women with cancer pay the bills. She started the organization soon after her own diagnosis, supporting herself by taking on freelance arrangements that could also be helpful: RatRaceRebellion.com, SnagaJob.com, On-Ramps.com (for part-time, flexible, and telecommuting professional assignments), HireMyMom.com, Flexjobs.com, Hourly .com, and UrbanInterns.com.

Some sites, like HireMyMom, cater to the growing number of women who are looking for home-based opportunities they can do while taking time out to raise children. Although they are targeting moms, most won't rule out working with others. Some of these sites are regional (such as NeedlestackJobs.WordPress.com, which serves Ohio) so you'll need to check carefully to see that your area is served.

Also check to see if there is a fee to post a profile because some of these sites require memberships. Before paying a fee for any job site, do some research online; if the site is reputable, you should be able to find some online reviews that will give you an idea of how satisfied users are and whether it will help you find the kind of opportunities you're looking for.

Of course, don't forget the obvious. Check the local paper, and look around you. Taking a retail job or fill-in positions during a holiday or seasonal rush could be just the thing to carry you over for a little while, and you could meet some useful contacts or pick up some unexpected skills even in a job that has nothing to do with your ultimate goal. Consider visiting a job fair if there's one in your area—they are particularly useful for retail jobs. Go to NationalCareerFairs.com to find job fairs near where you live.

writing and marketing consulting projects. "It so empowered me that I forgot about my own problems," McDonald said. She hopes to raise enough money to pay herself a salary and dedicate her full-time energies to the job. But until that happens, the Pink Fund is a side venture. This model also works well for people who don't see any income possibilities in their encore work or who don't want to burden themselves with finding a way to generate income in cause-related work.

Catalino Tapia, a Mexican immigrant who built up a business as a gardener, pursued his encore with no plan to abandon his primary work in the near term. He started the Bay Area Gardeners Foundation, a nonprofit that provides college scholarships to children of immigrants. He doesn't pay himself a salary at the foundation. Instead he runs his gardening business while working on the foundation evenings and weekends. He plans to dedicate himself full time to the nonprofit when he is able to retire.

Take Advantage of Tax Breaks, School Loans

If you are heading back to school, you may not be able to get your costs covered up front, but you may qualify for a school loan, school loan forgiveness after a period of work, or a tax break. The Education for Public Service Act reduces monthly payments on federal student loans for graduates who work in public safety, public health, education, social work, or the nonprofit sector. The law provides complete loan forgiveness for graduates who work full time for ten years in public service.

There is also a variety of tax incentives for education. Some people finance their return to school with after-tax 529 college savings accounts that were intended for younger family members but have no age restrictions. The accounts allow investments to be withdrawn tax-free, as long as the proceeds are spent on higher education.

Depending on your income, you may be able to take advantage of tax deductions for education expenses and loan interest. You may also qualify for a tax credit reducing the amount of tax you have to pay (as opposed to deductions, which reduce your taxable income). The Lifetime Learning Credit gives tax credits of up to $2,000 per year for courses to acquire or improve job skills. And the American Opportunity Tax Credit (also called the Hope Scholarship Tax Credit) is worth up to $2,500 toward the cost of qualified tuition and related expenses.

IRS Publication 970 has full details on all of these incentives. (Find it on irs.gov.) Keep in mind that the IRS doesn't allow "double-dipping," which means that you can't use both the deduction and one of these tax credits. Of course, speak to an accountant, if you can afford one.

You can also look into a low-interest Stafford loan, the main federal loan for students, which has a fixed interest rate of 6.8 percent. If you're working on an undergraduate degree, you may qualify for a Pell Grant, a federal grant of up to $5,350 a year available for those who demonstrate financial need. (For more on how to finance your education, see page 206.)

Apply for Scholarships or Grants

One of the benefits of being a student, being out of work, or working in the nonprofit or public sectors is that you can occasionally tap scholarships or breaks on tuition and other fees. So it's always wise to ask. RozeLyn Beck discovered this when she transitioned from a long career in insurance to a position with the YWCA in Hartford, Connecticut. One of Beck's greatest pleasures is the time she spends volunteering at hospitals and other places with her therapy dog, Cadbury. When Cadbury failed a certification training and needed to take it again, Beck considered just dropping it as she didn't want to incur the costs. But she discovered a scholarship for the training, applied, and got it. This time, Cadbury passed and Beck was able to get back involved in an activity that means a lot to her. "It was a humbling experience," she said. "I'd never have taken the scholarship if I didn't need it, and I wasn't going to let my pride get in the way."

Other Ways to Fund an Encore

Although most financial experts would advise against touching retirement assets before retirement, withdrawing some money as an investment in your future earning power might be a smart move. Of course, make sure that you understand any penalties for early withdrawals. (If you have a Roth IRA, you may be in a good position; contributions can be withdrawn without penalty since they are made with after-tax money.)

You could also consider doing a paid internship; a national service program like VISTA, Peace Corps, or Americorps; or a fellowship that includes a stipend or educational credit. I discuss these options in more detail in Chapter 8.

If you are over fifty-five, living close to the poverty level, and/or unemployed, you might qualify for government assistance. Benefits vary by state and some will even offer financial assistance for retraining or getting a minimum wage job in a community organization. You can learn more about options in your area at Benefits .gov, and your local One-Stop Career Center (find a location at careeronestop .org). The AARP Foundation website (aarp.org/aarp-foundation/) is another great resource to explore benefits (look for the Benefits QuickLink or visit Benefitscheckup.org).

Work from Home
If you're considering working from home to bring in extra cash, visit WomenForHire.com/ work_from_home/ where career expert Tori Johnson provides excellent ideas and resources as well as advice on avoiding scams. Though her company is focused on women, her advice is universal.

Common Financial Missteps

One of the most common mistakes people make is not starting to save early enough. Having some money you can tap into to pay for retraining or to support a period of time off is extremely helpful. Though it's not essential, building up a cash reserve can relieve some of the financial pressure of any career transition.

For those who don't have savings, it's crucial to ferret out ways to get financial assistance through stipends, scholarships, and grants to help you retrain.

Fred Mandell, a financial-adviser-turned-author, coach, and encore advocate, said he's seen many people stumble in the following ways:

- Taking Social Security too soon (see below).

- Failing to take into account those nonroutine events that require cash—replacing that furnace or hot water heater, buying a new car.

- Failing to plan for health care costs.

- Mismanaging 401(k) rollovers when leaving a job. (When you remove money from a 401(k), you have sixty days to roll it over into another plan without being taxed. Far too often, people miss that sixty-day deadline and suffer tax consequences that could have been avoided.)

- Investing in bonds under the assumption that you can get all your money out at any time. If you sell the bond before it matures, you may get less than you put into it.

- Making investment decisions based on every "great tip" you read or hear about rather than following a dull but sensible long-term approach.

Or you could just wait—until the kids are out of college, the mortgage is paid off, you're out of debt, or some other big financial burden is lifted. You could also consider abandoning life insurance as you age.

The Benefits of Working Longer

If you're nearing Social Security age, an encore career can help you to defer collecting so that when you do, you'll earn at a higher rate. Instead of dipping into savings or Social Security, the idea is to live off of your encore income until you can no longer work or choose to retire.

Mark Miller, a journalist and author who specializes in retirement and aging, explained it to me this way: "Every year that you work longer and don't file for Social Security translates into higher annual benefits when you eventually do file. Also, it means fewer years of drawing down your savings—and allowing savings more time to grow. Finally, it can mean more years of contributing to a retirement account."

The most crucial Social Security decision anyone can make is when to enroll. This can add up to hundreds of thousands of dollars, assuming you or your spouse lives many years beyond the break-even age. The website of the Social Security Administration has a comprehensive section explaining how your monthly payment will vary based on how old you are when you first elect to receive benefits. (Go to "Estimate your retirement benefits" at ssa.gov.) And if you want to get a quick look at how Social Security will work together with the rest of your financial inputs, have a look at AARP's retirement calculator (aarp.org/work/retirement-planning/retirement_calculator/).

If you plan to collect Social Security benefits before sixty-six or your NRA (your "normal retirement age," which varies depending on what year you were born) and you're still working, some of your benefits may be withheld. If you make more than a certain amount—$14,640 in 2012—$1 will be deducted from your benefit payment for every $2 you earn above that amount. This won't affect your lifetime benefits, though, because the withheld dollars are added to your benefits after you reach normal retirement age.

It's also important to understand Social Security's spousal and survivor benefits. These are incredibly important features of Social Security that can create powerful amplifying effects that can boost lifetime benefits. Visit Mark Miller's website retirementrevised.com for excellent resources on Social Security planning.

Wealth and Happiness

Having an understanding of the relationship between money and happiness is a useful backdrop for thinking about what trade-offs you're willing to make. I'm somewhat of a positive psychology junkie, so I tend to keep up with the latest research on what makes people happy. A favorite of mine is Gretchen Rubin's bestselling book *The Happiness Project*. Rubin's mantras—all based on research—have helped me considerably as I've thought about my own decisions about money.

Here are a few of the guiding principles that Rubin and others who have studied positive psychology tend to agree on.

First, doing good and giving of oneself are widely known to make you feel good; it's why we're often told that the best cure for a case of the blues is to go out and help someone. Volunteering and helping others contribute to what father-and-son psychologists Ed Diener and Robert Biswas-Diener call psychological wealth, which includes "life satisfaction, the feeling that life is full of meaning, a sense of engagement in interesting activities, the pursuit of important goals, the experience of positive emotional feelings, and a sense of spirituality that connects people to things larger than themselves." In addition, continuing to work, especially if it's in a role that brings you satisfaction rather than a feeling of oppression, has been tied to positive health outcomes. Put those things together, and it's easy to see why organizing your life around meaningful work, whether paid or unpaid, can provide a big happiness boost.

Second, experiences tend to provide more lasting happiness than the acquisition of material possessions. That's because you get the experience three times—in the anticipation of it, in the actual doing of it, and then through the memory of it. On the other hand, with the acquisition of stuff, you run into a phenomenon called the *hedonic treadmill,* which means we quickly adjust to things that once felt novel, so basically the happiness uptick you get from your flat-screen television wears off as you get used to it. Exceptions to this rule, as Rubin says, are things like a tent, skis, a camera, or a dining room table that lets you host dinners with people you love. These are all possessions that assist in the creation of experiences and contribute a lot to our happiness.

There's evidence that the hedonic treadmill works in the reverse direction as well. Studies on paraplegics and others who report similar happiness levels before and after a drastically changed situation show that we can adjust to just about anything. So, if you're considering trading some material goodies for work that gives you a deeper sense of meaning in your life, chances are you will adjust over time.

Third, relative wealth and social status may contribute more to happiness levels than absolute wealth. This explains why people who give up higher-paying work but surround themselves with others in similar situations can get used to having less to spend. It's easier to keep up with the

Encore Planning, Not Retirement Planning

Planning for your encore can look a lot like planning for retirement. These hypotheticals won't be relevant for everyone, but they give you a good sense of how people run the numbers.

• The Smiths, both sixty, intend to retire at sixty-six. They are earning a combined total of $75,000, with $100,000 in investable assets and $250,000 of equity in their home. They can expect Social Security, but no traditional pension. Together, they need to make $30,000 in earned income to be able to maintain their lifestyle.

For the Smiths, the half-dozen years before they leave their peak-earning careers can be a time to prepare for their satisfying, purposeful encores that will fit with their vision of their next stage.

• The Joneses are also turning sixty this year, and they intend to retire at sixty-two. They are earning a combined total of $75,000, with $100,000 in investable assets and $250,000 of equity in their home. They can expect lower Social Security benefits because they claimed early, and they'll have less time to accumulate additional preretirement savings.

For the Joneses, even a $30,000 encore career won't allow them to maintain their lifestyle—but it will help! Along with the psychic and social rewards, it will make it feasible for them to sustainably downshift and better manage their income, for example, by maximizing their Social Security benefits.

• Down the block, the Browns, also sixty, have roughly the same income and assets as the Smiths and the Joneses. But the Browns plan to work till they're seventy. They'll maximize their Social Security, accumulate additional savings before they retire and, actuarially speaking, not have to cover as many years of post-retirement expenses. As a result, they won't have to earn continued income at all after they retire from their peak-earning careers.

For the Browns, switching to an essentially full-time, ten-year encore career is an appealing option, and investing time and money in a one-year results-based transition program is a solid proposition.

Smiths when the Smiths take their vacations camping in national parks rather than jetting off to St. Barts for the weekend.

Less clear is the question of whether increasing levels of income or wealth make people happier. A widely cited 2010 study from Princeton University found that one measure of happiness—people's broad evaluations of their lives—tends to increase with increasing wealth. That said, it found that day-to-day reports of emotional well-being topped off after earnings above $75,000. It's kind of confusing to parse out the difference between these two concepts, but here's the takeaway from the researchers: Higher income doesn't necessarily make one happier, but it might bring you a life that you think is better.

More interesting to me than how much money a person needs to be happy—which seems awfully hard to measure—is research showing that

Navigating the Minefield of Health Insurance

What's the one thing keeping many people in a job they're ready to leave? Good health insurance. It's one of the reasons there is a spike in self-employment when people hit sixty-five and are eligible for Medicare.

Moving into a full-time encore job that comes with health benefits could be an unexpected financial perk of doing work that matters. But what are your options if your plan involves starting your own venture, working part time, or working for an organization that doesn't provide health benefits?

- Hold on to your job. Work as long as possible while building your encore on the side. (Or, find a stopgap job. See page 94.)

- Reduce your hours. Work the minimum required to maintain your employer's health insurance. (See page 148 for why employers want to keep older workers and tips on how to negotiate a reduced or flexible schedule while still keeping your health benefits.)

- Join a group plan. You may be able to find coverage through a trade association, community group, or professional association. (As a writer, for years I got a very reasonable health insurance plan through a writer's trade group I belonged to.)

- Use COBRA coverage. Under federal law, employers are required to offer healthcare coverage to an employee and that employee's dependents for eighteen months after a job ends. This may not be cheap, but it can be a good transitional option. Note: Federal COBRA only applies to employers with more than 20 employees, so if you work for a small business, you'll need to see if your state has similar COBRA coverage. Also, keep in mind that if you have money in a Health Savings Account (or HSA), that can be used to pay for COBRA premiums.

- Buy a private policy. These can be expensive, especially if you're over sixty. One way to keep costs down is to consider a low premium/high deductible plan. You'll pay out of pocket for routine expenses, but you'll be covered in case you have a very big hit like surgery or hospitalization. Make sure to read the fine print so that you understand the coverage caps (e.g., lifetime limits on certain categories) and any exclusions (e.g., aspiring to a lifestyle that is out of your financial reach is a certain path to *un*happiness. When you think about taking a pay cut, either in the short-term or for the long haul, the key is figuring out whether living at your new income level will make it possible for you to lead the life you want to lead or whether you will continually be feeling the pinch of sacrifices you have made.

preexisting or certain types of conditions). If you have a high deductible plan, consider setting up a Health Savings Account (HSA), which allows you to put aside tax-free money to pay for uncovered medical expenses. Starting in 2014, assuming the Affordable Care Act survives legal challenges, Health Care Exchanges will arrive on the scene. These exchanges will be the main vehicle for individuals to shop for insurance. Many states will be creating their own exchanges; residents of states that don't will be able to shop in a default federal exchange.

- Check out your state's high-risk pool. If you have a preexisting condition (and who doesn't at this point) and have been denied insurance for that reason, and you've been uninsured for at least six months, you may be eligible for insurance under the Pre-Existing Condition Insurance Plan, a new program available under the Affordable Care Act. You can apply at HealthCare.gov.

- Take turns. If you're married or have a domestic partner, take turns with your partner on who takes the job with health benefits.

- Check out veterans' benefits. Tricare (tricare.mil) has options for retired military personnel under sixty-five.

- Explore Healthcare.gov. This is a site created by the federal government in 2010 to remove some of the mystery around shopping for health insurance. The site is an easy-to-use starting point for assessing options given your family situation, your health, and where you live. In a matter of minutes you can input a few details and see a variety of plans that you can narrow down by premiums, deductibles, doctor choice, and other criteria. Because the site is maintained by the government, there's no advertising and no favoritism. It also means you're seeing all the options available, which can be overwhelming.

- Check out the Freelancers Union (freelancersunion.org). This union offers health insurance plans for independent workers in a growing number of states.

- Take good care of your health. The best way to keep your health care costs down and preserve your energy for your encore career is to eat well and exercise.

Which brings me to an idea touted by Laura Vanderkam in her recent book, *All the Money in the World*. Vanderkam approached the money-happiness connection as an investigative journalist rather than as a scientific researcher and, though she didn't do any double-blind studies, her reporting led her to some compelling conclusions. She argued persuasively that rather than cutting out the small pleasures (such as the proverbial latte), you'd be better lopping off some part of a major expense like housing. Her reasoning is that if you can successfully cut your housing expense, you'll be making a one-time mental adjustment. But if you focus on constantly clipping coupons and denying yourself lattes, you'll be setting yourself up for a lifetime of daily sacrifices. "A one-time adjustment might be easier than constant self-discipline," she told me. Seems worth thinking about if there's a way to downsize your housing or give up your car that you don't think would make you feel like you're sacrificing day to day.

Finally, Vanderkam argues that rather than focusing on constantly cutting costs, more people should be thinking about where they can increase their income. Clearly, figuring out how to earn a living from doing work that you love would fit into that way of thinking.

Your Bottom Line

By now you should be ready to figure out your encore number—the ideal income you'd like to generate in your encore to fulfill the financial obligations you have and lead the life you want to live.

First, you'll need to figure out your expenses, including any debt you have. You can use the budget worksheets provided on pages 280–282 or use a site like Mint.com.

Second, get a handle on what sources of income you have in addition to what you'll earn in your encore work. Do you have investments or real estate that provides income? If you're close to collecting Social Security or a pension, will that be part of the mix? The budget should help here as well. You may also want to complete the income statement (a financial statement reflecting both your income and expenses) provided on page 280 to give you a more complete picture of where you are financially.

Third, ask yourself whether you are interested or willing to reduce your expenses to dedicate your time to work that pays less than you wanted. This is where the trade-off exercise comes in. You may not have to make any cuts, but knowing what you're willing to do will tell you what kind of flexibility you have to work part-time, take on an unpaid or low-paid role, even take a gap year or time off to retrain.

Finally, consider talking to a financial planner so that you can get an objective view of your financial situation and create a plan to accomplish your goals. (Before talking to a financial planner, try to run the numbers on your own, so that you'll be using a planner to verify your own results.) A financial planner will have access to software that allows you to see the results of various scenarios, such as what your situation will look like with different investment choices, or what it will look like if you make more or less money, if you save more or less, and if you work full time or part time for two, five, or ten more years. Even if you don't plan to work with a financial planner on an ongoing basis, you might get a lot out of one or two meetings where you do an audit of your finances and come up with a basic plan.

> **"The additional income has enabled me to reinvest rather than spend the required minimum withdrawal from my IRA."**
>
> –Don Tarbutton, hospice chaplain

If you are only looking for advice rather than someone to actually manage your money, you'll want to use a certified financial planner (CFP) who will be able to give you advice, usually for an hourly fee. (The national average, according to the Bureau of Labor Statistics, is $44.) The CFP designation is an instant sign of credibility, so focus on people who have that credential.

FAQs

I'm concerned about moving from a job with a regular paycheck to a life where my income may fluctuate over time. What are the best ways to manage an erratic income?

This is where good planning comes in. I spoke to freelancing guru Michelle Goodman, who offered these tips:

- Do whatever you need to do to have at least several months of savings. Make sure one late check isn't going to make or break you.

Working with a Financial Planner

If you've never worked with a financial planner, here are a few things to think about.

• Start with referrals from trusted friends or professionals who have worked with financial planners. Lawyers and CPAs are good people to ask. If you have no one to ask or want to find someone on your own, you can search cold at these organizations where you can find CFPs by zip code: NAPFA.org (National Association of Personal Financial Advisors); FPAnet .org (Financial Planning Association); and GarrettPlanningNetwork.com (which has a searchable network of planners who charge by the hour).

• Plan to interview a few people before you settle on someone. Some planners strictly focus on tax planning or insurance, so make sure that the planner you use has experience in helping people come up with a financial plan for the future and running through various financial scenarios. Someone familiar with retirement planning would likely be able to give you the right kind of perspective, because they are accustomed to helping people think about planning for the future and moving into periods of potentially lower income.

• If you're hiring someone without a referral, do some research on the person's background. Check to see who administers the planner's credentials and verify that those credentials are current. You can check on discipline records for CFPs at cfp.net/learn/disciplineactions.asp.

• Make sure you understand the fee structure of any arrangement you enter into. Although you may have said you are just looking for some planning, certified financial planners get paid in a few ways. If the planner also ends up working with you on investments, he may charge a fee that is a percentage of your invested assets or take commissions from products he sells. Financial planners who get paid on commission are making money from the financial products you buy if you invest with them, so keep in mind that they may not be objective about your investment strategy. If you're just looking for a one-time assessment, your best bet is to work with someone for an hourly rate; see if you can negotiate that in advance.

• As with any professional, find someone who makes you feel comfortable. Many planners will offer free initial consultations.

If you want to play with various scenarios on your own, try FireCalc.com. Again, putting together your budget, balance sheet, and income statement beforehand will make this tool easier to use.

- When you're flush, make sure to pay any big bills.
- Take the time to understand contracts and to make sure that you are covering yourself by asking for the right amount of money. Don't forget to ask for reimbursement for expenses.
- When taking on a big assignment, invoice for a percentage (say, 25 percent) up front; then invoice again at various milestones during the project. This way, money comes in on a regular schedule.
- Invoice as soon as you are able to under your agreements and don't be shy about asking when you haven't received a check in a timely manner. Often your contact isn't the person in charge of cutting checks, so make sure to know who that person is and how to get in touch with him or her.

You talk a lot about cutting expenses in this chapter. What about those who can't do anything about their housing costs because they've either borrowed too much against their homes or their home's value has disappeared?

That's a tough situation. Many of those who are underwater have thought about just walking away from mortgage payments. "There's no easy way out without taking a big bath," financial journalist Chris Farrell told me, "and we don't know how long the bad times will last." That said, the one thing you have in this situation is a home. So think about whether there are any ways you can use your home to your advantage. Do you have grown kids or parents you want to take in? Can they contribute to living expenses? Could you rent out part of the space? Could you start a business out of your home or invite others to cowork with you, charging a small fee for the space?

Can I support myself on a nonprofit or government salary?

Nonprofit and public sector salaries are usually lower than salaries for comparable roles in the private sector, but pay varies dramatically depending on the type of organization, geography, and role. Nonprofit headhunter Laura Gassner Otting told me, "The pay is typically higher the further away you get from the cause, meaning the people, animals, or environment your work touches. So frontline jobs where you are actually serving people or working in the field will likely pay less than management roles in an organization." The type of organization will also dictate the pay. "Hospitals, universities, think tanks, and foundations tend to pay more than direct service or advocacy organizations," Gassner Otting said.

What if I have a lot of debt?

You're not alone. Millions of people are approaching retirement or considering encore careers while still paying off debt from mortgages, school loans (theirs and their children's), home and line-of-credit refinances, and credit cards.

If you've got an extreme amount of debt, you might be looking at bankruptcy, which is way beyond the scope of this book. If you're in that camp, contact your local or state bar association, which should be able to connect you to a lawyer for some pro bono (free!) legal advice.

Assuming you've got a reasonable amount of debt, you can check free online tools (such as the one at bankrate.com) to determine how long it will take to pay it off. One rule of thumb: If you double your monthly payments on most types of debt, you will cut the time in half.

There are two schools of thought on how to tackle debt. One approach is to pay down the debt with the highest interest rate first and continue to pay the minimums on others, if you can. When that debt is finished, go after the next highest rate. And so on. Using this method minimizes interest payments.

The other option is to list your debts by size and then pay off the smallest first, proceeding until you've reached the biggest one. This method will have you paying more interest, but you might get a psychological benefit from knocking off one debt at a time.

While you're getting your debt to a manageable place, you might not be in a good position to make a career change, particularly if it requires a reduction in income. This is an ideal time to pare down, said financial journalist and author Chris Farrell. "Get rid of clutter, get rid of stuff, transform some things you no longer want or need into cash and put that money—however trivial— toward debt." If moving to a lower salary is going to be part of your encore plan, getting comfortable with less will be an important part of your process.

Experts seem to agree that the only way to get out of debt is to stop accumulating it. Personal finance expert Manisha Thakor calls it "a fiscal fast" and recommends cutting up credit cards and swearing off new debt.

If there's one thing I should focus on first, what would it be?

Debt. It's very hard to move forward in life if you are weighed down by debt. Spending the time to eliminate debt and recalibrating your life so that you can live comfortably without taking on new debt will give you the freedom to explore what you want to do next.

Is it possible to see your savings grow significantly if you're starting in your fifties, rather than your twenties?

"To some extent, there is no difference," Farrell told me. "True, the person in his twenties or thirties has more time. However, psychologically you have a better reason to save in your forties or fifties. With less time ahead of you, you'll have to try to save more. But even if you can't, in those years you are still young." Whenever you start, you can see a nice buildup in savings after ten years. And by midlife, you have nonfinancial assets, too, such as a better sense of how to use the money you have. Having a cash cushion will give you the freedom to explore new things and indulge your curiosities. Most of personal finance is developing good habits, said Farrell. "The trick is to get started, worry less about time, and make it as automatic as possible."

If I have a choice to save for my own retirement or save for sending kids to college, what should I do?

It's entirely possible that you'll be thinking about paying for your own education and retraining at just the same time you're thinking about how to help your children with theirs. Most financial advisers caution against funding your children's education in favor of saving for retirement. Manisha Thakor, an expert on personal finance for women, explained it to me this way: "If you can afford only one, always save for your retirement before kids. The reason is that you have no other option for your retirement savings. Kids can take out student loans. They can live at home, work to save money, or extend how long school takes," she said. "But if you lose your job and can't get more work, you'll need that money." Basically, you can get a scholarship or grant to go to college, but you can't get one for retirement. "If you choose to fund your children's education rather than saving for retirement, what you've basically done is put the financial burden of your retirement or your eldercare onto your kids," she said.

We've all heard that women need to set aside more money for retirement than men. Is that true—and why?

Yes, it's true. A few factors come into play here. The simplest is that women tend to live, on average, about five years longer than men. And the expenses of caring for a partner in later years can eat up a lot of savings. For couples, this often means that the survivor (often a woman) is left with less money after paying the expenses of caring for an ill spouse.

The situation is also changing as men suffer the effects of the current recession, which many experts say has hit men harder than women.

Then there is the earnings gap—women still only earn, on average, 77 percent of what men earn. Women also spend, on average, eleven more years out of the paid workforce than men. Of course, all of this changes for women who haven't had children, a group that now constitutes about 40 percent of women over the age of forty.

Manisha Thakor calls this the 77/11 effect. Here's how she explained it: Let's assume women earn 77 cents on the dollar and spend an average of eleven more years than men out of the workforce. If you take two individuals starting right out of school at age twenty-five, a guy who earns $50,000 and saves 10 percent a year ($5,000) until he is sixty-five will have about $1,000,000. Given the 77/11 effect, a woman at age twenty-five who earns $38,500 and saves 10 percent each year, then spends eleven years out of the paid workforce, goes back, and still saves at the same salary and pay rate, will have $500,000. Of course, this is less true for women without kids or for those who haven't taken time out of the workplace. But either way, after you add in the longevity issue, women still need to save more.

Any advice for couples trying to figure out how two people can coordinate reductions in income and the costs of retraining?

One way to do this is to take turns. Taking turns on who has the job that provides health insurance, for example, can be a good way to allow one person to move into an encore without concern about those expenses.

This is another good reason to spend a few hours with a certified financial planner who can give you and your partner's financial situation a holistic look and help you review different scenarios.

I can't afford to not be working. What are your thoughts about temping as a means to discover what's next? Or about taking a job that doesn't interest me at all but pays pretty well?

Both of these are excellent strategies if you need to earn money while you're in transition. Having a job that isn't too taxing can also be a way to free your mental energy to do the planning, research, and networking that will help you move forward.

CHAPTER 6

Networking: It's Not a Dirty Word

"We are caught in an inescapable network of mutuality, tied in a single garment of destiny. Whatever affects one directly, affects all indirectly."

—MARTIN LUTHER KING JR.

A fter being laid off from his job as a real estate project manager, David Buck finally had a moment to think. He was forty-six. Most of the major pieces of his life were in place—he had a solid marriage, two children, a home in Minneapolis. But when it came to finding new work, he couldn't get excited about returning to real estate. "The world already has too many buildings," he remembers telling his wife while visiting Chicago. "Why create more?"

In his quest to discover a new path—journaling, reading lots of books, meeting with his minister and friends—Buck zeroed in on his interest in older adults, but that's about as far as he got. On a lark, he called Warren Wolfe, a reporter at the *Minneapolis Star Tribune* who covered issues relating to aging.

"I just called him out of the blue," Buck said. "I told him I was interested in working with older adults and wanted to learn about what was going on in the community." Wolfe spent an hour on the phone with Buck, giving him the lowdown on everything relating to aging issues in the Twin Cities, along with the names of all the key players.

One of the people Wolfe suggested Buck call was Jan Hively, then seventy-five, who had created the Vital Aging Network, a positive aging group affiliated with the University of Minnesota. Hively agreed to meet with Buck, and when his designated half hour came to an end and her next meeting was to start, she said something to Buck that stayed with him: "You're no different than 76 million other baby boomers who are at a new stage, looking for meaningful work. What we need here in the Twin Cities is a community to help people through this transition." Buck was immediately attracted to the idea. "It was like a little diamond that fell out of her pocket at the end of the conversation," he said.

Discussion Prompts
What's your natural style of connecting with others? • Do you prefer to get together in small groups or one-on-one or do you enjoy parties and other social outings? • What kinds of groups do you belong to? • Are you getting enough out of them or might it be time to shake things up and start connecting with some new communities?

After that meeting, Buck went up to a family cabin and started thinking about creating a new organization. About a month later, he asked Hively to get involved. "She meets a lot of people with ideas, but she was impressed," he said. Before long, the two were working on a business plan that ultimately led to SHiFT, a Minneapolis-based network for "people in midlife transitions who seek greater meaning in life and work." The two co-led the group for five years.

I'm taken with this part of Buck's story because it shows that meeting and clicking with the right people can be crucial for transitioning into new worlds. Buck's idea to call a newspaper reporter to ask for contacts was a straightforward and simple way to learn more about something that interested him.

People aren't just sources for ideas or sounding boards, they are also links to other communities, organizations—and opportunities. Connecting yourself to new webs of ideas, people, and organizations is fundamental, not just for moving into a new stage of work but also for ensuring that you're effective in your new role when you get there. Expanding your circle also helps you find support along the way from like-minded folks who understand what you're going through and from those who can help you get there.

Yes, we're inching over to that dreaded, cringe-inducing word: networking. It's okay to hate the word—and, whatever you do, please don't say to someone, "I want to network with you." That says instantly that you don't get it. Instead, if you approach people with genuine interest and curiosity and are open about what you want to do with your life, you will likely find that good things happen.

If you're resistant to networking, don't feel authentic doing it, or just don't think you're good at it, read on: I hope to give you some new ways to think about it. If at any point you think, "I could never do that," move on and see if something else feels more comfortable for you. The best connections happen when people are relating in a natural way. If you could never make a cold call, for example, try one of the other approaches.

If your problem with networking is that it makes you feel like the focus is too much on you and your needs, it's time for some reframing. Think of networking as a way to increase your capacity to give, not as a way to get others to do you a favor. You're looking to move into a position where you can have some positive impact on the world, not where you can make the most money or have the biggest corner office. Isn't it worth it to create new relationships or rely on old ones if they can help you to do something worthwhile?

People who care passionately about the work they're doing are often open to helping others. Often, but not always. People doing good work and getting results can also be very busy, and they may not always be accessible or receptive. But you can improve your chances of having good results by making sure that you're smart about how you make and maintain connections.

First, Know Your Story

One of the hardest parts of reaching out to your network is knowing what to say. If you've left your prior identity, who are you? Do you hold on to your old job title as long as possible ("I've just left a job as . . . ")? Or do you talk about where you're going ("I'm moving into a career in . . . ")? Do you tell people you've retired if, in fact, you're looking to find another job? Does it feel right to say that you're looking for your encore career? How do you talk about a layoff? Depending on the situation, you'll tinker with the details. But thinking in advance of a few ways to present yourself can make life easier.

David Buck needed a quick story about himself when he made that call to the reporter. When I asked him what he said, he couldn't remember verbatim but said it went something like this: "Hi, David Buck here. I'm hoping to get a few minutes of your time. I'm thinking of a career transition, am interested in working with older adults, and was hoping you could tell me a bit about what's going on here in the Twin Cities and who the major players are." For his purposes, brevity was key, and he didn't need to focus too much on his background. All he had to do was say enough to get someone's attention and sound reasonably sane. In other instances, it might have been helpful to talk about one's professional background or relevant work experience.

Think about how you'd introduce yourself if you're trying to make a quick introduction on the phone. What would you do if you had a little more space to explain, such as an in-person meeting at a party or event? And what if you're approaching someone by email? Can you craft a few sentences for each of these situations? See the box (right) for some sample scripts.

Who's in Your Network?

Reaching out to your network can be as simple as sending out an email to a group of friends with a question: "Do you know people who have gone back to school after fifty who'd be willing to talk to me?" Or writing a status update on your Facebook page saying, "Looking for a volunteer opportunity this weekend. Any suggestions?"

Networking doesn't mean contacting everyone you know. When Dale Peterson was downsized from his private practice architecture job, he made a handful of calls to people he had worked with on projects throughout the years. Those calls led him to his new job at a city agency. "It wasn't about volume," he explained. "It was about calling the right people."

If you're going to be strategic, you first have to take inventory. Think about the various strands of your life—friends, extended family, work,

"Hello, my name is . . ."

Here are some quick, effective ways to introduce yourself.

Brief exchange at an event.

Hi, I'm Linda, nice to meet you. I'm looking into working overseas, helping expand access to health care. It's so great to be in a room full of people all doing good work in far-flung locations. What are you focusing on these days?

Networking call to a cold contact and getting a receptionist.

Hi, I'm Bob Schultz, a former journalist trying to move into education reform. I've been following your organization's work with the school board here and was hoping to set up a call with Pam Jones to see if there's a way I can get involved as a volunteer. What's the best way to do that?

Email to a friend of a friend.

To: Mary Smith

From: Jim White

Re: Referred by Jane Black

Hi, I'm Jim White, a friend of Jane Black. I'm in the process of transitioning out of real estate sales and looking at opportunities in land conservation, and Jane thought you might be willing to chat with me for a few minutes to help me get a sense of what's going on in the field in Kansas City.

Would you have time for a brief telephone call in the next week or so? If so, what would be convenient for you?

I'm available most weekday mornings until 11:30 a.m.

By the way, I read that great story in the *Gazette* about your new round of funding. Congratulations.

All the best,

Jim

Forwardable email.

To: Jill Brown

From: Bill Green

Thanks so much for your offer to introduce me to Jenny Kim at Helping Hands. The following is a note you can forward along to her. Let me know if it would be easier if I sent it as a separate email that you could forward without any cutting and pasting.

All the best,

Bill

Dear Jill,

I recall you saying that you know Jenny Kim. As you know, I just finished my ESL certification at Minnow Community College, and I'm trying to meet as many people as possible who work with immigrant communities. Would you mind asking Jenny if she'd be open to a quick conversation as I try to learn more about the needs in our area? I've attached my résumé, and I've included a link to my LinkedIn profile.

Thanks in advance for your time.

Best,

Bill

neighborhood, community, faith, hobbies—and identify people you've clicked with whom you haven't been in touch with in a while. Is your contact list current, or do you need to reconnect with people from prior parts of your life to see what they're doing now? Are there people you really enjoy whom you'd like to see again? Are there others you'd like to meet? If so, spend some time building a list. Scroll through old address books, Rolodexes, and online contact lists. Or you can use LinkedIn or Facebook to automate some of the process for you. (For more on how to use your digital network, see page 126.) This fundamental step will get you thinking about people to talk to about the ideas you're exploring.

Focus on Weak Ties

Social scientists have discovered that when we're looking for new information, or people to help us find a date, a petsitter, or a job, it's not our closest relationships that yield results. Rather it's the weak social ties, the more distant or casual relationships, that deliver. So when looking for new opportunities, it's important to mine those weak ties.

It pays to think intergenerationally. When young people want to make a career move, they scour their parents' LinkedIn connections to get introduced to people in high places. The same idea works in reverse. Find mentors who are just getting their footing in the workplace (they tend to clue you into new technology trends and how young people see a particular field), as well as those with decades of experience (they know who's who in high places and often have the kind of big-picture, long-term perspective that comes from living through many business cycles).

Forming a group around an interest or hobby can also open up a new set of relationships. For nearly twenty years, I've had a monthly book club, and for about ten years, I've cohosted an almost-monthly poker game. Both have turned out to be great sources of comfort and inspiration—and they've connected me to many new networks.

If you don't want to make such a big commitment, plan a one-off activity. If there is something you want to do—go on a particular hike, organize a cooking class, catch a show at a museum—invite a handful of friends and ask each one to bring someone new. You'll have an interesting afternoon or day and will likely add one or two people to your circle.

How to Talk About Being Laid Off

According to career coach Michael Melcher, one of the biggest mistakes made by people who have been laid off is overexplaining. "What you think they want to know isn't really what they want to know," he told me. Melcher encourages clients to control the urge to "lay it all out there." After a layoff you may be feeling wounded or betrayed, and these are not the right feelings to lead with. It's just like dating, said Melcher. "Do you really want to start a date by talking about what went wrong in your past relationship?"

If you feel the need to address a layoff, Melcher suggested what he calls a "yes and . . ." construction. As in, "I really enjoyed my work at XYZ until it ended and now I'm hoping to . . ." or "I moved on and now I'm getting involved in . . ." You can be certain that the person you're meeting has had plenty of exposure to layoffs, either in her own life or through people close to her. So if you have a good perspective on what happened, Melcher said, it will be noticed and appreciated.

Of course, there are moments where you'll have to address a layoff or other difficult part of your career history head-on. This is one where I've had some personal experience. When *The New York Times* cancelled my "Shifting Careers" column and blog, it wasn't exactly a layoff (I was a freelancer, not an employee), but it felt like one. I felt I had to put my story out there because my work had a public element to it—and I wanted to maintain a relationship with readers and sources. So I decided to use my final two posts of the blog to write about it—with the permission of *The Times*. It was risky because I was opening myself up to all kinds of criticism (and there was some of that), but in the end it proved to be a good decision. By being open about what happened, I opened the door to lots of opportunities. And I was approached by someone from Yahoo! to create a new blog for them within weeks of writing my farewell.

(You can read my last post here: nyti.ms/FarewellPost.)

Don't forget about friends of friends. Social networks such as LinkedIn and Facebook are built on the idea of letting people have access to friends of friends. One outcome of this is that the whole "do you know anyone who works in such-and-such-a-field?" game has become far more direct and efficient.

Practice Often

Successful networkers find ways to cultivate their connections on a daily basis. Randal Charlton is a serial entrepreneur who now runs BOOM! The

New Economy, a Detroit-based initiative to help people over fifty change careers, start businesses, and find meaningful volunteer work. When he launched this venture, he made sure to find a place to have his office that would put him in proximity with other organizations working on similar issues. That's the same philosophy he used when he decided to launch a tech venture in a business incubator at Wayne State University, where he would be surrounded by scientists and others working on start-ups. "Even in this connected world, there is no substitute for old-fashioned human interaction on a daily basis," he told me. "I could literally go down the elevator, walk next door, to a coffee shop, or in the car park, and talk to world-class scientists and researchers."

For years, my main exercise has been taking morning power-walks along the Hudson River with a rotating group of other writers. These walks have kept me fit, but they have other benefits. I get fresh air every day (which is important for a writer who works from home). I stay in touch with my friends. And I have a regular way to brainstorm ideas with people I respect.

Stewart Friedman, a management professor at the Wharton School of Business, writes about four-way wins in his book, *Total Leadership*. A classic example is the time-strapped corporate employee who organizes a charity bike ride for her company and involves her partner and children in the ride. In one fell swoop, she's helping a cause that she cares about, spending more time with her family around a shared activity, doing training rides to stay fit, and becoming more of a leader at work. It's multitasking at its best.

One of my favorite methods of "multitasking" is to bring someone every time I go to an event. This has several benefits. If you don't think you'll know anyone, going with another person can ease your anxiety about walking in alone. It can also ensure that even if the event is a bust, you can enjoy spending time with someone who has a shared interest. If you're cultivating new relationships, inviting someone to an event is an ideal way to stay in touch and get to know someone better. You'll also maximize your chances of meeting people because two people can work a room more easily than one. And if you're itching to leave early, you'll have a handy excuse if you say your friend needs to get going. That's a five-way win!

Expand Your Network

Bill Pace traveled the world for twenty-five years as a management consultant. By his mid-fifties he decided he wanted to get involved in one or two well-run nonprofits in the San Francisco Bay area near where he lived. After years on airplanes, the last thing he wanted was more travel.

Pace did some research and identified three areas that interested him: education, community engagement, and economic development. Next, he approached key people in his network and asked for introductions to people who might be helpful to his search. When he had a sizable list, he set up meetings and phone calls. He had two goals for each interview: to learn as much as possible about that person's experience in the sector, and to get a few more names of people to talk to.

In a period of four months, Pace talked to about 120 people, much in the same way he would have done scores of interviews to learn about a new industry for a consulting client. By the end of the process, he had discovered the three organizations among which he now divides his time. He also managed to build an entirely new network in the process.

Get Your Karma Going

One of the most challenging things about moving into something new is the feeling that you are always asking others for help. Flip this dynamic around and get on the giving side of networking.

Get in the habit of asking people about themselves, and don't limit that habit to formal "networking" events. If you're volunteering, taking a class, even waiting in line at the grocery store, you may meet someone who can turn you on to a new idea or possibility.

Look for ways to help others each day. We all get emails asking if we know someone who'd be appropriate for a job or some opportunity; take the time to scan your contacts and forward the message to a carefully chosen list of people in your network. If you've had a great professional experience with a colleague, write a recommendation for her on LinkedIn. If you've read a book that has influenced you, post a short review on Amazon. Get in the habit of closing your day by asking whether there is anyone you can thank for something that happened that day. Then hop onto your email or, better yet, take out a pen and paper and write an old-fashioned note.

Flexing your "giving" muscle will help with that "always asking" feeling.

Pace's 120 conversations might be more than you had in mind, but informational interviews and networking meetings are an essential tool in moving into a new kind of work so you should get comfortable with them if you aren't already.

You can use these meetings to help figure out what you want to do (and what you can rule out); what roles would be good fits for you given your talents, skills, and interests; where the greatest needs and opportunities exist; and what trends are driving any given field. They also come in handy when you're settled into a role but taking on a new challenge or project such as giving a keynote speech, running a big event, or starting a blog. And if the meeting goes well, you'll have a new person in your network who might just lead you to your next position.

By now, you probably have experience meeting people for all kinds of reasons. But there is something about moving into a new kind of work that can bring us right back to feeling like complete novices. That's why having a strategy is key. First, figure out what you're trying to learn; then think about what kinds of people would be ideal to talk to. After you've got a sense of what and who you're looking for, reach out to your network. You can do a group email, post a status update on your Facebook page, or call up ten of your go-to people (think of that personal board of directors) for leads.

A few caveats here: Don't be offended if a friend isn't rushing to introduce you to someone you're dying to meet. There could be many reasons for that. Your friend may not have as close a relationship to the person as you think she has. Your friend also may not be comfortable making introductions to that person because she hasn't replied to similar requests in the past. Keep in mind that not all attempts to connect will succeed.

> **"It wasn't about volume; it was about calling the right people."**
>
> —Dale Peterson, on networking after a layoff

If you're hesitant to approach new people, here are a few ways to make it easier and to improve your chances for good results.

- **Start small.** Practice with people who don't intimidate you or who you already know from another context. There's no need to start with the person who is in the exact role you want to play or who runs the biggest organization doing work that interests you.

• **Be respectful.** Recognize that people giving informational interviews are being generous with their time, so suggest meeting near them
or by phone if that's more convenient. Assume that a meeting will be
brief (a half hour perhaps) unless the person suggests longer. And if
you're out for a coffee or meal, offer to pick up the bill (yep, even if
you're out of work). If you encounter someone who's too busy to talk,
just move on to the next person on your list.

• **Use connections where possible.** Before approaching a person or an
organization you don't know, see if you know someone who can make
an introduction for you. Though it's possible to get good results with a
properly done cold call or email, you will probably get a quicker response
if you can have someone vouch for you, especially if you're reaching out
to someone who is especially busy or of some stature in her field.

   You may know right away if you have a common connection.
If no one comes to mind, one of the easiest ways to find a connection
is by using LinkedIn. (I go into this more on page 129.) Ideally, you'd
like to have someone introduce you in a brief email that includes some
lovely things about you. But if the person you're asking is too busy, ask
if you could use her name when reaching out. When doing this, I like
to write "referred by Sally Smith" in the email subject line. (For sample
language, see the box on page 117.)

• **Know why you're meeting.** When someone offers you an introduction to a good contact, don't rush to set up a meeting before you know
what it is you'd want to talk about. You may still be refining your ideas,
and it may make sense to learn more before initiating contact with a
person who may be more helpful when you have a clearer picture of
what you want.

   An open-ended fishing expedition session can work, as long as
you're clear that's what you're doing. That's exactly what David Buck
did when he first contacted Warren Wolfe and Jan Hively.

• **Study first.** Learn as much as you can about a person you're contacting so that when you do get in touch, you can be as informed as possible.

A quick Internet search will give you some idea of whether the person has a big presence online or if the person's work has been covered by the media. If either of those is true, read enough so that you understand that person's public positions about issues in the field. Ask the introducer about the best way to approach the person—email, by phone, or over coffee or lunch. Knowing that kind of information in advance can make all the difference between a smooth interaction and an awkward one.

> "I was not used to informational interviews. I felt like I was bothering people. But when I approached them, they were unbelievably helpful and gave me ten other people to contact."
>
> —Jeri Janowsky, former college professor

- **Don't assume that your request is a burden.** It's entirely possible that your request to chat might be the highlight of someone's day, if you've caught them at a convenient moment and approached in a way that works. (See page 117 for sample language.)

- **Follow up.** If you said you'd send an article or do some other thing, do it. Remember to send a thank-you email or note. And if you hit it off, find a way to stay in touch.

What's Your "Leave Behind"?

It's a good idea to have something you can leave behind to help people remember you after the meeting. Do you have a business card? If so, does it feel current, or is it too tied to a former identity?

When Ruth Wooden left her post as a nonprofit president, she found herself stewing in that place author Suzanne Braun Levine calls "the fertile void." As she was drifting through the uneasy threshold to a new stage of life, one of the first things she did was "throw away old business cards and order new ones. Just my name, address, telephone number, and email address. No title, no affiliation, no silly description. Just me."

Wooden was ready to move away from her prior identity, but you may find that you're clinging to yours. After all, we live in a society that sizes us up by what we do and who we are.

When you're connecting with people by email, you can add information about yourself by adding a link or attachment—a narrative bio, a LinkedIn

Informational Interview 101

The more specific you can be in a meeting, the better. Here are some questions you might want to ask:

- What is a typical day in your role?

- What do you like most and least?

- How's the pay?

- What kind of training would it take to get into this kind of work?

- How would you describe the kind of people you work with?

- What do you think are the greatest needs and opportunities in your field?

- Can you think of any roles that are ideal for someone with years of work experience, even if in a different area?

- What skills or training might someone like me need to transition?

- Is there anyone else you think I might want to talk to?

- Any events you think I should attend?

- What books, blogs, or newsletters do you read to keep up with the field?

- Do you see opportunities for flexible or part-time work in your field (if that's of interest to you)?

- What have been the biggest changes in the field since you entered?

profile, a résumé. (More on these tools in Chapter 7.) Your email signature is a handy place to reveal a little about yourself. If you've recently published a blog post or article you want people to know about, you can include a link to it. If you've spent time helping out with a conference or other event you need to promote, consider linking to that.

In some cases, you might even have a sample of your work that will help get a conversation rolling. When RozeLyn Beck (see page 180) finished a fellowship with the Encore Hartford program and started networking in the nonprofit sector, she always brought along a prop—a portfolio containing the development strategy she put together for the nonprofit where she had her field placement. "It was a very visual example of how my skills were transferable to the nonprofit world," she said. "I can't tell you how many people told me that it was impressive. It helped skeptical people in the nonprofit world to see that I get it." Another person I spoke to used writing samples from an internship in much the same way.

Expand Your Reach Online

You may long for the days where networking just meant going through your address book and picking up the phone. And though it's possible to manage your network and find encore opportunities without spending much time online, you can dramatically increase your reach by taking advantage of online tools. It is increasingly difficult to keep up with what's current (and to look like you're keeping up with what's current) if you don't have at least a minimal presence online, and it can also create some awkwardness when reaching out to other people if you're not familiar with the dominant ways people are staying in touch.

Laura Gassner Otting, the nonprofit recruiter, told me that she has never thought less of a candidate because that person didn't have an online presence. "But I have judged someone for using online tools poorly," she added. So if you're unwilling to take the time to learn how to use social media or other online tools, you would be better off communicating in ways that make you feel comfortable.

However, according to Gassner Otting, there is another reason to consider spending a little time online: "Age discrimination is real, and one of the best ways to combat it is to look like you've mastered new technology."

If you've played around with social media but haven't gotten too far, consider ramping up your presence on one site. Maybe you've got a LinkedIn profile but have barely filled it out. Or you've checked out Twitter but couldn't get past wondering why everyone is Tweeting about their lunch? Don't feel you have to conquer them all at once. Read through the section and decide what might work best for you.

James Robinson got pushed into understanding social networking after entering his nonprofit—which helps gay, lesbian, bisexual, and transgendered (GLBT) youth in Huntsville, Alabama—into an Encore.org Launch Pad contest to win $5,000. Robinson realized that social media would be crucial for getting online votes for his organization. So, in twelve- to fourteen-hour days on his laptop, he taught himself everything he could about Facebook, LinkedIn, and Twitter so that he could build a list and share messages. His strategy worked. He was one of the contest winners. And his social media immersion paid off in other ways. Robinson is now plugged into a network of people working on GLBT issues all over the country. His online life has also boosted his spirits. "Every time I get discouraged or tired, I'll get a message from a kid or an adult somewhere thanking me for what I'm doing."

Dig into Facebook and Twitter

Facebook and Twitter have transformed the way people share information online and interact with their social networks. And they are huge. Both have hundreds of millions of members and add new users by the second. You may already be one of those users but have you tapped into how social media is being used to try to change the world? Twitter has played a key role in spreading news during world events, such as the terror attacks in Mumbai and in social movements like the Arab Spring. Governments, nonprofits, and thought leaders of every type use Twitter daily in their work to have public conversations, reach the media, and move their agendas forward. And Facebook is a standard channel of communication for all kinds of companies and organizations.

One of the best ways to wade in is as an observer rather than an active participator. A sizable percentage of people on Facebook and Twitter are considered "lurkers," meaning that they read the posts of people and organizations that interest them without ever sharing anything of their own.

Each site has some particular benefits. Facebook is fabulous for reconnecting with old friends and doing some of that work around weak ties. It's also a good place to find organizations that interest you and keep up with

My big obstacle is technology. What are the best ways to get up to speed on social networking and computer skills?

Many community colleges and public libraries offer programs to help you get up to speed on computer skills and social networking. But that's just the beginning. Courses are everywhere—community centers, alumni groups, faith-based organizations, and more. Check trade associations for courses specifically tailored to your field (for example, social media for teachers, nonprofit professionals, journalists, and so on).

Another option is to find someone who can tutor you—and, without lapsing into stereotypical age-based assumptions, you may want to try someone in her twenties who lives and breathes technology. I don't recommend reaching out to a family member unless you know he or she will have the patience needed to tutor a relative!

> **"I've met countless smart, young people the same ages as my kids, and they don't dismiss me."**
>
> —Linda Bernstein, writer/ social media consultant

their work. And after you figure out how to tune out your grating friend from fourth grade (easy to do once you master the Hide feature and no one will know!), the nuisance factor is greatly minimized. For James Robinson, connecting with like-minded activists on Facebook was a way to feel less alone in his work.

Twitter has a lot of appeal to news junkies because news breaks on Twitter sooner than in traditional media. It is also a great place to learn about trends and ideas that are shaping a field and to find links to articles, videos, or other news you might have missed. You can attend a conference by reading live posts from people who are there. And because you can follow people who are not following you, you can eavesdrop on public conversations between industry leaders. Linda Bernstein, a journalist who saw her industry transformed by social media, took a class and got hooked on Twitter, where she now has a whole new network of people who know her as @Wordwacker. "Twitter has brought me out into the world in a way I haven't been in ages," she said.

Google Plus is gaining in popularity, but even those entrenched in other social media channels are waiting for it to become more mainstream before investing time in it or relying on it too heavily. There are also specialized social media sites catering to particular groups, like Govloop.com, a site just for those working in or interested in working in local, state, or federal government. And there are bound to be others vying for our attention. A quick online search of "social media" and a keyword like "teachers" or "nurses" will give you a sense of how social media is being used by people in that field and will produce a list of links to any specialized social media networks. Among the social networking sites that cater to nurses, for example, are NurseGroups.com, which helps prospective nurses find the right training program; MyNurseBook.com, which is working toward a collaborative approach to solving the global nursing shortage; and NursingLink.com, a Monster.com-owned site focused on job opportunities and ongoing professional support. As you learn more about fields that interest you, ask people you meet which sites they find most useful—and be aware that sometimes premium features will have a fee.

The best way to better understand social media is to dig in. Take a workshop or arrange a tutorial with a tech-savvy friend. Ask others who they follow on Twitter and what they like on Facebook. And then do some lurking online, testing out one network at a time. As you refine your ideas about what to do next, talk to people about whether and how they use these tools in their work. (See page 300 for some good resources.)

Master LinkedIn

When LinkedIn came on the scene in 2003, it was as a mash-up between a résumé and an address book. Load up your résumé, scout around for contacts, and in six-degrees-of-separation style, you could take stock of your network and connect with the contacts of your contacts. Those features were revolutionary at the time and made it an invaluable tool for anyone looking to make a career shift.

During the past few years LinkedIn has rolled out so many new features that it has become as valuable for people wanting to excel in their work as it is for people trying to move into new kinds of work. And with more than 100 million members and new people joining at a rate of two per second, it has become an essential place to visit for all kinds of work-related reasons. If you're looking for a job, it's essential to be on LinkedIn because that's where most recruiters go hunting for candidates.

LinkedIn is a logical place to start if you're doing research on an organization. It can also be helpful with work you'd do for an employer, such as finding an independent contractor with a particular background or talking to someone about a joint venture. I'm happily employed, yet I can't seem to go a day without popping over to LinkedIn for one reason or another. I subscribe to an email that delivers a weekly roundup of top news stories from the nonprofit sector. When I want to make introductions, I often send along someone's LinkedIn profile. The list goes on and on.

The following are some smart ways to use LinkedIn. (As of the writing of this book, all of these features were available on the free version of the site.)

- If you've been sloppy about keeping up with people through the years, LinkedIn can help you sort through the mess and keep you up-to-date on people's whereabouts. After you start filling in your profile,

LinkedIn will suggest people you might know based on your other connections.

• Identify people at organizations that interest you.

• Follow organizations to learn about the latest developments. This is especially useful when you're trying to get familiar with a field or when you're going to meet with someone and want to know what's happening in their world.

• Create a customized news feed with top stories of the day in a specific industry or sector.

• Try LinkedIn's résumé builder (resume.linkedinlabs.com), which removes the drudgery of formatting and spits out a spiffy résumé in a variety of styles.

• Fill out the volunteering and causes sections to showcase unpaid work you have done and highlight issues you care about.

• Check out who has recently looked at your profile (and keep in mind that unless you change the settings from the default, people will be able to see if you've looked at their profiles).

• Ask for recommendations from people with whom you had a good working relationship, and write recommendations for others. It's a relatively easy way to acknowledge someone else's good work in a public way.

• Create a vanity URL with your name so that you can easily share a résumé with anyone. Here's mine: linkedin.com/in/marcialboher.

• Search the one million (yes, that's right, one million!) groups on LinkedIn by issue; then join a few online discussions with people interested in similar issues or members of communities to which you

Stay in Touch

Salespeople have long understood that the best way to make a sale is to make sure that people think of you when they have a need for your product or service. Which is one of the reasons people try to find creative ways to stay top of mind. Hosting or organizing events or gatherings are time-tested ways to do this. As are sending birthday greetings, newsletters, or clippings of relevant articles.

With the arrival of email, blogging, and social media, there are new ways to be on someone's mind in a fairly regular way. Experts call it "ambient awareness," which is that feeling of being in touch with someone because you have a sense of their activities from reading their blog or following them through some kind of social media. Ambient awareness allows us both to share information with large numbers of people and to follow the activities of others without physically running into all of those people. Or even talking! You can keep up with what people in your network are doing and working on by logging onto a social networking site and spending a few minutes doing what I call "walking the hallways."

Just sending an update by email can have a big impact. A lawyer I had used years ago included me on a mailing he sent to raise money for his cause, a local Ronald McDonald house. We hadn't spoken in two years, but his letter was so heartfelt that I not only made a donation, I called to catch up with him.

Finally, don't discount the value of picking up the phone. With so many hours of our day dedicated to email, it can feel refreshing to talk.

belong. As an example, check out the Encore Careers group and connect with others exploring or already in the midst of their encores. Poke around: You may also find groups for prior employers, schools you attended, or organizations you belong to.

• Explore the Answers section where you can pose questions to experts and answer questions when you have relevant expertise.

As a bonus, consider this: If you don't have any other online presence, your LinkedIn profile will show up when someone searches online for your name. For step-by-step instructions on setting up your profile and doing the various things on this list, visit LinkedIn's Learning Center (learn .linkedin.com).

Be Savvier About Email

Because of the nature of my work, I spend a lot of time answering people's career questions or introducing people to one another. These days, a lot of that happens by email.

Here are some tips to make your emailing more effective:

- **Have a professional email address.** When someone wants to write an email to you, usually they start typing your name and the email program will fill in the rest. That works well if your email address is some logical variation of your name, like sandy.smith@gmail.com or even something with part of your name. But if your email address is shared with your partner, such as thealberts@aol.com, or a cutesy variation on your pet's name, such as fido58@hotmail.com, you may give someone the impression that you don't take your work seriously.

- **Master the forwardable email.** If you're asking someone to make an introduction, you will be doing that person a great favor if you include some sample language they can use to describe you and what you're looking for. (See the box on page 117 for ideas.)

- **Put some thought into your signature.** Even if you're between things, it could be useful to include some identifier below your name so that people you correspond with have handy access to your contact details or a brief bio. An abbreviated URL to your LinkedIn profile works well for this purpose. And why not include a line in your signature about your stage in life—"Ask me about my encore career," or "Searching for my encore." It might just spark a useful conversation.

Take an Online Relationship Offline

A lot can happen when you take a relationship that began online and turn it into an "in-person" connection. Michelle Block, a fifty-six-year-old teacher in Chicago, was thinking about a shift to a new kind of work and began searching online for information related to midlife career reinvention. Her search led her to Encore.org and the Encore Careers LinkedIn group and Facebook page.

For months Block engaged in conversations with various people online, and then she heard about a gathering of encore leaders taking place in San Francisco. She decided to go to the conference and, while there, she discovered a large group of people working—many in paid roles—to advance the idea of encore careers on the ground in local communities. Block was not only surprised to find so many people working on these issues, but she also said she was "amazed that people were interested in what I had to say."

On the plane home, she got the idea of contacting libraries to see if she could do something to help people with encore career transitions. Block had taken eighteen hours of graduate-level library courses twenty years ago, and she started to see an idea coming together—to help libraries develop career resources. She is still exploring, but meeting in person with people who had created community-oriented programs to help others through encore transitions was the spark she needed to get started.

FAQs
All this online stuff has me worried about my privacy. Should I be?

You have to decide on your own how much of your personal life you want to reveal online. Every social networking site has privacy settings, so take the time to understand how those work, especially if you're concerned about who is watching your activity. On Facebook, for example, you can control who sees your photos, your wall posts, and the posts of your friends.

When it comes to having a professional presence, it is important to have at least some kind of information about yourself online, if only to ensure that you know what people will find when they Google your name. The easiest way to do that is to create a LinkedIn profile or some other public profile where you choose how much you want to include. Posting a photo has also become fairly standard.

It is true that social networking sites know a lot about us through the information we share. If you're worried about identity theft or other dangers of online activity, think carefully anytime you're asked to share your Social Security number or a credit card. That information is more likely to come up with online shopping, online banking, online tax preparation, and financial sites than it is for social networking sites (unless you are paying for a premium service, when you might be asked for a credit card).

I'm reluctant to post a photo online because I fear it could invite age discrimination. Should I be?

Again, that's a personal choice. But there are some good reasons to think about getting comfortable with using a photo in an online profile. Miriam Salpeter, an expert in online social networking and the author of *Social Networking for Career Success*, said having a photo online can be a big part of whether people will find you if they are searching online, particularly on the site LinkedIn, where photos are fairly standard. "Not including a photo may discourage someone from clicking through," she told me. "It also distances you and your profile from the community." Salpeter said the photo is important not just in situations where people don't know you. "Haven't we all been in a room full of people, collected business cards, and then can't remember exactly who someone is by name alone? Using a photo online can make all the difference. If someone doesn't have a photo on LinkedIn and asks to connect, it's possible that the person won't remember meeting you."

Of course, if you're posting a photo, make sure it's a good one—current enough that it's reflective of "today," more or less, and nicely balanced between casual and professional.

I want to contact someone who is known to be busy (or is quite well-known in a particular field). Any tips for how to do that?

If you're approaching someone of some stature or someone who isn't easily accessible, this task gets more complicated. People who have a public presence can be overwhelmed with requests to connect. There can be gatekeepers who make it harder to get to them. Your request may even end up in a communications black hole.

When you don't have an affiliation or a standard pitch, it can be hard to get someone's attention with a phone call or cold email.

A few ideas include:

- Look for a mutual contact. Emails beginning with "referred by [fill in the blank]" in the header often get a quicker response than one that comes with no connection, assuming that the person referring has a good relationship with the person you're trying to reach.

• Know how to identify yourself quickly in a way that establishes your credibility and your respect for the person's time.

• Try to figure out how the person wants to be contacted by asking a mutual friend or by checking a website, blog, or Twitter account. If someone is exceptionally busy or traveling a lot, email may be preferable.

• Be respectful when approaching assistants or gatekeepers. In fact, if you're having trouble getting in to see the person in charge, it's possible that you may learn a lot by asking for a meeting with that person's assistant instead.

Someone isn't calling me back. Should I be offended?

So much of networking is about timing. And if you're not getting a response from someone, it probably says more about the state of the person's email inbox or life than it says about you. It's also possible that the person isn't open to making new connections. So, first things first, don't take it personally.

Before writing the person off, follow up after a reasonable period of time to make sure that your message was actually received. If you try again and still don't get a response, it may be time to move on.

Forming new relationships involves some chemistry. So even when you try to meet someone with a common goal or interest, you may find that you just don't click with that person—or worse, you can't get a response at all. If that's the case, simply find other ways to accomplish the task. If that person holds the knowledge you're seeking, find another way to learn it. If that person is involved with an organization you want to be connected to, try to find another way in.

If you notice a pattern and several people aren't responding to your requests for making a connection, you may want to take a look at your approach and see if you should tweak what you're doing. If your emails are going unanswered, for example, ask someone whose opinion you respect to give you some objective feedback.

I don't have time for all of this. What should I do?

Cultivating and staying in touch with your network shouldn't require a lot of time if you can weave it into activities you're already doing. The best way to do this is to look at your calendar for a few weeks and see what kind of things you do regularly. Then think about whether there is a way to connect with people while you're engaged in day-to-day activities. If eldercare is consuming your time, can you involve some other people in those responsibilities, or make a point of meeting a friend for coffee to relieve some of the stress after a caregiving session? If you like to cook, consider hosting a potluck for people interested in helping one another with various transitions. If you're planning to volunteer, invite a friend you're eager to spend time with. If you like to exercise, can you take a walk with a friend? (See page 120 for ideas on how to multitask.)

Remember to give yourself permission to take small steps. There's no need to do everything that's suggested here. Find one or two suggestions that fit into your life now. A single coffee date or phone call may be enough to spark an idea for something you want to explore further.

Finally, monitor your TV and Internet time. If you're losing hours in front of one of these screens, consider swapping some of that viewing time for reading something instructive, visiting suggested websites, or working on your LinkedIn profile.

What if I'm an introvert?

When people hear the word *networking,* they tend to imagine a gadfly zipping around at a party, chatting it up with everyone in sight. The truth is that shy people or introverts can be just as effective at networking as extroverts, who get energy from being around other people. In fact, introverts are often adept at building relationships one-on-one or in small groups.

The trick is to network in ways that fit your natural inclinations. Susan Cain, author of *Quiet: The Power of Introverts in a World That Can't Stop Talking,* is an authority on how introverts should think about networking. "We often think of a situation like a cocktail party as being daunting for introverts," Cain told me. "The key is to rethink it and treat it like nothing more than a series of one-on-one conversations, which is something that introverts are quite good at." When Cain goes to an event, she said she considers it a success if she has made one new, authentic relationship with someone whose company she enjoys. That kind of quota system relieves the pressure of having to "work a room." And because her tolerance for events and parties isn't high, she also gives herself a quota on how many events she has to attend in a week or a month—and makes sure that it is a number that feels comfortable.

Many of the tips in this chapter, such as mastering social networking tools and using email, are things that should come just as easily to introverts as to extroverts.

How do I create a network when I don't know anyone in the field I want to join?

First, scan your own network to see if you know anyone who works in the field. If you're a member of an alumni association, for example, see if there's a way to put out a note to the group expressing your interest in meeting people in that field. This is another instance where online social networks can come in handy. You can put out a note to your network on Facebook or LinkedIn. You can search LinkedIn for groups that have relevant keywords and get involved in online conversations.

If you're inclined to get out and meet people in person, do some research and ask around as you do your informational interviews to see if there are any professional associations that you can join or conferences you can attend.

I'm interested in doing something related to government. How can I start making contacts?

This is one area where showing up can be a great way to both meet people and immerse in the issues. The easiest place to start is where you live. Heather Krasna, author of *Jobs That Matter*, gives these suggestions: "Go to a town hall, city council, or other public meeting. Sit in on a hearing. Listen to what's being discussed. That's where the action is, and you can even listen to some meetings via podcasts."

All government offices have websites, so you can see who is in charge of various agencies. And most of these offices now have a presence on Facebook and Twitter, so you can also keep up with the issues—and potentially even start conversations with like-minded people—by engaging with social media.

Again, online groups can be a real shortcut. Check out Govloop.com, a social networking site solely for people interested in or working in government (you don't need to work in government to join). You can also find people you may want to approach on LinkedIn if you search by region and the names of various offices. It's possible to even find people who have a certain degree, such as a master's in public policy, if you're deciding whether you need a credential to do the kind of work you want to do.

I've been out of the workforce for a decade or more, and my prior professional experience has no relevance to the work I want to do. How can I get started?

Figure out how to package any volunteer and community work in a way that makes sense. You can even find a way to show your passion and transferable skills through roles that you've played as a caregiver in your family or for a friend. Often, it is those very personal experiences that shape what people want to do in their encore years.

Career coach Belinda Plutz shared this story with me: "A client was reentering the workplace after nineteen years. She'd got some advice to focus on her last so-called *real* job, which was nearly twenty years old. She didn't take that advice. Instead, she focused on what she did in her family and her community, compiling a résumé using action verbs to describe her activities as a committed volunteer and fund-raiser, a skilled family manager, and an expert in child- and eldercare. She got a job within a few months despite the fact that she didn't have a college degree." (See page 271 for sample résumés that address this and other encore challenges.)

CHAPTER 7

Present Yourself

"It's never too late to become what you might have been."

—GEORGE ELIOT

Y ou've stumbled across the perfect job listing on Idealist.org and you're ready to apply. You have a meeting with the head of an organization you admire and you've made a date to meet. You're starting your own consulting practice and looking to build a client list. Before you click send, sit down for coffee, or pick up the phone, it's essential that you are well armed with the ability to present yourself as a strong prospect. That means the right set of tools—whether a résumé, bio, or online presence—and a clear sense of what you have to offer and how you'll talk about it. It can also mean getting comfortable talking about your age—and coming to terms with being the new kid on the block again. Yes, you may know a thing or two about a thing or two, but when you're taking on new challenges, it pays to be humble. It's a delicate balance. You need to convey that you're someone who has volumes to offer, but also that you're eager and willing to learn new things. This is true as you move into an encore as well as once you get there and begin to develop relationships.

Old Tools, New Spin

Résumés, cover letters, and interviews have long been the hallmarks of looking for work. And for the encore seeker in today's market, they still matter—but with some twists. For example, your encore résumé will likely be one way you introduce yourself—but your LinkedIn profile or narrative bio might serve you better depending on the circumstance. You'll still be writing cover letters, but this time they may be in the form of email. And you'll find it necessary to expand your definition of "job interview" to include more informal exchanges. In short, it's about presenting the best "you" for the opportunity you're chasing. You need a résumé that provides a profile of your skills and talents, a résumé that tells your story.

Building an Encore Résumé

An up-to-date résumé is a useful thing, and not just for job applications. You'll want a strong résumé on hand for other purposes—if you're considered for a board position, if you're applying to an academic program, even if you're trying to get hooked up for that coffee date. Sure, in some instances, a LinkedIn profile is enough, but old-fashioned résumés still have a place.

But maybe not your *whole* story.

Discussion Prompts
Do you have a clear sense of what you have to offer? • When's the last time you took a look at your résumé? • When was the last time you had an interview? • Have you faced any questions about your age?

"A résumé isn't an autobiographical history of everything you've done," explained Miriam Salpeter, a résumé coach and author. "Its job is to showcase what you can do for a specific someone. So the key is to identify your target someone and then write your résumé to show how you can solve that target's problems."

In practical terms, that means a few things:

- **Don't cover your entire career history.** It's acceptable to focus on what you've done in the past ten years—unless there's something much earlier that feels relevant. If there is something from a while back you want to highlight, you can do it with a phrase like "early work history includes. . ." Highlight work that is unpaid if it's relevant to what you want to do. It may be valued just as highly as something you did for compensation.

- **Don't fret too much about dates.** Experts go both ways on whether to include your age if you're over forty, fifty, or sixty, but most of the ones I consulted didn't see much benefit to removing ages. "Removing your age just puts up a red flag," according to nonprofit recruiter Laura Gassner Otting. "I end up assuming more years are missing than not, which just makes you appear older." In the end, you're probably not going to be a good fit for an organization that doesn't value experience. At the more senior levels, having some extra years can be an advantage.

- **Don't try anything too flashy.** Use a basic template and make sure to customize it for different situations. Unless you're some kind of word-processing geek, the hair-pulling part of writing a résumé is getting it formatted and proofed in a way that passes muster with the chief copy editor in your household or circle of friends (you are having someone review it, right?). There are some free online helpers to do some of that work. If you've filled out your LinkedIn profile, try the site's résumé builder (resume.linkedinlabs.com), which spits out a spiffy PDF résumé in a variety of formats. VisualCV.com is another easy and free tool you can use to create a résumé. The site allows you to embed videos, photos, and other links, making it ideal for creative professionals or others who want a résumé with some show-and-tell aspects. Résumés on VisualCV can be shared as a link or a PDF.

- **Use keywords.** Résumés sent in cold are often scanned by computers to sort out candidates, so savvy résumé writers make sure that their résumés include some of the language that a computer searches for. The best source of keywords is the job listing itself. Are there any industry-specific terms used? Do they mention necessary training, certification, or skills they would like a candidate to have? Those are all hints at the keywords you'll want to use. I almost hate to bring up the issue of keywords because if you take this too far, you'll have a résumé loaded with jargon. But if you're submitting a résumé for a process where you don't have a contact to help you stand out, make sure to include a handful of these terms so that you at least pass an initial screening.

For a growing swath of the workforce and in a growing number of situations, the résumé has been replaced by a narrative bio. If you've ever seen someone introduced at a conference, you have a sense of how important it can be to help others tell your story. Written bios show up on websites and in the summary section of a LinkedIn profile, and snappy short ones are used for Twitter or email taglines. So take a little time to work on yours. It's a good idea to craft bios of various lengths, in addition to your résumé. These will come in very handy as you have to present yourself in different ways.

Feel free to show some personality. Darrell Hammond, the CEO of KaBOOM!, a nonprofit that partners with corporate sponsors to build playgrounds in low-income areas around the United States, uses just these few sentences for the "about the founder" section of KaBOOM!'s website: "I grew up with seven brothers and sisters at Mooseheart, a group home outside of Chicago. The Mooseheart community instilled in me the power of volunteerism and helping those less fortunate. My journey would eventually lead me to co-found KaBOOM! in 1995 and begin a lifelong commitment to give all children the opportunity to play. KaBOOM! has raised over 100 million dollars to build over 1,500 playgrounds, skateparks, sports fields, and ice rinks, and improved thousands of others across America in just twelve years." For more examples of résumés and narrative bios that address common encore challenges and situations, see page 271.

> **"Now that I'm out of the tech industry and into teaching, the students are my customers—I have to be able to sell them my goods."**
>
> —John Kostibas, executive-turned-math-teacher

Finessing the Cover Letter

Old-school cover letters were formal notes printed on the highest-quality bond paper and accompanied a résumé sent by mail.

Cover letters still exist, but now they are sent by email and the only person printing them is the recipient. Too bad for the manufacturers of bond paper. My preferred method is to paste a cover note right into the body of an email so that people have fewer attachments to open. If you want a little more formality, which sometimes works for letters you expect to be forwarded along to someone else, you can attach a cover letter along with your résumé. You may be writing to introduce yourself and express interest even though there isn't an actual job opening that you know of. You may be trying to get a meeting to learn more about an organization's work. You may want to explain something on your résumé (e.g., a gap between jobs), or you may want to highlight some relevant experience so it isn't overlooked. You may be pitching your services as a consultant or introducing yourself as a potential volunteer, board member, or for some other purpose. Whatever your goal, a cover letter should:

- **Mention a connection if you have one.** My favorite place to put this is right at the top, either in the email header ("referred by Marci Alboher") or as the opening line of your note ("I'm writing at the suggestion of Marci Alboher, who told me that you were searching for an interim development director").

- **Get the name of the person you'll be addressing.** And then tell that person a story.

"When I was a teenager traveling in Guatemala, I saw a woman who was badly burned from cooking over an open fire. I have never forgotten that image. On hearing about Stove Team International's work to create safe cookstoves, I went immediately to your website to learn more and see if there is a way I could support your work."

- **Explain exactly what you want *and why*.** I've seen lots of cover letters that serve as job applications but never explain why the applicant wants that specific job. When applying for social purpose work, use your cover letter to explain why you're drawn to the organization's mission and what experience you have that will help the group achieve its objective. Do your homework and make it clear that you understand what the organization does.

Follow the News

If you're hoping to enter into a new field, learn to stay on top of relevant trends and developments. Read the news with a critical eye. If a new law is passed or the government is investing in an area that you're considering, think about the implications. Read trade publications so that you know which organizations are getting funding, who is expanding and hiring, and where there are opportunities for people with your kind of background. Monitoring job sites like Idealist.org and Indeed.org can tell you more than what specific jobs are available; they can also tell you which organizations are flush with cash and where they see needs. (These sites can be just as valuable for the freelancer or consultant as for the job seeker.)

- **Make your points quickly, then close.** This is especially true if you're applying for a specific job because hiring managers may scan hundreds of letters for one position. If you're using the cover letter to highlight your relevant skills and experience, consider using bullet points, which make for very easy reading. (I'm walking the walk here!)

- **Include all your relevant contact details.** Do this in your email signature and as part of the actual letter if the two are separate.

Nailing the "Interview"

Interviews have always been an important part of how we get screened for opportunities, but these days you are always on an interview—even when that's not what it's called. You're interviewing when you get involved in public conversations regarding issues you care about—in old-school ways like writing op-eds, and newer ones like posting comments or sharing articles on Facebook or other social networking sites. In the new workplace, someone is your boss or subordinate one moment and your client or collaborator the next. So as you get out there and do things, recognize that you are building your reputation through every interaction.

I like to say that I had two years of dating Encore.org before we got hitched. While I was writing for *The New York Times,* I frequently called Marc Freedman, the founder, to get his opinion about stories I was working on. He invited me to speak at a Purpose Prize conference, and while I was there I met several other staffers as well as a couple of board members. We had many chances to see each other in action. By the time we got to the official interview, we were so comfortable that our conversations were about whether my joining the organization would be a good fit for both of us, not whether I was qualified.

That said, there are plenty of situations where you'll find yourself in a more traditional interview. Here are a few tips to keep in mind for those:

- **Show your passion.** "Mission-focused organizations want to know you're going to be in the foxhole with them," explained nonprofit recruiter Laura Gassner Otting. That means it's critical to talk about why you're interested in an issue and why it feels important to you. At the same time remember that you need to show how you're able to solve a problem the interviewer is facing. So even if you haven't done the exact same thing being discussed, find ways to show that you've done something similar.

- **Hone your story and tailor it to the setting.** Just as you'll want to tailor your résumé to the particular opportunity, you'll want to talk about your background and experience differently based on the situation. You may even find it helpful to practice aloud at home or with a friend. "It's important that you get to say what you want to say even if the perfect question isn't asked," said Gassner Otting. "Channel a politician with a set of talking points and make sure you hit all of yours regardless of the questions asked," she suggested. "I always tell people to have three key points they want to make. If they get them during the questioning, great. If not, try to inject them at the end or in a thank-you note or follow-up email. Also consider making a bit of a closing statement. Something like: 'I think the work you do is so important, and I want to be a part of it' or 'I think I've got the passion and experience to really make a difference here.'"

- **Anticipate sticky areas and be prepared to address them.** For example, if you've never worked in the nonprofit sector, be ready to allay concerns by pointing to your pro bono or volunteer experience and your willingness to learn. If you're overqualified for a position, talk about why the role is appealing to you at this time in your life. Don't be too concerned about being in transition—one of the hallmarks of the new workplace is that everyone has been through one transition or another. "Just talk honestly about where you've been and where you want to go," said Gassner Otting. "Don't overcompensate for what you're doing now, and don't say that you're consulting if you're not."

> **"I went across to the president's office at Wayne State University and asked him if he had a job for an old soldier."**
>
> –Randal Charlton, encore entrepreneur

- **Expect hypotheticals.** "What would you do if . . ." is a common beginning to an interview question. There are no right answers to this kind of question. The interviewer is more interested in your thought process and whether you can think on your feet than what you end up concluding. Use hypotheticals as a way to highlight a time in your past when you did something you are proud of. Anticipate this one: What changes would you make if you get this job? Be careful here not to assume that you know enough to answer. Instead, build into your answer the steps you'd take to get up to speed and the process you would use to make informed recommendations.

- **Ask good questions.** The interview is your time to learn things you weren't able to learn anywhere else. It is also another chance to show that you've done some research. Come prepared with some genuine, clear, smart questions. Spend time on an organization's website and study its latest news. If a program doesn't seem aligned with an organization's mission, ask about it. If you're wondering how secure funding is going forward, that's fair game. Think of some questions that will get to the culture of the organization, like how do people communicate with one another and how are decisions made.

- **Dress appropriately.** There are no longer norms about what to wear to work. And it can be as awkward to show up overdressed as it can be to be underdressed. When I left the law business and started meeting with editors, I was shocked to find that anything dressier than jeans made me feel wildly out of place in a newsroom. When I travel from New York City to meet with my San Francisco colleagues, I'm routinely the only one not wearing fleece. The only way to know for sure about how to dress is to ask in advance; doing so can go a long way to making you feel more comfortable in an interview.

• **Don't forget to look around and observe.** Remember that you are also interviewing the person and organization you're meeting. Unless an interview is happening by phone, use the experience to see if you'd feel comfortable working with the people you meet. How do you feel about the work environment? Do people look like they are happy, or do they look excessively stressed? Do they treat each other kindly? How are people dressed? How are they interacting with one another?

One of the most useful resources for interview prep is Glassdoor.com, a site where people post real interview questions from specific companies. A quick tour around the Internet will also turn up countless resources on specialized interview processes such as telephone or group interviews, as well as ways to approach various kinds of interview questions. In the end, be sure to be yourself. Don't parrot a script suggested by anyone else.

Worried About . . . Your Age

And then there's the matter of those accumulated years. By now you've probably had at least a few incidents where someone treats you differently based on their assumptions about "someone your age." Or your own feelings about age may be bubbling up. Even those who are fully acclimated in their encore careers will tell you that work can feel different once you hit a certain age (and that certain age is different depending on whom you're talking to). There comes a time in all of our working lives when we realize that the way we learned it isn't the way it's done anymore. And when we learn new things, it's just as often from someone younger than from a peer. We also start to worry if our age will be held against us.

The age issue crops up in a bunch of ways.

Transitioning While Still on the Job

Many people hang on to a prior job or identity while laying the foundation for an encore. So if you're working in one role while trying to move into another, one of the most important conversations you'll have is with your employer.

As Cali Yost, author of *Work + Life: Finding the Fit That's Right for You,* explained to me, you have some leverage in this situation because most managers don't want to lose good, experienced people. Here's what she recommended: "Go in with a well-thought-out plan about how your encore will benefit your employer. Show how your job will get done, what you'll do, and what you'll delegate." That doesn't mean you'll get exactly what you're asking for, but you stand a good chance of at least starting a conversation. Another critical piece, Yost told me, is to come up with a proposal and suggest implementing it for a fixed trial period, which may be easier for your employer to approve.

During Susan Burket's encore transition, she spent one day a week volunteering for Habitat for Humanity. "My schedule was nine to four, five days a week, and I proposed working nine to five, four days a week," she said. "I just went into my boss and said I'm interested in helping this nonprofit." It helped that Burket worked at a small company run by good people who weren't concerned about setting precedent.

At bigger companies you may not be the first to have negotiated some flexibility; in fact, there might be policies around flextime that make this kind of negotiating easier. When Judy Berry, a regional sales manager for a barbecue company, decided she wanted to contribute to the cause of better dementia care, her boss was her biggest champion. He was supportive of Berry's requests for time off to care for her mother, who was suffering from dementia.

He recommended her for an executive-on-loan program, which allows employees to collect a full-time salary while taking time to do community work. Berry used her life savings to start a residential dementia care facility and a nonprofit in rural Minnesota that focuses on providing dignified care to dementia patients and special assistance for low-income seniors needing help.

When you get to the point of accepting a position, make sure to revisit the things you identified as important to you in your ideal work setting (as figured out in Exercise 8 in Chapter 3). Are there ways you can suggest trading something you don't need (like health insurance if you are on your partner's plan) for additional time off or a salary bump? Does title matter to you? If so, that may be an easier thing to negotiate for than things that cost money.

Age Discrimination—It's Real

There is no question about it—age discrimination exists. But the best way to prevent your age from holding you back is to focus on two things that you can control: your attitude and your qualifications for the work you want to do. None of this is about erasing the added years. Instead, it's about ensuring that you defy the stereotype of an older worker unwilling to embrace new ways of working.

That all said, if you're convinced your age is the reason you're being discounted, you likely won't be able to prove it—and it's probably not worth your time to try. It's also a good sign that you may not be a good fit for an organization's culture. If that's the case, invest your time and energy in places where you feel experience is valued. For example, if you're interviewing at an organization's offices, look around. Is there anyone your age on the team? Do you get a sense that the organization has figured out how to integrate people of different generations into its work?

> "Academia is a place where maturity doesn't go against you the way it does in the corporate environment. The more you've done, the more you're respected."
>
> —Veronica Buckley, corporate-administrator-turned-college-instructor

What if you're asked head-on about being overqualified? Career coach Maggie Mistal recommends acknowledging it up front and being ready to explain why you want the role. There are plenty of good reasons why you'd take a job for which you're overqualified. You may want a chance to return to something you did earlier in your career that you missed as you gained seniority. Maybe you want to minimize your work stress. The main thing you want to avoid is the perception that you just need a job, any job, and that you'll move on the minute you find something better.

Looks Matter, but Ability Matters More

I've talked to hundreds of people about their encore transitions and it's clear that how people feel about the role of aging varies widely. Some don't give the slightest thought to whether their age will be held against them. I spoke to one woman in her seventies who works in education and says gray or white hair is common. She told me that not coloring her hair seems to give permission to others around her to let theirs go, too. (She happens to have one of those elegant heads of smooth, white hair that could make a thirty-year-old want to go gray.)

If you feel that your appearance may be holding you back, ask a friend with a good sense of current trends for some objective feedback. If it's been a while since you've updated your wardrobe, consider adding a couple of new pieces.

Tough Questions, Good Answers

There are some common ways interviewers ask about age. Below are a few sample questions and ways to answer them that should satisfy any concerns. Of course, you should always answer honestly and tailor to your own situation.

The Overqualified Question: You're such a strong candidate, but to be frank, I'm worried you'd be bored in the job.

Answer: First off, I get a lot of satisfaction in doing something well—whatever the job. And second, I see many challenges in this role. (*Then name them and mention that finding the opportunity to mentor is one of the things you're hoping to achieve.*)

The Are-You-Going-to-Retire-Any-Minute Question: Where do you see yourself in three or five years?

Answer: I want to be doing work that matters to me and to the world. I've learned how hard it is to predict where one will be in the future, but I understand myself and my priorities. I want to have purpose. I want to have challenges. I want to learn from colleagues and friends. I want to give back.

The Are-You-Too-Old-for-Us Question: Do you think you'll feel comfortable in our work environment? Most of the people here are under thirty and communicate largely by text and instant messaging.

Answer: Working in an intergenerational group is one of the reasons I'm drawn to this environment. There's so much to learn from young people—and I hope they'll also see that they can learn from me. If you're worried that I won't be able to keep up with the pace, let me put your mind at ease. (*Then provide some examples of your energy, enthusiasm, and ability to work with younger people.*)

The Can-You-Teach-an-Old-Dog-New-Technology Question: How do you feel about learning new technology?

Answer: I'm game. (*Then provide an example, like "I recently got an iPad and have been having a hard time separating myself from it." Assuming, of course, that this is true. If you're not willing to learn new technology and it's a requirement for the position, you may want to reconsider.*)

But rather than focusing on looking young—after all, in the age of full-body tattoos and nose rings, young people today haven't exactly made a name for themselves on the appearance front—focus on whether your skills and your methods of communication are up-to-date. Knowing the latest trends in your field and being adept at social networking could make you look a lot more current than focusing on some aspect of your physical appearance.

Here's a test: If someone asks you to be available for a Skype call, is your reaction: 1.) "Sure." 2.) "Sure, can you help me set it up?" or 3.) "What's Skype?" If it's the last one, I'd recommend you spend some time on a technology tune-up.

Working with—and for—Younger People

Working alongside younger people doesn't have to be hard. You probably have memories of enjoying when it was the other way around—having an older office friend or mentor who was able to show you the ropes. If you haven't worked or spent a lot of time with young people, you may want to read a little or chat about it with some younger people you know about the work styles of the GenY or millennial group (those born in the late 1980s and early 1990s), because there are some interesting differences that have been well documented.

A few things to expect: Younger workers want a less hierarchical, more collaborative approach. They also tend to use technology in some different ways (which you know well if you live with anyone under the age of thirty). Texting is a given, for example. And they like a lot of positive feedback. (Note: Expect to encounter people who disprove every one of these statements!)

To get off on the right foot, try to understand the culture of the workplace you're joining and convey an attitude of willingness to try new things even if they aren't what you're used to. Also, see if you can find some ways to cross-mentor. It's entirely common these days for mentorship to run both ways, with an older person sharing contacts or life wisdom, for example, while the younger one helps to demystify technology.

Howard Johnson, sixty-nine, had thirty years of experience as a consultant in the fishing industry when he became the director of global partnerships for the Sustainable Fishing Partnership, an independent non-governmental organization (NGO) working on ways to advance sustainable seafood and marine conservation. At the Partnership, nearly everyone, including his boss, is significantly younger than he is. "Most are in their late twenties and early thirties," he said, "and the old people have just turned forty." Johnson said being a mentor to younger staff has been one of the most rewarding aspects of his job. "We hired a young woman in China who comes from a nonseafood background. She's like a sponge, soaking up information. She made her first presentation at an international conference and was so good. It was almost like watching one of my children, but she's younger than my children," he told me. "These young people give me energy."

Finally, don't assume anything. There are plenty of work environments where the oldest person around is leading the way on technology advice or managing the triathlon training team.

Being the Rookie . . . Again

You have years of experience in an area such as finance, accounting, communications, marketing, or technology. You have probably managed people, perhaps run whole departments. Yet people aren't racing to hire you. What gives?

You may be facing the skepticism many employers have about people who have worked extensively in other sectors or fields. They're not sure your experience is transferable. They're not sure you'll fit in their culture. For those moving into social purpose work, employers may wonder how you'll deal with an environment where mission matters more than money, where resources are tight, and where decision-making processes may be slow attempts to achieve consensus.

Successful reinventors recognize that though they bring a lot of talent and experience, they also have a lot to learn. It's a delicate dance between touting what you know and acknowledging where you might have gaps to fill.

You may be able to manage these things with some fairly simple steps, or you may find that you need a deeper experience like a course, an internship or fellowship, or some other training to feel more prepared.

Practice Humility

"When I interview potential fellow candidates, I look for a learning, rather than a telling, stance," Leslye Louie, national director of the Encore Fellowship

Network, explained. "Someone who has eyes and ears open, rather than someone who said, 'I'm going to show them how to fix things.' If you're used to being in an environment with resources and a title, you have to be humble about where you fit in. You may not have a staff, and you have to do whatever comes your way."

> "If you ask the right questions with the right attitude, people are ready to help you."
>
> –Nancy Burkhart, encore entrepreneur

Karin Hazelkorn thought a lot about humility when she took leave from a senior position with Cisco Systems to explore her interest in fair trade textile manufacturing. As part of her learning, Hazelkorn talked to countless people in the industry and took classes. With every meeting, she set herself up to learn from others' expertise and made sure to be respectful. "I don't wing it, and I don't want to waste anyone else's time," Hazelkorn told me. Slowly, she got the lay of the land, learned the jargon, and in time she had met so many people that she was able to make some connections for others. "That's when it really started to be gratifying," she said. She is still working on her transition. When I last spoke to her, she was thinking of returning to the private sector to get some relevant experience and sock away some money before moving into her encore.

Identify Transferable Skills

As you explore situations, try to identify how your skills and experiences might translate to the position you're considering. When Terri Ward (see page 23) interviewed for her copywriting position at Shenandoah University, she realized that, whatever the product, marketing is marketing. "The biggest challenge was learning a new vocabulary," she said. "I went from writing for a precast concrete manufacturer that built parking garages to adopting the mind-set of an eighteen- or nineteen-year-old thinking about college. That's where my perspective as a mother came in. With four teenagers at home thinking about their futures, it wasn't that much of a stretch."

Show Your Willingness to Learn

Though you want to highlight your transferable skills, you'll help both yourself and any organization you're considering working with by acknowledging where you have gaps and what you would do to address them. Lester Strong was a television news anchor when his interest in meditation led him to get involved in the Siddha Yoga (SYDA) Foundation, a nonprofit that teaches yoga and meditation around the world. He started by anchoring international broadcasts on meditation and later joined the organization's board and was eventually offered the job of president and chief executive officer. Strong accepted, but he and board members agreed that he needed to fill in some gaps. He enrolled in a nine-month nonprofit management course at Columbia University. "I had never managed an organization so it was quite an act of trust and faith," he told me. "I was a reporter and a great producer. But I needed to learn things like strategic planning, people management, and other things that were core to running a nonprofit." Strong said he still had a lot to learn on the job, but taking that first step equipped him to make the transition. Today he's CEO of AARP Experience Corps.

Expect Some Culture Shock

Differences in workplace culture can show up in all kinds of ways, so be prepared. "As a reporter," Strong continued, "my job was to see something and go make it happen. I had gratification within 24 hours, whether it worked or didn't. But helping to shape an entire international organization was a very long, deliberative process. It took time to understand and appreciate it," he adds. "I also didn't have to worry about fund-raising as a broadcaster. I worried about ratings, but I never had to sit down and explain what we were doing and why we were doing it to funders and supporters of the work. It was all very new."

Learn to Bounce Back

There will always be stories of the nearly instantaneous transition that appeared to happen with almost no effort, but for most people the transition to an encore is a process of exploring, building a network, learning about the role and field you want to be in (especially if it's a new one), getting any necessary training, and then finding an opportunity that fits what you want to do. Often there are a series of stops along the way—roles that get you closer to what you want to do or help you hone your skills, build your connections, and figure out where you fit in.

Mistal said it's important to remind yourself that your last career didn't happen overnight. "Landing the job isn't the only measurement of success," she said. "Try to recognize and celebrate some things that you've learned along the way."

George Wolf has pounded the pavement well into his seventies, facing age discrimination countless times. He said he mined the most obvious episodes of discrimination for their comic value as stories he could use to entertain others, then just picked up and kept going. "There's no sense in getting pissed or getting depressed," he said.

RozeLyn Beck said she had to keep reminding herself that whatever you're feeling comes through in an interview. Her trick: Take some time and internally focus on your best moments, the situations where you shined. By doing this, you can be really clear when you need to talk about your accomplishments during interviews. Ask the people around you who you value and trust what they think your best talents are. That could give you the ego boost you need.

If your search is taking so long that you're starting to wonder whether you are doing something wrong, take a good look at the situation and your strategy. This is where coaches and mentors can be helpful. Is there someone who can give you an objective perspective on how you're presenting yourself and whether you're looking at the right kinds of situations?

FAQs

Is it possible to convince an employer that I can do a job even if I might not have all of the qualifications listed on the job posting?

This happens all the time, according to nonprofit recruiter Laura Gassner Otting. "Most employers realize that not every candidate will have all the specific characteristics requested in a job description," she added. "Strengths in one area can negate a lack somewhere else."

If you feel that you have the chops for a particular job, don't be put off if your background doesn't match up perfectly with what's listed in a job posting. Use your cover letter to explain why you're qualified for the job. If you get called in for an interview, you'll have a chance to talk about your credentials. Be prepared to answer questions about any qualifications you don't have.

If you make a good impression, the job could be tailored to your strengths—and aspects of the job that don't match up could be assigned to someone else. You could also offer to get training in an area where you don't have experience.

What are the best ways to determine an organization's culture and whether I would fit in?

Laura Gassner Otting, the nonprofit recruiter, suggests starting by looking at the kinds of information the organization shares with the public. Visit the organization's website, as well as their LinkedIn profile, Facebook page, and/or Twitter feed, if available. Then ask yourself some questions. What kind of vibe are you getting? Is the organization staid and stodgy, or up-to-the-minute hip? Under the About Us tab you can usually find bios of board and staff members. Do these sound like people you'd like to work with? Is there anyone with a background like yours? Does the organization have a blog or a Recent News section? What do the posts there tell you about the organization? Notice how the organization talks about its work, its successes, and its challenges. Can you meet the team at any public events? If so, definitely do that.

If the organization is a nonprofit, Otting suggests taking a look at its IRS form 990, available on Guidestar.org (you have to register on the site but it's free). On that form, you'll be able to see a list of board members, a list of staffers, and the salaries of the top five employees. Keep in mind that you are looking at a snapshot from a year ago, even two, so things might be different. "If there aren't a lot of matching names, then there's a lot of turnover, which could say something about what it's like to work there," said Gassner Otting. "Then again, if you look at a 990 from ten years ago and there's no change, maybe the organization isn't open to change."

Don't forget to talk to people as part of your research. This is one of the best uses of informational interviews. Try to find out not just what the organization does, but what it feels like to work there. What's the management style? Do things move fast or is it a slow and deliberate kind of place? How many people does it take to get a decision approved? Do people communicate largely by email or do they walk into each other's offices? Is there even an office culture or are people working virtually from remote locations? When you start hearing the same things from multiple, unrelated sources, you can begin to decide if it's right for you.

What if a potential employer or client asks me to come up with a proposed budget or marketing plan for their organization to show them what I can do? Should I do it?

If you're interviewing for a significant position, employers may want to do more than question you about what you've done in the past. They may want to see you in action and get a sense of how you would handle the unique issues they're dealing with, which is where requests like this come in.

How much is too much to ask? You'll be the ultimate judge of that, and you should make your decision by examining how much you want the work, and how much you trust that the request is a sincere attempt to evaluate you and not just a way to have interview candidates tackle projects for free. You might ask people you know what's standard in your field.

Maggie Mistal, a career coach, said she has had clients who have gotten burned by being too willing to accommodate excessive requests to produce materials for an interview. If you feel a request is excessive, she recommends that you refer the interviewer to the most relevant samples of your best work, sharing copies (free of any client names) and highlighting what you would tweak or change if you were doing this for the organization requesting it. You could also offer to do some work at a discounted rate.

It should be possible for an employer to discover your ability to perform without putting you in a position where you feel exploited. If you feel exploited, perhaps this isn't the employer for you.

CHAPTER 8

Go Do Things!

"To try and fail is at least to learn.
To fail to try is to suffer the loss of what might have been."

—Ben Franklin

So you've been *thinking* about a couple possible encore paths for months —maybe years—but you still haven't done anything about it because you're just not sure if you're ready to commit. Or maybe you've gone after a few opportunities but they didn't pan out because you don't have the right background or enough experience in the new field. If either scenario rings true, consider investing some time in unpaid (or low-paid) "experiments."

Experiments can be small immersions—visits to an organization where you want to check out the vibe, coffee dates with people working in fields that interest you, or an afternoon volunteering at a soup kitchen or a reading hour at a library. They can also be much deeper experiences—a long, pro bono consulting gig, an apprenticeship, internship, or fellowship. Even serving on a board in an organization that will give you exposure to an issue area you want to know better.

With each experiment, you will almost certainly learn something about what you want (or don't want) as part of your encore—your experiment may even end up being your encore. Each experiment adds valuable experience to your encore résumé, expands your network, and can lead to long-term opportunities. They are also a great way to get out of your head and into the world—whether you're still figuring out what it is you want to do or after you've zeroed in on an idea and nothing seems to be happening.

Test, Learn, Repeat

When I was trying to leave the legal profession, I knew I wanted to teach and write, but I had no idea what shape either of those activities would take. So I did a few experiments. The first one was a day as a substitute English teacher in a private high school. From the moment I arrived I felt trapped. I couldn't believe (gasp!) that a teacher can't freely leave the room to make a private call or visit the restroom. After years of making my own

Discussion Prompts
Reflect on any times in your life when doing something helped you hone in on an interest or rule out something you thought you were interested in. • If you wanted to try something out, what kinds of available time do you have to do that— weekends, vacation time, evenings, playing hooky for an afternoon?

schedule and coming and going as I pleased, I couldn't fathom staying inside one building for an entire school day. And I couldn't imagine how I'd ever get a group of hormonal teenagers to get excited about *Hamlet* on the first day of spring. Eventually I found a better fit: evening writing classes at a community center in my neighborhood, where the adult students were thrilled to be in the classroom. My one day of teaching in a high school helped me realize I wanted to teach adults, and I wanted to teach in a place that was open to the public.

Lauri Grossman, a homeopath, used this technique when she went to Haiti after the earthquake in 2011 to work with the nonprofit group Homeopaths Without Borders. Traveling to a country in the immediate aftermath of a national disaster confirmed her belief that she wanted to be involved in relief efforts. Those trips also helped her refine her ideas about how she could have an impact in a way that's compatible with her life. After studying what worked and didn't work during her Haiti experience, she decided she could do as much good consulting from the United States as she could working overseas. She had another motive for wanting to avoid excessive travel. After two decades of raising her kids as a single mother, Grossman had started a serious relationship in her fifties and wasn't so eager to leave home. "I waited this long to have someone in my life who means so much. What good is it if I'm never around?"

When Suwon Smith left Citigroup, one of the first things she did was start a small business baking desserts for organizational events. Although the business brought her joy, she couldn't see herself doing it full time because it kept her from other things she was still yearning to do—coaching, teaching, and helping people become more financially literate. So when a fire in her home essentially put a halt to Smith's small business (sometimes you have to listen to the fates!), she decided that while she would occasionally bake on request, she would not actively seek new customers. Immersing in the baking business for a while helped Smith figure out how to better balance her passions.

As you think about what to do, recognize the power of taking a small step toward something that interests you. Author Peter Sims calls these moves "little bets" in a book of the same title. Little bets are low-risk experiments that can help you refine ideas. The idea is to get a firsthand look at life in a particular role with an immersion of a few hours, an afternoon, or even a week where you get to observe and ask lots of questions. Spending time in the environment where you'd be working—or a similar one—can be invaluable for illuminating realities, dispelling misconceptions, and seeing if something appeals to you.

Try It On: Volunteer

If there is one surefire way to get started on an encore, it's through volunteering. Volunteering, in its many incarnations, shows up in just about every encore transition story, even when people don't get involved with the intention of moving into paid roles.

When you volunteer, you learn about the issue from the inside, make contacts, and get yourself plugged in. If you're a valuable volunteer, board member, or pro bono consultant, chances are an organization will try to get more of your time, which often leads to job offers.

Young people often volunteer or serve to learn. It's different when you've got years of work experience behind you. At this point you know a lot and you may be volunteering purely to share what you know. But you might need to learn, too. You may need to know how to use the technology that's prevalent in a field you want to break into. You may want a close-up look inside an organization working on an issue you care about. You may just want to give your time because it feels good. These are all valid reasons.

Young people are trying to form connections and get experience. You are probably loaded with connections and experience, which will shape the way you find your volunteer opportunities and what happens when you're there. Susan Gilson (see page 26), a youth-services worker in Oregon ready for a change, gave herself a year to explore and then developed three volunteer experiences to help her find the best way to match her skills and interests with a career focused on aging adults. First, she called an acquaintance who owned an assisted living center. She played cards with the residents, and when she learned they needed someone to take residents to appointments, she did that. Next, she volunteered for a hospice, spending time with an older man in his home, providing relief for his wife and daughter who were caring for him. Finally, she helped serve meals in the dining room of a senior meals site. In the end, she liked the work at the meal center so much that she applied for an opening there and got the job.

On the flip side, volunteering can be a good way to figure out what you *don't* want to do. Susan Burket had a vaguely unhappy feeling at work after years as a computer programmer. She decided to use her free time to volunteer, thinking there must be a nonprofit that could use her skills. She quickly found a project, creating a database for the Montgomery County Volunteer Center, a neighborhood organization in Maryland. "I thought maybe this would scratch the itch," she told me. She spent six months on the project. And when it was over, she came to two realizations. First, although she loved the general feeling of helping, doing more of what she was doing all day wasn't satisfying. Second, she decided it was time to change what she did all day. She started looking for an opportunity that involved writing, an interest she had been exploring through some classes.

One of the first points to consider as you look into volunteering is whether you want to be on the front lines, working with the people (or animals, or natural environment) being served. Susan Gilson's experiments were all examples of direct-service roles, something that a caring,

> "I hear three common themes when I talk about volunteering with people over fifty. First, no one asked me to volunteer. Second, if I volunteer, will I be trained? And third, after they train me, will they stay in touch? If you are giving your time, you should get #2 and #3."
>
> —Carlos Campos, executive director, YouthBuild USA

Technology and Volunteering

Technology has changed some things about volunteering, but not everything. Sites such as VolunteerMatch .org, Idealist.org, and AllforGood.org have become a standard part of the volunteer experience. And online is a good place to start. With sites like Catchafire.org and Sparked.com, you can even find ways to be a virtual volunteer—doing projects like grant writing, web design, or social media assistance—without even leaving your home.

What technology hasn't changed is the need for a volunteer experience to be well managed so it's satisfying for the volunteer and useful to the organization. Whether you find an opportunity through a site or use your own ingenuity, you'll want to get a few basic questions answered.

• What kind of training or orientation will you receive?

• Who will be managing you, and what kind of access will you have to that person?

• Will you be working with and learning from other volunteers?

• Is there some method for keeping you informed about organizational progress or decisions that are relevant to the project you're working on?

If you're creating the arrangement on your own, you want to formalize what is expected of you, possibly even draw up something in writing. If you're doing high-level work or representing an organization externally, you may want to ask for a title—and business cards.

responsible person could do with a little bit of training or orientation. Typical direct-service roles include delivering meals to ill or elderly people, answering calls for a rape crisis center, tutoring or mentoring kids, cleaning up a park, or building a house for Habitat for Humanity.

Direct-service volunteering makes sense if you are itching to get your hands dirty, connect with other people who share your interests, be out in your community, get to know an organization from the ground up, or get a close-up look at the work being done by an organization.

Skills-based volunteering (also called pro bono service) draws on your specific skills or professional training. Examples include medical personnel who volunteer at clinics, lawyers who volunteer their services, or professionals who create databases or business plans for nonprofits—even musicians who volunteer their time performing in schools or hospitals. But despite your expertise, you may still need a reboot.

Recently retired from a twenty-seven-year career in development for the federal government, Carla Barbiero, then fifty, went to a seminar led by AARP Experience Corps, a tutoring and mentoring organization that was seeking volunteers to work with schoolkids. Barbiero was impressed with the Experience Corps model but had no desire to work directly with children. So she approached the leader at the end of the seminar and asked if there was someone she should talk to about helping the organization with fund-raising. That led to a meeting with Elizabeth Fox, founder of the Washington, D.C., chapter of Experience Corps. The two, who had mutual friends, immediately hit it off. Barbiero had years of experience in giving away money from the U.S. government, but needed to learn about the new world of fund-raising. Fox provided background and mentoring so Barbiero could start bringing in donations.

If You Want to Help Far from Home

Use some vacation time to volunteer abroad or travel to a country that interests you. This idea has become so popular it even has its own name, *voluntourism*. As with domestic volunteering, you should think about whether you're interested in direct service or offering your specific skills.

Read about what's going on politically in the country. Talk to people at organizations doing work on the ground. Then travel there and spend some time, either as part of an organized trip or on your own. Talk to as many people as possible, both casually and through planned informational interviews, so that you can get a sense of where you think there are needs that you could help meet.

If you'd prefer to do something that has already been organized, you've got ample choices. Faith-based and community organizations frequently offer missions to travel to other countries as part of a group. Two of the best-known organizations serving people of all ages are Cross-Cultural Solutions and Global Volunteers. Idealist .org also offers extensive international volunteer postings and you can search by country.

Habitat for Humanity offers brief trips throughout the year for people who want to work on home-building projects; there is no age limit as long as you're physically able. The Sierra Club is a great choice if you want a well-organized experience on an environmental project overseas (check out their domestic trips also). FlyforGood.com partners with nonprofits around the world to create volunteer travel experiences that have been vetted by Guidestar, a reputable nonprofit evaluator. The benefit of these trips is that someone else has given some thought to creating an experience meant

As you think about the various ways to give your time, you may want to explore where your urge to volunteer is coming from. Knowing the answers to these questions may help you figure out what kind of activities to consider:

- Are you interested in giving your time simply because you care about the cause and have no other motivation?

- Do you want to update your résumé?

- Are you interested in meeting new people, networking, or getting out in your community?

- Are you hoping to learn something new?

- Are you looking to test out something to see if you like it?

- Are you learning on the way to starting your own venture?

- Are you hoping to volunteer as a pathway to a part- or full-time job?

---

to make it a good one for you and the communities being served.

If you want to use specific professional skills, you'll need to network in your field a bit. Doctors Without Borders is an example of a great pathway for doctors who want to offer their services in parts of the world where they are needed. If you're looking for opportunities abroad in your profession, start by contacting your industry trade association and Googling "volunteer abroad" or "volunteer overseas" together with "lawyer," "teacher," "social work," or whatever your profession.

- Be wary of traveling with an organization you haven't heard of or whose fees seem excessive. Though there should be some administrative costs to sending volunteers overseas, fees shouldn't be very high and organizations should be transparent about how they are using funds.

- Do your research before you go. Visit online forums and sites like AbroadReviews .com and GoOverSeas.com where people share their thoughts about overseas programs. CharityNavigator.org is a useful site for vetting nonprofits.

- There is some debate about whether paying hundreds or thousands of dollars for a week or two of direct service is the greatest way to have an impact in a country with serious needs. It is unlikely that a week of your help will make a dramatic change in the lives of the people you serve, but it could spark an interest that you want to deepen. And if you work with a reputable organization that has vetted the project carefully, you can have a meaningful service experience much in the same way that you would have if you gave your time locally.

- Are you hoping to use the same skills you've honed in your primary career, or are you hoping to flex some different muscles?

- Do you have an urge to do something hands-on with a population or area you're helping? Or do you want to be working on a more strategic level, helping an organization be more effective?

- Do you want to contribute a few hours a week, a few hours a month, half your time, or even more?

- Are you looking for something at set times or more ad hoc (e.g., as an on-call adviser)?

- Do you want a connection to a new community or group with which you identify (e.g., your faith, veterans, a women's organization)?

- Are you inclined to join an organized program, or find or craft your own experience?

- Are you looking for a way to serve your country or local community?

Try Pro Bono Consulting

If you have skills in law, technology, design, or some other area in demand, consider volunteering your services pro bono for a nonprofit as a way to learn more while doing some good. One place to look is the Taproot Foundation, which assembles teams of skilled volunteers for projects like building a website or creating a marketing plan or human resources strategy for nonprofit clients.

Taproot isn't intended to be a pathway to a new career; it's a way to weave pro bono service into your everyday life. Yet lots of people use a stint with Taproot as a way to get a glimpse of nonprofit culture and see if it's a good fit. "If you've never worked in the sector, you may have fantasies and stereotypes," explained Hurst. "Pro bono is a good way to try a shoe on, maybe even try a few shoes on, because not all nonprofits are the same. You may even realize that you don't want to work in a nonprofit."

The Taproot Foundation operates in five cities around the United States (Los Angeles, San Francisco, Chicago, New York City, and Washington, D.C.). If you don't live in or near one of these cities, there are many other options—find a local organization you're interested in and then offer pro bono consulting on your own.

Experienced entrepreneurs and business leaders may find that mentoring growing businesses or consulting nonprofits is a great way to volunteer. A few organizations to investigate include:

- SCORE (score.org), which has 364 chapters nationwide, pairs experienced businesspeople as mentors with those trying to get new businesses off the ground.

- The Executive Service Corps Affiliate Network (escus.org) is a nationwide network of organizations that provides low-cost consulting services to nonprofits. The consulting is done on a volunteer basis by people with senior management or professional experience.

- The National Executive Service Corps (nesc.org), which works in New York, Connecticut, and New Jersey, is similar to the Executive Service Corps model and matches experienced businesspeople as consultants to nonprofits.

"Nonprofits say they want volunteers, but often they don't know what to do with high-quality volunteers. You need to make sure it's a high-quality experience."

–Barb Quaintance, senior vice president, AARP

Whatever your field, there is likely an organization that offers a way for professionals to serve on a pro bono basis, including several that involve going overseas to serve in less-developed countries. A few well-known ones include Doctors Without Borders, Architecture for Humanity, and Geekcorps. If you're trying to find pro bono opportunities in your field, check your local or national professional associations.

If you've served in the military, check out MissionServe.org and Serve.gov, both of which have opportunities specifically designed for veterans interested in civilian service. Returned Peace Corps volunteers and others with similar international experience can also visit Servicecorps.com to find organizations specifically looking for people with experience in other countries.

If you'd like to get paid as a mentor, consider signing up for PivotPlanet.com, where you could be matched with someone seeking your particular expertise.

Serve on a Nonprofit Board

Board service can be a great opportunity—a way to share your talent and skills, have influence, and even benefit from some of the halo effect of an organization doing good work. A great opportunity, yes, but also a great responsibility. As a nonprofit board member, you will be accountable for making sure that the organization fulfills its mission and lives within its means. You will also be responsible for key personnel decisions such as hiring and firing the executive director. In smooth times, these may not seem so serious. In difficult times, being on a board can be a huge test of your fortitude. As Ruth Wooden, former chair of the Encore.org board and a board

Volunteer Websites

Deciding which volunteer website to use can be as daunting as figuring out which online dating site is best for you—and some of the same logic applies.

You're likely to find some of the same listings on a variety of sites because nonprofits post their opportunities in multiple places. Second, sites vary not just in the opportunities listed but in the way they're set up. It's best to explore a few of them and see which ones you like.

Here's an overview of the biggies:

SERVE.GOV, a government-supported volunteering portal, highlights White House initiatives, including projects supported by the First Lady and Second Lady and nationally observed days of service (e.g., Dr. Martin Luther King's birthday and September 11). It offers both ongoing opportunities to serve in your own community and ways of getting involved with nationwide efforts. The site also offers a toolkit of resources to help you design your

own volunteer project and recruit others to help you.

VOLUNTEERMATCH.ORG has one of the largest databases of volunteer opportunities. It also has a lot of partnerships with corporations wanting to make volunteering easier for their employees and nonprofits trying to improve their online recruiting of volunteers. It lets you search geographically and has profiles of individual volunteers that may give you ideas about what you'd like to try.

ALLFORGOOD.ORG was inspired by President Obama's 2008 call to create a clearinghouse of volunteer opportunities all in one place. It's free for nonprofits to use in all kinds of ways, so it may contain some postings you don't see elsewhere.

Whether you have five minutes, five hours, or five days, CREATETHEGOOD.ORG, an AARP-sponsored site, can help you find an opportunity near you. It also has simple how-to guides for creating your own short-term project, whether it's holding a winter veteran, advised me: "Don't do it to set yourself up for an encore career. Do it because you're passionate about the issue."

Board service can be an invaluable way to expand your network and get a firsthand look at how an organization handles all kinds of strategic and operational issues. If you're already in the nonprofit sector, joining a board can be a way to connect with a new set of people, contribute to an issue that's new for you, and develop new skills and perspectives.

Whatever the impetus, you're probably not going to start a relationship with a nonprofit by talking about board involvement. "Usually board members come through an informal network of contacts," said Steve

---

coat drive or helping your community prepare for a natural disaster.

IDEALIST.ORG is a hub for all kinds of nonprofit activity, not just volunteering. It has extensive online listings for nonprofit jobs and internships, consulting jobs, and even postings for opportunities outside the United States. Plus, you can subscribe to a daily or weekly update that monitors job postings and events happening in your geographic area or in your field.

HANDSONNETWORK.ORG, an enterprise of Points of Light, is a network of 250 volunteer action centers. These centers help people find and engage in volunteer activities in their local communities. Local action centers offer a calendar of ongoing group-based volunteer projects that are easy to sign up for, in addition to longer-term national service programs.

CATCHAFIRE.ORG matches individuals who want to give their professional skills to nonprofits and socially minded businesses that need help. The projects can be done

virtually and on a flexible schedule so there is no requirement to be in the same city as the organization being served. If you get involved, you'll be trained through a webinar and matched with an organization for discreet projects that would normally be done by an outside contractor. This is ideal for those with skills in marketing, communications, design, social media, fund-raising, human resources, technology, finance, or strategy who are looking to work independently on a finite project.

SPARKED.COM takes the idea of flexibility and convenience even further by offering opportunities for *microvolunteering*—giving back that can be done online, often in a matter of minutes or hours. The site caters to the person who is so jammed that the only way to fit in volunteering is during a few spare moments here and there. Projects are suitably bite-sized and include product brainstorming, participating in focus groups, social media, IT, and design.

Villano, whose firm Social Vision Productions helps nonprofits build better boards.

Lawyers and other professionals often get asked to join boards after doing a pro bono project for a nonprofit. Sometimes boards are looking for people who have a personal connection to an issue or are a part of the community they serve—so a treatment facility may tap a person who has overcome addiction, or a group working with immigrants of a certain culture may want people from that background.

The more time you spend with an organization—showing up at events, volunteering, or doing pro bono work—the more you will know about whether joining the board is the right move for you.

If you're new to boards and considering joining one for the first time, do these things first:

- Get to know the organization as well as you can. Go to its events. Take on a serious volunteer or pro bono project to see what it's like to engage with the organization from the outside.

- Meet as many staffers and board members as possible. Ask to see the minutes of a few prior meetings.

- Review the IRS 990s, the tax forms that all nonprofits must file, to make sure you know as much as possible about the organization's operations and financial health.

- Consider joining an advisory board first. Advisory boards are groups of people who lend their time and counsel to an organization without taking on the fiduciary responsibility of being on an official board of directors.

- Find out if there is a "give-get" requirement—does joining obligate you to either give or raise a certain amount of money each year?

- Ask if it's possible to join with a three-month probationary period to see if it's a good fit on both sides. If you don't like what you're seeing

Getting on Board

Here are some useful sites with information about training for board service, as well as board service opportunities:

- Bridgestar.org

- Boardsource.org

- Boardnetusa.org

Some organizations also hold board fairs. Look at the following sites to see if anything is happening in your area:

- UnitedWay.org. Find your local chapter and attend its next board fair.

- National Council on Foundations (cof.org/locator). Use this link to find your local community foundation.

- National Council of Nonprofit Associations (ncna.org). Look for your state chapter.

Sites like these are useful as you learn more about board service and explore opportunities in your area. But as with job sites, they should not be a replacement for showing up, getting to know the people involved, and rolling up your sleeves.

after a trial period, investigate other organizations until you find one that's a good fit. Usually, there are many organizations working on the same issues. If you're ready to make a board-level commitment, take the time to find the best match you can.

Consider National or Community Service

At a moment when our country is facing enormous challenges, you might find it gratifying to spend your time serving in one of the government-supported service programs. Like traditional volunteering, national service comes in several different forms. Some service programs are designed purely for people over fifty-five. These include the federally supported Senior Corps (seniorcorps.gov) programs—Foster Grandparents, Senior Companions, and RSVP. Others, such as AmeriCorps and the Peace Corps, are open to people of all ages. Some AmeriCorps grantees, such as AARP Experience Corps (go to aarp.org and search for "experience corps") and OASIS (oasisnet.org), offer opportunities exclusively for people over fifty-five.

National and community service programs offer a spectrum of commitment, from a few hours a week to full time. Senior Corps may be a good fit for you if you are over fifty-five and want to make a part-time, flexible volunteer commitment through RSVP; or if you are over fifty-five, have a limited income, and are interested in modestly paid direct service with children or the elderly, try their Foster Grandparents or Senior Companions programs. Most AmeriCorps members serve nine to twelve months and require a commitment of ten to forty hours per week.

> "One of the best things for me being an older AmeriCorps member was being surrounded by a group of young people who were still idealistic and believed that the world was going to change."
>
> —Carolyn Glass, development comanager, donor relations, Sisters of the Road

AmeriCorps engagements pay a modest living allowance, cover individual (not family) health care benefits, and offer a Segal AmeriCorps Education Award that's worth about $5,000 when applied to tuition costs or college debt. If you are over fifty-five and earn an AmeriCorps Education Award, you can transfer its value to a child, foster child, or grandchild.

The most intense experiences, such as AmeriCorps VISTA or Peace Corps, require a full-time commitment of one to two years. AmeriCorps VISTA serves low-income areas of the United States, offers a living allowance that's indexed to the current federal poverty level, and requires that VISTA members not have any outside employment during their year of service. It's not easy, but it's an opportunity worth considering if you want to help solve the problems created by poverty. The Peace Corps requires a two-year placement overseas, which can be a great fit if you are bold, adventurous, in good health, and considering work with a global impact.

For Carla Kelley, service was a way to refine her ideas. Having returned to college in her fifties after her third child was out of the house, Kelley was thinking about doing some kind of work to fight bullying and increase tolerance. She spent a year working as a full-time, salaried educator for the Anti-Defamation League, delivering anti-bias curriculum to youth and adult audiences. Then she joined a local AmeriCorps program focused on providing classroom support to teachers. Kelley asked her AmeriCorps manager if she could try out her program, and he gave her the green light to test it out first on the AmeriCorps team and then later with students in various schools. The experience was so rich she signed up for a second year. Soon afterward, she started the Human Rights Education Center, which addresses bullying and discrimination in schools, online, and in workplaces. The AmeriCorps education award came in handy in paying off Kelley's student loans. Here are some other opportunities:

- **Corporation for National and Community Service** (nationalservice.gov). Individual program selector allows you to put in eligibility parameters like age and income, and preferences such as direct versus indirect service.

- **Peace Corps** (peacecorps.gov/50plus). Through a recent partnership with AARP, the Peace Corps is trying to interest more people over fifty to become Peace Corps Volunteers.

- **ReServe** (reserveinc.org). An excellent option for those over fifty-five who want to serve part time in nonprofits or government agencies. Pays a small hourly stipend. Currently only available in New York and Miami, with plans to expand to other cities. (For more, see page 177.)

- **The Center for Music National Service** (musicnationalservice.org). This organization has a few different service opportunities for musicians. MusicianCorps trains and places musicians to serve full time as teachers and mentors in low-performing public schools, youth centers, and other high-need community settings. MusicianCorps mentors receive a living stipend, health care, and professional development in exchange for a year-long service term.

"I was assigned to one school where a lot of kids were giving up. For a while I was the only reason they were coming to school. The principal found a lean-to and created a music room. We taught and played music in there. We had a choir, a guitar class, a jazz band, a wind instrument class. We rocked out for a whole year."

—Robert Frazier, musician/teacher, on his MusicianCorps Fellowship year

- **International Senior Lawyers Project** (islp.org). A nonprofit organization that delivers free legal assistance to developing communities around the world from experienced lawyers. Programs are primarily focused on three areas: Human Rights and Social Welfare, Access to Justice, and Equitable Economic Development. For attorneys at or near retirement.

- **NPower** (npower.org). NPower provides nationwide IT training and services to nonprofits and young adults. Opportunities vary in time commitment.

Internships? At Your Age?

Getting a great internship has long been a rite of passage in the early years of a career. So it's not surprising that older folks want in on the meaty experience of on-the-job learning and networking.

The recession has made internships for adults increasingly popular, and some employers have jumped at the chance to bring on experienced people who realize that internships can be great résumé enhancers. In 2010, the U.S. Labor Department cracked down on some rarely enforced rules that require unpaid internships to be primarily for the benefit of the intern, not the employer. As a result, companies—even nonprofits—have been revamping their internship programs to make sure they don't run into legal problems. So don't be surprised if a nonprofit would prefer to call you a volunteer, not an intern.

Susan Burket (see page 162) was intrigued by an internship opportunity at Habitat for Humanity. She knew it was a well-run organization with a great mission. Then she read the description, which said something about welcoming "juniors or seniors" with a certain GPA. At the time she was forty-nine, not a junior or a senior no matter how you define them! Still Burket decided to go for it. When she arrived, she walked into an office filled with young people and said to the interviewer, "I'm not sure I'm what you had in mind, but hear me out." Burket convinced the interviewer that she would be a good fit for what they needed—writing for the newsletter, organizing luncheons, and helping to set up a speakers bureau. Burket worked at Habitat one day a week, spending the other four in her existing job as a computer programmer. Like any good intern, she did a combination of high- and low-level tasks, and she made a point of not acting proud when doing the literal dirty work. While washing dishes after luncheons, she would pepper the head of fund-raising with her questions.

When I was in my twenties, I had time for a long internship. Is spending the time worth it at this stage of life?

That depends. If you plan to work for five or more years in a new field, or even a new role, spending several months or a year in an internship or some other kind of training is probably worth it.

You may bristle at being called an *intern* at this age. If you're not being paid, you may have some ability to set your own job title. I'm running into lots of *senior advisers* and *senior interns* these days. SHiFT, a community organization in Minneapolis focused on the encore stage, started something called *midternships,* which are just what they sound like—midlife internships designed to expose people over fifty to a new experience in a new field. *Consultant* or *senior adviser* carry some weight and could feel right, depending on your arrangement.

If you're going to apply for internships, be prepared. Most internships won't have an age requirement, but some will likely be limited to students.

Find Someone to Shadow

Shadowing someone for a day can be a great glimpse into a potential new career. In an ideal scenario, you'd also find a person willing to serve as a mentor, sharing his or her perspective on what it feels like to do the work.

Brian Kurth was so convinced that shadowing is a great first step for career seekers that he wrote a book, *Test–Drive Your Dreams,* for do-it-yourselfers and built the company Vocation Vacations, which pairs people curious about a particular job with a mentor for a vacation-length immersion experience. He helped me think through some tips on making your own shadowing experience happen.

- Identify a few organizations and a few people within those organizations doing work that you think you may want to do. LinkedIn is a great tool for finding organizations and people in specific jobs. You can also identify people who are playing a leadership role in the field by finding out who's speaking at conferences and who's blogging. (These people may be more approachable than your average leaders.) Keep in mind that people who run smaller organizations and entrepreneurial ventures might be more flexible than people in large institutions or government agencies, where an individual may not have the authority to invite visitors.

- Contact a few people with a brief and gracious email, explaining that you are interested in the kind of work they do and would welcome the chance to do an informational interview by phone or Skype. If it goes well, you can ask about job shadowing later.

- Select a person who seems receptive. One of the beauties of mission-focused work is that people are doing the work because they care about it, and they tend to be thrilled to hear that others want to work on the same issues they feel passionate about. Still, be prepared that not everyone will be open to this idea, which is why you want to identify several people to approach.

- After you've identified a willing mentor, schedule a mutually convenient time when you can shadow the person in his or her job for anywhere from an afternoon to several days, ideally in the days leading up to a big event critical to the organization's functioning or an important board meeting. If the person or organization is concerned about liability issues, offer to sign a waiver or release.

If you like this approach, have a look at Kurth's book, which provides extensive detail and advice about every step of the process, and find a way to shadow several people.

Consider the New Hybrids

There are a handful of organizations across the country that are working to help people in the second half of life find experiential learning opportunities that can help them transition into encore careers. These new organizations are hybrids, combining service, training, part-time work, and consulting.

ReServe

ReServe is an organization that matches professionals over the age of fifty-five with part-time, paid placements at nonprofits and public agencies. It's now operating in New York City, Westchester County (NY), and Miami.

In 2012 I attended a ReServe orientation session at the New York City office. Ruth Blackman (a ReServist herself) welcomed the group, then warmed up the room with a get-to-know-you exercise. Each person was asked to explain to their tablemates why they came, what they used to do, and when they'd last been on the Internet.

People came from a wide variety of occupations—a social worker and lifelong activist; a graphic artist; a couple of teachers; one with an advertising background; and several whose résumés defied easy classification. Their reasons for showing up were varied. They were retired, laid off, wanting to give back, wanting to get out of the house (or out of someone's hair). At least two mentioned wanting a break from caregiving responsibilities. They wanted a way to use their talents and experience. Some, like Maria Pacheco, had very specific reasons for attending. She wanted on-the-ground job experience to add to a recent certification as a community health worker. Nearly everyone had been online within hours of showing up at the meeting—a good thing, because all ReServe placements require computer literacy.

Moving beyond introductions, Blackman explained what ReServe offers—a way for people to use their time and skills in part-time jobs at nonprofits, with a nominal stipend of $10 an hour, and a way for nonprofits to add some experienced people to their teams to help meet their public service missions. With a bit of training, ReServists are placed on the front line with direct exposure to clients—helping first-generation college applicants, for instance, or recruiting new adult literacy tutors for a public library. As Blackman explained, "It's exciting. It's fun. You get paid, but not a lot."

ReServe isn't designed as a pathway to something else. In most cases, a ReServe position is an end in and of itself. But occasionally a stint with ReServe leads to a part- or full-time position. In fact, ReServe itself has been known to hire ReServists into staff positions.

Encore Fellowships

Fellowships are another way to immerse deeply, with the added benefit of a title that denotes a certain level of prior experience or accomplishment. There is no single model for a fellowship, but they tend to describe an affiliation with an organization as well as a fairly intense experience involving some kind of contribution, learning, study, or training. Often there is a community of other fellows in the same or similar roles. The application or nomination process is typically rigorous, and as a result, fellowships can carry a lot of prestige.

Laura Gassner Otting, the nonprofit recruiter, is a big fan of fellowships for people on their way to an encore. "It sounds more like graduate school, continued education as opposed to glorified filing," she told me. "Plus, you're part of a pipeline that you can access for introductions and knowledge."

Although fellowships tend to have an academic ring, they don't necessarily have a connection to an academic institution. Often they are affiliated with think tanks or research institutions, and more recently, with social entrepreneurship organizations such as the Ashoka Foundation. Some fellowships involve a stipend or other perks, such as gatherings with leaders in the field.

Similar to internships, most fellowships cater to young people or those early in their careers. But that is starting to change. There's a new breed of fellowships cropping up with the sole intention of creating a bridge for people interested in encore careers. Started by Encore.org (then called Civic Ventures) with just ten people in Silicon Valley in 2010, Encore Fellowships match professionals finishing their midlife careers with nonprofits in their geographic area looking for a certain kind of expertise. Encore Fellows typically work 1,000 hours over a six- to twelve-month period, through either a part- or full-time schedule, and earn a stipend of between $20,000 and $35,000.

Everyone benefits. Nonprofits get access to senior-level talent at a fraction of the cost. And fellows make a high-impact contribution to a local community organization, get an intense exposure to a new kind of work environment, plus a chance to try out a different role and build a professional network.

An Encore Fellowship helped Mark Judge move into the nonprofit world after his twenty-two years in children's publishing ended with a buy-out. Although he had worked at nonprofits earlier in his career, Judge didn't have much of a network in the Bay Area and that was holding him back. So he started volunteering for twenty-four hours a week at Resource Area for Teaching (RAFT), a local nonprofit that provides mentoring to teachers, along with activities and ideas they can use in their classrooms. On a recommendation from his supervisor, a former Encore Fellow himself, Judge applied to become an Encore Fellow and worked for a year at RAFT. Today he divides his time between paid positions at two youth-serving organizations—RAFT, where he is under contract to work on the organization's national expansion, and Youth Science Institute, where he's a "half-time" marketing director.

A key ingredient to the Encore Fellows model is peer support and community. Fellows meet regularly for panel discussions and to spend time with other fellows in their group (usually around ten to a class), and they are also part of the Encore Fellowships Network, fellows and alums of the program around the country who communicate online.

Although there are only a few hundred Encore Fellowships across the country now, the program is expanding. In 2011, Intel offered any U.S.-based employees eligible for retirement the chance to apply for Encore Fellowships. Intel will pay the cost of the stipend and provide six months of health insurance. If more companies follow suit, Encore Fellowships could eventually become a commonplace option for corporate employees interested in moving from the business to the nonprofit sector.

Also in 2011, the California HealthCare Foundation funded a program to place Encore Fellows in community health clinics to help improve the quality and efficiency of service provided to some of the state's neediest residents. In 2012, based on recommendations from clinic operators who hosted fellows and the demand from others who want fellows, the foundation

Encore Fellowships aren't yet available in my city. How can I create something similar?

The essence of the Encore Fellowship is a meaningful, structured, paid opportunity to contribute your skills and experience to a social purpose. Although it could be challenging, you may be able to create an independent consulting project that has some of the same attributes— a high-impact assignment with a fixed duration, access to senior decision-makers in an organization, and a stipend to indicate the value of your work.

You may also be able to create a peer support group where you can compare notes about your experiences and even invite guest speakers to meet with you to discuss topics you'd like to learn more about. With some creativity, you should be able to craft something that will provide value to the organization, expose you to its culture, and fit nicely on your résumé.

If title is important to you, consider proposing something like "encore consultant" or "senior adviser." Learn more at Encore.org.

announced that it would double its investment. Other philanthropic organizations may follow suit and begin offering experience to help the organizations they support.

Encore Hartford

Encore Hartford, which is affiliated with the University of Connecticut, launched a program in 2010 to help experienced professionals move from unemployment into nonprofit jobs, while at the same time helping Connecticut's economy by putting people back to work.

Created to assist people who have been displaced by the recession, the program consists of twelve weeks of classroom learning followed by placement in a nonprofit. The fellows learn in environments as varied as the basement of a church that houses a soup kitchen to the palatial offices of a science museum. "The idea is to taste and feel the work environment," said David Garvey, who designed and now heads the program.

RozeLyn Beck discovered the Encore Hartford program after her position at the Hartford insurance company was eliminated in 2009. After twelve years with one company, she decided it was time for a change. "Continuing to move up the corporate ladder wasn't all that I'd thought it would be," she said. So she took a package and started to work on a plan.

As part of the outplacement offered by the Hartford, Beck filled out a worksheet (much like the ones in Chapter 3) where she had to rank the three things most important to her in her next move. Earlier in her career, when doing a similar exercise, she put "financial security" at the top of the list. This time, financial security didn't even make the top ten.

Beck was matched with a small food bank in Connecticut where she worked closely with the executive director. "I grew up in an entrepreneurial family, so I could relate to it," she said. "In the nonprofit world, you need to become a jack-of-all-trades. I emptied trash cans on Friday afternoons, yet at the same time the executive director was willing to have me involved in anything I wanted to be involved in. I worked very independently, figuring things out, providing recommendations, and moving on. My executive director looked to me to decide things. I bounced ideas off my colleagues, but it felt like this was my job. I got a chance to go to a funder with a grant discussion, and I did one-on-one interviews with every member of the board. It's the grown-up version of an internship." Today Beck is the director of marketing and development for the YWCA Hartford Region.

The Hartford program costs about $2,500, with opportunities for scholarships. Participants can collect unemployment while in the program.

The Encore Fellows Network and Encore Hartford are two examples of programs that help people with long careers in the for-profit sector transition into roles that are filling important needs in nonprofits. Although the names and particular details will likely vary, expect to see more variations on these kinds of bridge programs as the encore idea takes hold.

Craft Your Own Course

Organized programs can make it easier to use your time and talent to have a positive impact in the world. And they can relieve some of the pressure of having to figure out everything on your own. But if you have the right combination of research skills, creativity, persistence, and patience, you can craft your own course. And many people are doing that.

First, you'll need to put all your energy into researching what's out there, and then seeing if there are ways to get yourself in a position to do and learn—both to hone your ideas and to try things out. You'll probably use a process similar to the one outlined in "Go for a Test Drive" (see page 64). These explorations take time, so don't be surprised if you're exploring quite a few positions before it all comes together.

Seminary professor Alice Marie Graham's DIY journey was launched just after Hurricane Katrina ravaged the Gulf Coast of Mississippi. "A pastor friend had been assigned to Mississippi, and I learned through her what the clergy were dealing with and how overwhelmed they were," she told me. Graham immediately put together a course on pastoral care in the midst of a community disaster, and as part of the course, she brought ten students with her to Mississippi for a week.

Before teaching the course, Graham didn't have any expertise in the subject. "I thought it would be a good opportunity for me to learn alongside the students," she said. To prepare, she did a lot of reading and took a class on crisis intervention and stress management during disasters.

That trip turned out to be the push Graham needed to deal with the restlessness she was feeling at work. The next year, she took a three-month sabbatical from teaching in North Carolina and went to Mississippi, where she put together a combination of paid and volunteer projects. "I worked with seniors, leading caring conversations where people talked about surviving Katrina," she said. "I worked with clergy who were unprepared to respond to such an overwhelming disaster. It was exciting to feel engaged and useful in a way that spoke to my spirit."

Graham was so invigorated by this new work that she decided to retire three years early and return to Mississippi, not knowing what she would do when she arrived. "When I told the president of the seminary that year would be my last, he thought I'd lost my mind." Months of sleepless nights followed, yet Graham didn't waiver in her resolve, convinced that she would be able to find an interim role through the web of contacts she now had in Mississippi.

"Every time I panicked, something would happen to calm me down and I would know I was on the right course," she said. A friend offered a rent-free home. Others volunteered to come to North Carolina and help her move. And then, a week before her scheduled move, she got a call from one of her new contacts about an interim executive director position at the Mississippi Coast Interfaith Disaster Task Force, an organization she had worked with during her sabbatical. She is now its executive director.

The Benefits of Showing Up

Sometimes the best way to make things happen is to just walk through the front door. Although a lot can happen while sitting in front of your computer, don't spend all your time reading online or sending emails. At some point, it's critical to get out in the world, meet other people, and see things firsthand.

Carlos Campos, a retired Army colonel with a post-graduate degree in instructional leadership, got a job as a teacher after literally walking through the front door of a middle school in the Bronx and asking to meet with the principal. He knew he wanted to work with difficult kids and asked if there was an opportunity to help with the students no one wanted to teach. It turns out that an eighth-grade special education teacher had recently quit, and they were desperate to fill the position. He stepped in and ended up staying for three years.

The walk-in-the-door method worked for a handful of other people I spoke to. Old school, but still effective. In the end, nothing beats face-to-face. If you've sent in a résumé or had your name floated in front of an organization, that doesn't mean it's time to sit back and wait. Take advantage of any ways to make a personal connection or show your interest. Show up in all the various ways you can.

FAQs

I need a job, and the organization I volunteer for isn't hiring. How can I use my volunteer experience to get a job somewhere else?

Volunteering can be taken just as seriously as paid work if the experience is on point for what you want to do. In fact, this phenomenon is so widely accepted that the social networking career site LinkedIn added a section on its profile form where people can list volunteer positions. According to LinkedIn, one in five hiring managers say that they have hired a candidate because of their volunteer work. The key is identifying what you accomplished in your unpaid role and communicating how you could similarly help another organization to meet its goals.

How does pay affect how people view what has been traditionally called volunteer "work"?

Whether money changes hands definitely matters. Often, the existence of payment elevates a role—and makes everyone feel more invested in the project. Modest pay was a critical design element in the Encore Fellows model, for example. "It was important to us that everyone—the fellow and the nonprofit work host—had skin in the game," said Leslye Louie, the program's national director.

Some people feel just as strongly that their contribution should be unpaid. Amy Avergun had that feeling when she volunteered on a project for Discovering What's Next, a community organization in the Boston area that helps people explore the encore life stage. She intended to volunteer her services, but then the organization got a grant to cover the work and insisted on paying her. "I took it, but I didn't like it," she told me. "I wanted to make this contribution. For years I have been giving money in various ways, but this was a way I could give of my time." After that experience, Avergun found lots of ways to give her time to the organization. In fact, she is now on the board.

Organizations may have their own reasons for wanting to classify you in a particular way. Pay can turn a volunteer or intern role into a job, and the lack of it can create problems for an organizations' compliance with various labor laws. Keep these points in mind if an organization doesn't seem willing to craft the kind of relationship you're hoping for.

What is the value of an organized service opportunity?

You probably know by now whether you do better with some structure or if you like to figure things out on your own.

One of the benefits of finding an organized program is that someone else has thought through the various pieces of a particular kind of transition. For example, EnCorps Teachers trains math and science professionals to become educators in underserved public schools in California. Unlike many academic programs, they get participants into the classroom right away; one of the key ingredients in this transition is understanding that students today have a very different way of acquiring knowledge than when we all went to school. EnCorps Teachers also helps people navigate the often confusing certification requirements for teachers in California.

Another benefit in finding an existing pathway is having a ready-made group of peers who understand what you're going through. Career transition can feel isolating, and you may find that even the most sympathetic family members and friends can't give you the kind of support that you'll get from others in the same situation. Antoinette La Belle, East Coast director for the Encore Fellowship program, often refers to the cohorts as "fellow travelers." I can see why.

Then there's the credential aspect of it. Just like graduating from a recognized school opens doors, so too does completing a program that has some recognition in the field you're trying to break into. One nonprofit director likened the value of having an Encore Fellow to winning the "golden ticket of maturity, work ethic, and experience" that has stretched his organization's work and boosted everyone's accomplishments.

Finally, as programs graduate more people, there's the alumni benefit. I stopped keeping track of the number of people who told me they were hired because an encore program alum put in a good word. That will only increase as more of these programs sprout up.

I have no interest in stuffing or licking envelopes. How do I make sure that I'm getting a volunteer experience that actually uses my skills?

Volunteering has come a long way since the days when the only way you could help was to stuff envelopes or answer phones. But that doesn't mean you should assume that every organization seeking volunteers knows how to use them properly. Shirley Sagawa, the author of *The American Way to Change*, said it is critical to have the answers to a few key questions before you commit to a volunteer role:

- What exactly will I be doing?
- Will I be trained?
- To whom will I be reporting?
- How will I be evaluated?
- How can I share ideas if I have them?

If an organization has given a lot of thought to how it uses volunteers, you won't even have to ask these questions. The answers will be given to you in an orientation session or even on an FAQ page of the website you visited to learn about the opportunity.

I'm interested both in direct, hands-on experiences and helping on a strategic level. How can I achieve both goals?

It's possible that you'll find a way to do that in one place, but it could be tricky to navigate multiple roles in the same organization. You may have an easier time going in one direction for your paid work and keeping something else as a volunteer activity. RozeLyn Beck went that route. Before she left her job, she got her dog, Cadbury, registered as a therapy dog and started making visits to nursing homes and rehabilitation centers. She so enjoyed that work that she thought she might find a staff position at one of the organizations working in that area. But she ended up finding a role better suited to her professional skills with the YWCA and, at least for now, she's keeping her pet therapy activities as part of her volunteer life, serving on a board and continuing the visits with her dog in her free time.

CHAPTER 9

Back to School

"It is utterly false and cruelly arbitrary to put all the play and learning into childhood, all the work into middle age, and all the regrets into old age."

—MARGARET MEAD

Pamela Harris vividly remembers being one of the only women in her law school class back in the seventies. Now she's the only one in her sixties in her master's program for library science. "Libraries are the most democratic institutions we have, and librarians are universally committed to growing and maintaining access to information for everyone," she tells friends who are surprised by her late-career move. And besides, she adds, "What's so great about settling into a trailer and playing bridge?"

Don Tarbutton, seventy-four, has been the "oldest guy in the class" three times in his life. When he was in his mid-forties, he got a master's in health care administration from the University of Washington. Then, in his sixties, Tarbutton trained to become a Buddhist chaplain at the Salt Center for Buddhist Studies in Santa Cruz, California, and did his clinical pastoral training at the Veteran's Hospital in Seattle. Tarbutton now works part time as an associate hospice chaplain, doing work that provides the extra income he needs, along with some pretty great rewards. The work, he said, "is without a doubt the most meaningful work of my life." (For more on his story, see page 42.)

Before Priscilla Santiago returned to school (fifty years after dropping out of high school)—first to get her GED, then for her associate's, and ultimately a bachelor's—she never thought she'd get a degree. It was scary, but having a network of support—friends, family, and a raft of mentors and counselors along the way—helped her through. Now sixty-five and eyeing a master's degree, Santiago uses her example to illustrate that it's never too late. She also recommends persistence: "If you can't get in where you want to go, just keep applying." (For more on her story, see page 7.)

In the jargon of higher education, Harris, Tarbutton, and Santiago are *adult learners* or *nontraditional students,* meaning they are over the age of twenty-five. The language is more than a tad imprecise, as there's a lot of ground between twenty-five and seventy-five. "It's also insulting to eighteen-year-olds," quipped Mary Beth Lakin of the American Council on Education. "And once we get to the point where we recognize that the nontraditional learner is traditional and that everyone is learning across a lifetime, terms like *adult learner* will vanish."

The U.S. Department of Education estimates that 90 million individuals participate in some form of adult education (that's another one of those fuzzy terms but, for our purposes, just know that people of all ages are showing up in all kinds of educational settings) each year, and 40 percent of American college students, or almost 6 million people, are twenty-five years of age or older. A survey by *U.S. News and World Report* in 2007 found that the number of college students ages forty to sixty-four had increased nearly 20 percent to almost 2 million over the previous decade.

The latest research from Encore.org shows that 31 million people ages forty-four to seventy are interested in encore careers, and a good chunk of them will need some kind of education or retraining to move into their encores. So expect those adult learners to have even more company.

Older learners aren't a new phenomenon. In 1975, Elderhostel, now called Road Scholar, pioneered the idea of educational travel for people over fifty. I remember when my grandmother was in her seventies (she's now ninety-seven), heading off to college campuses all over the country with groups of friends to study classical music and watercolors. So-called enrichment courses, like the ones offered by Road Scholar and Osher Lifelong Learning Institutes, are still well attended, as are a slew of new, free online courses from top universities. But adult learning today is as much about job training as it is about expanding horizons.

When you're looking to retool in midlife, some education or a new credential can help level the playing field and give you a better shot at a new job.

It can be a fill-in, as in picking up a few classes to give you the latest skills, or an extra credential that will allow you to do something new. Or it can be full-on, like a multiyear program for an advanced degree. And it can definitely be the key to discovering what it is you want to do next.

There's no shortage of options. There are the usual suspects—community colleges, public and private four-year colleges and universities, and community centers or organizations. You'll also find a growing number of for-profit education providers. And within all these categories, you'll find courses catering to people of all ages and interests. What surprised me most when talking to people about their encore educational choices is how unpredictable they could be. I've met people with fancy degrees who trained for their encores by getting a quick certificate at a community college and people who had never finished college who went back to finish a four-year degree and continued on well past graduation.

> **"An associate's degree today is like a high school diploma. Education plays a very big role in anything you want to do."**
>
> –Priscilla Santiago, on getting a degree in her sixties

A Taste of What's Out There

A small but growing crop of programs has emerged to serve people in midlife or beyond who are searching for meaningful work with social impact. Community colleges have taken the lead by partnering with nearby employers and training people for in-demand jobs in health care, education, social services, and the green economy. Backed by venture capital and launched in 2012, Empowered UCLA Extension offers online certificate courses specifically designed to provide baby boomers with marketable skills for later careers. Empowered offers training for careers in such fields as environmental sustainability, college counseling, nonprofit management, and patient advocacy.

Encore Hartford, a program affiliated with the University of Connecticut, offers a twelve-week course for unemployed professionals interested in moving into the nonprofit sector. Through a combination of classroom experience and field placements, students learn about the

Discussion Prompts

- Is going back to school necessary for the work you want to do? Talk to people in the field about the skills and credentials employers are looking for in the roles that interest you.

- If there are multiple levels of credentialing, how much of a commitment are you willing to make?

- How much leisure time are you willing to sacrifice for classes and studying?

- Might you benefit from a formal program to explore what it is you want to do before going back for more training or education?

- Do you have the flexibility to travel, or do you need to keep your options local?

- Do you have the discipline for an online program? (Find out on page 208.)

- How much can you afford to spend?

nonprofit sector while experiencing it first-hand. More than half the students attend on scholarship, thanks to an arrangement with the federal Department of Labor. (For more on Encore Hartford, see page 180.)

Harvard University's Advanced Leadership Initiative was created in 2009 to help experienced business leaders take on challenges like poverty, global health, environmental degradation, and education in their encore careers. A husband-and-wife team, both alumni of Stanford's Graduate School of Business, recently created Beacon Stanford, a four-month program to help alums explore ways to plan their encore careers and have a greater impact on the world.

You can find educational opportunities offered by entities that aren't "schools" at all. JVA Consulting, a nonprofit consulting firm in Denver, trains people around the country in grant writing and social media skills for nonprofits via its low-cost webinars. Wellcoaches, a coach training school in partnership with the American College of Sports Medicine, offers training (mostly for nurses and personal trainers) for new roles as health and wellness coaches entirely through teleclasses (in effect, instructional conference calls).

Whatever your interest, there is likely some combination of old and new ways to get training—in person, online, by phone, through fieldwork, or via a hybrid model. You could fold school into your existing life, with night or weekend classes. You could go away to school like an eager freshman flying the coop. Or you might discover an executive education-style program where you travel to be part of an orientation session and attend periodic gatherings but do the rest of the learning at your home computer.

Why Go Back to School?

Before you can even think about where and how to go back to school, it makes sense to think about *why* you want to. Which brings us to a few fundamental questions: Is going back to school necessary for the kind of work you want to do? Or might going back to school help you figure out who you are at this stage of your life and what you want to do next?

What follows are a few common reasons why others in midlife and beyond have elected to go back to school.

Finish a Degree

More than 40 percent of those who started at four-year institutions haven't finished, according to the Department of Education. Not finishing a degree can haunt you, and it can hold you back from many opportunities. Finishing a degree can set you on a completely new life course. It can also lead to a quest for a lot more education. That's how it was for Veronica Buckley.

Even though Buckley was an excellent student in high school, she was pushed away from the idea of college because she was told she was "only going to get married anyway." Buckley did a one-year college program to improve her secretarial skills but never continued after that. She married, raised two children, and worked all along the way, thriving in increasingly senior human resources roles, first in financial and then legal firms. Still, the lack of a degree dogged her. "I felt a sense of inadequacy," said Buckley, now sixty-four. "I just didn't have the ticket." When her kids were older and she was in her late forties, she decided it was time to fix that.

Buckley researched various programs near her home in Chicago and decided that DePaul University had the most appealing program for returning adult students. Classes were long and met once a week in the evenings. Every student had an academic committee that provided guidance until graduation. And Buckley was even able to get some college credit for her work experience. "I just loved what it was all about," she explained. "The environment was collaborative. And because

Collect Unemployment? If you're out of work, you may be able to get some financial assistance for your education or retraining while still continuing to collect unemployment benefits. The rules vary by state, so check with your local unemployment office.

> "When I get out of the subway and walk up the steps to my classes, it's a metaphor for entering another world. It's like going to Hogwarts."
>
> –Ruth Wooden, former nonprofit executive director

everyone is an adult, the student is teacher and the teacher is student."

Find Your Way

You may decide to take classes not to learn any specific subject but to rediscover who you are and figure out what you want to do next.

After twenty-seven years in the federal government, Mattie Ruffin retired with a good pension and the goal of taking a full year of total relaxation—a long vacation, as she puts it. After her break, Ruffin said she was eager for something new. A friend told her about Envision 50+, a ten-week reinvention program at Prince George's Community College in Largo, Maryland. The program was a combination of guided self-assessment work and career-planning work such as updating résumés and honing job search skills.

For Ruffin, the self-assessment process reinforced what she already knew—that she liked being around people and helping them. Soon after the program ended, Ruffin applied for and got a part-time job at the college working in a department that teaches English and math to non-English speakers who are working on their GEDs. She registers people in the program and collects data for the government agencies that cover its costs. "I'm working because I want to, not because I have to," she said, and the job meets her needs. "I'm a people person; I like to help people," she said. "That's what this is doing—helping people. That's the story of my life."

Explore an Interest

Ruth Wooden had some ideas about what she would do after "retiring" from her role as the president of a major nonprofit. She started out with what she no longer wanted to do—be anyone's boss, handle "adminishit," work full time, and focus on policy rather than people. She likened the process to paying attention to dreams. "I started seeing little flashes of images that were appealing," she explained. "I frequently saw myself in a room full of people sharing tough stories and helping each other without judging, which is the model of family-supported therapy." She also started remembering how much she enjoyed counseling people and giving advice, but what form that would take now was not clear.

Then through a random connection, Wooden was introduced to Serene Jones, the president of Union Theological Seminary at Columbia University, who wanted to know if Wooden would teach a class on public engagement at the school. As they started exploring the class idea, Wooden learned that only half of the school's students were on track for ordination—the others would go into counseling. "A lightbulb went off," she said, "and I immediately went through the course catalog and discovered an incredible program called Psychiatry and Religion. I realized that what I'm thinking about is some kind of spiritual counseling."

Wooden is starting slowly, taking one class at a time. "We're still dating," she said of her relationship to the program. And she likes to joke that she keeps her student ID right next to her senior-discount metro transit card—a riff I've heard from three people going back to school at what they think others will find to be "shocking" ages.

Get Spiritual

Enrollment of boomers is soaring in divinity schools. More than 60 percent of new clerics are over thirty. A third are over forty. Students over fifty made up 12 percent of divinity school students in 1995; 20 percent in 2009.

Fill in a Gap

Sometimes a few classes or a short certification program are all you need for a move into a new field or to remain current in your existing field.

Diana Meinhold, a travel industry executive, was drawn to working with aging adults after managing the affairs of a friend suffering from Alzheimer's. She thought she would be taken more seriously if she got an official credential. Initially she thought she might become an executive director at an assisted living facility, so she took an administrator training course through the Care and Compliance Group, an organization recommended by several people she met as she built contacts in the industry. In the in-person, five-day, forty-hour course, Meinhold said she got an introduction to "the nuts and bolts of running a community—food and beverage, special diets, medication management, wound care, degrees of wounds, hospice, death and dying issues, as well as financial management." At only a few hundred dollars, Meinhold said it was an incredible value. (For more on her story, see page 43.)

Formalize Your Training

Many of us stumble into careers in our twenties and thirties, responding to instincts and opportunities as they arise. That happens later in life, too. Nancy Weiser was reading *The New York Times* one Sunday and stumbled onto a wedding announcement of a woman who was a health counselor and had graduated from the Institute for Integrative Nutrition. At the time, Weiser had no intention of going back to school. But she was intrigued when she read about that program. She tracked down the woman and asked her some questions about what exactly it meant to be a health counselor. Then she contacted the school, which invited her in for an orientation. The next program started in three weeks, and Weiser signed up.

The decision felt quick, but Weiser had been moving toward it ever since she was in business school nearly twenty years earlier, when she feared she was heading down a path that wouldn't allow her to live a healthy lifestyle. All around her she saw a pattern—"the faster you go, the faster you have to go, like a hamster in a wheel, on the route to corporate workaholism," she said. That's when Weiser decided that whatever she did, she would be mindful of her health. In time, she became a dispenser of advice on all things holistic and natural to her entire social circle.

When Weiser learned about the Institute for Integrative Nutrition, her reaction was immediate: "Someone made a school to teach what I'm already doing." At that moment, she decided there was potential to turn her obsession into a career, with a credential.

Plan for the Future

As Jennifer Douglas, a nurse, inched toward retirement age, she knew she would not be able to continue the pace for much longer—pounding cement floors, working nights, days, weekends, and holidays. But full retirement wasn't her answer. Douglas knew she would need some income, and she knew she wouldn't enjoy slowing down completely. "I needed to reevaluate, and decided I needed an *intervention* rather than a *reinvention*," she told me.

Douglas saw a flier in her hospital advertising a course at Westchester Community College that trained nurses to be adjunct instructors, and then she learned that two nurses from her hospital were already signed up for the course. Both the program and the timing seemed perfect. "What a great way to guide nursing students and at the same time help shape the future of nursing," she said. "It's a way to give back to a profession that has kept me gainfully employed for decades."

Because the classes and clinical sessions were only one day a week, Douglas was able to organize her work schedule so that she barely missed any time. The program included a résumé-writing session, which came in handy because Douglas had not worked on a résumé in years. After the program, she applied for two teaching positions and got offers from both. Because she is still working full time, she is easing into teaching, just taking on one course at a time. She expects to work another six years at the hospital, while ramping up the teaching and building her experience.

"My husband and I plan to move to a college town—a place with coffee shops, bookstores, culture, and vibrancy," she explained. "And doing the adjunct teaching in a part-time way is now part of the plan."

Nurses Needed
According to the U.S. Bureau of Labor Statistics, registered nursing will be the top occupation in terms of job growth through 2020.

Retool for Something New

As an engineer and a veteran executive in a series of telecommunications companies, John Kostibas noticed "a huge decline in American engineering students, all stemming from a math phobia they had in middle and high school," he said. "My thought was that if I could help them get over the phobia, I could direct more students into engineering and technology careers."

With years of start-ups and high-stress business deals behind him, Kostibas, at fifty-four, decided the time was right. "I was ready to do what I always wanted to do, which was teach math in high school."

To make the switch, Kostibas did his research. Eventually he chose Collin College in suburban Allen, Texas, because it offered a fast-tracked certification program aimed at those transitioning to second careers in teaching. Students took one semester of courses, and then worked one semester as student teachers. Kostibas also liked the combination of pedagogy and in-classroom experience. "There was a lot of focus on how you deal with kids. Plus there was a refresher in math, which was great since I hadn't taken a

Get to Know Your Community College

Whether you've had limited education or have degrees from elite universities, community colleges have a lot to offer. Hotbeds of practical learning and vocational training, they offer a growing number of programs specifically designed for encore seekers. And according to the American Association of Community Colleges, 90 percent of Americans live within easy distance of at least one community college.

The beauty of community colleges is that courses are inexpensive and they are open to everyone, regardless of age or educational background. And they are prepared for nontraditional students, if that phrase even means anything anymore, as well as people who have been out of school for a long time.

Their connection with the community and their sense of responsibility to help local employers find qualified employees nearby means they are plugged into volunteer and work opportunities. Often, community colleges offer classes online, so if you find a course that's not conveniently located, there might still be a way to do it.

Other things to know:

• Half of all new nurses in this country and the majority of other new health care workers (radiology techs, for example) are trained by community colleges.

• Almost half of all teachers receive at least part of their education at community colleges.

• Computer training courses are almost always available because these are in demand pretty much everywhere.

• Many community colleges offer self-assessment, career-planning assistance, and even mentors to help you along. In fact, you may be able to tap some of that career assistance before enrolling.

Because community colleges rely on government funding and play so many roles in their communities (training displaced workers, offering associate's degrees to prepare people for four-year college degrees, and more), they often have to make difficult decisions when budgets are slashed. The same is true for any institutions that receive public funds. Which means that even popular programs sometimes get cut.

In the event you are interested in a program that is oversubscribed or cut, you'll need to be dogged about finding other ways to get the training you need. Go back to your contacts in the field and ask for suggestions. Ask the college's career office if they know about offerings through other colleges or institutions that would get you the same training. And check in often to see if the program returns.

To find a community college near you, use the American Association of Community Colleges community college finder (aacc.nche.edu).

math class in thirty-five years, possibly more," he said. "We even learned how to use a graphing calculator. Thirty years ago we didn't even have graphing calculators."

Other programs Kostibas considered lasted only four to five weeks and didn't include a student teaching component. "I don't care how smart you are or what your experience is, you're dealing with teenagers," he explained. "The big factor is can you communicate what you know to them?"

Today he teaches algebra and geometry at Marcus High School in a suburb of Dallas. In time, he hopes to move to an inner-city school, but only after he feels like a "master teacher." He said his education is far from over.

Do Your Homework

B egin by reaching out to people in the field you want to enter. Laura Gilbert, author of *Back to School for Grownups*, suggests talking both to people who have been in a field or job that you're interested in for a long time and those who have entered more recently. Ask questions like "What has changed since you started out?" "Where do you see this field moving?" "What trends are you noticing?" "How would you get credentialed now if you were to do it over again?"

Belinda Plutz, a veteran career coach, agrees with this approach. "Start with the role models and the market," she told me. "If you want to be an ultrasound technician, talk to the head of that department at a hospital or get out in the field and talk to people." If possible, meet with someone in a hiring or human resources role at a place similar to where you'd like to work.

Professional and industry associations are also great resources for finding out what credentials are necessary to do different kinds of work. When speaking to someone at a trade association, also ask about trends in the industry—that will help you to determine where the opportunities and needs are.

O*Net (onetonline.org), the free site run by the Department of Labor, has an overview of the level of education people tend to have in a particular role. As you search by occupation, you may also notice a little sunny face with the words "bright outlook." That's the government's way of saying job prospects are looking up for people in that field. For health care jobs, the Virtual Career Network (vcn.org/healthcare), a new site sponsored by the U.S. Department of Labor and the American Association of Community Colleges, has even more detailed information on what kind of training is needed and where and how to get it for countless jobs. You can also research whether you'll be able to get credit for any prior learning you've done. (See the box on page 202 for more on getting credit for prior experience.) This site may be expanded to include other industries as well.

You may want a degree because of the status it confers, but it's entirely possible that, in some fields, you can land a desired job with less than a full degree. That's where certificates come in. Certificates are usually measured in hours of class time or fieldwork required for completion rather than semesters or academic years. Even within fields that involve certifications, some roles require certificates and others don't. As you narrow your interests and begin networking, the distinctions will become clear, and so will the credentials which are most valuable.

Up-to-date training is often the most important thing. "A college degree isn't always the key to success," according to Anya Kamenetz, author of *DIY U: Edupunks, Edupreneurs, and the Coming Transformation of Higher Education*. "A bachelor's degree from twenty years ago isn't as relevant as a certificate from last year," she told me. "Most important is the connection to the education program you're choosing and the job you're hoping to get at the end of it."

It's also possible that you may need a government-issued license for some roles. If you do, you may take a course to prepare for or to meet the educational requirements for a licensing exam. If licenses are required for a particular field, you need to be sure that a program prepares you to pass any required exams.

Don't forget to tap the resources of any schools you are considering. Good college career advising staff help perspective students sort through the requirements needed to work in a given field. Many colleges will offer

> "My first move when school started was to cancel the weekday part of my *New York Times* subscription, because I needed to study every morning before work instead of reading the paper."
>
> —Pamela Harris, on being a graduate student/ full-time lawyer

preenrollment forums or orientation sessions to share this kind of information with groups of interested students to help them figure out if the program is a good fit.

Open Education and Independent Study

If you're a self-starter, you may be able to learn what you need to know on your own—through reading, a webinar, online courses, or study groups—without any formal education or training.

In recent years, there has been an explosion of high-quality, free online courses and lectures, usually called some variation of *open* education (*open courses, open source,* and so on). These offerings are an attempt to democratize education by making learning available to all—as long as you've got enough broadband to stream video. Players include the Kahn Academy, MITx, Stanford, and even iTunes University (where you can download open courses from NYU, Stanford, and other universities right to your iPhone or iPad).

Historically these courses—or one-off lectures—have been free, noncredit, purely academic offerings (e.g., lectures in physics, biology, or statistics), but some of these initiatives are now offering badges, certificates, and other credentials for a modest fee. Watch this space; it's developing and evolving quickly.

Around the time this book went to press, there was a flurry of news on MOOCs (Massive Online Open Courses), a new acronym to describe this space, and Coursera.org, a social venture created in 2012 which enables top universities to offer free online courses and lectures.

Open learning could be useful in a variety of ways. You can enhance your knowledge about something, such as Introduction to Databases, a popular course offered free by Stanford in 2011. You can test out one class for free to see how you like online learning before making a bigger commitment to a program with a significant online component. You may even be able to find free open courses—such as a math class through Kahn Academy—that will help you meet requirements for a certificate or degree program. To do that, you will likely have to pass a test to show that you know as much about the topic as someone who passed a traditional college class.

Anya Kamenetz's book *The Edupunk's Guide to a DIY Education* and website EdupunkGuide.org are excellent resources for charting your own educational course.

Finding the Right Program

You can discover academic programs the same way you found out what kind of training you need—by asking people in the field. After you've identified a few programs, it's time to see how they stack up against one another. Most programs will have a brochure or website that covers the basics. Some will even have videos, podcasts, or profiles of recent alumni talking about their experiences. Set up an appointment with someone in the admissions or career advising office and ask if you can connect with one or two current students or recent graduates.

Through formal or informal channels (or both!), make sure to get answers to a lot of questions:

- What are the admissions criteria, if any?

- Don't forget to ask if student evaluations are available.

- How many hours a week can you expect to spend on coursework or other projects?

- If the program isn't specifically designed for older students, does it do anything to support people who may need extra assistance or special support?

- Some schools have mentors or peer advisers for older students. Is anything like that available?

- What's it going to cost? Don't forget to include fees for books, technology, and transportation in your estimates.

- Are there any grants, scholarships, or other kinds of financial aid available? Are there any work-study options?

- Are classes offered at convenient times for you?

- Is it mostly online, in person, or in some combination (often referred to as a *hybrid*)?

- Are there any opportunities for internships, field study, or other kinds of experiential learning?

- What kind of technology will you need, and does the school offer a computer lab you can use if you don't have your own computer or want to work on campus?

- What's the age breakdown of students (if that matters to you)?

- If you have a disability, will the school be able to accommodate you?

- If you would be traveling a distance to attend classes, does the program support commuters in any way or provide housing?

- Is it possible to observe a class or talk to graduates or alumni?

- Is it easy to get into all the classes offered in the program or might there be waiting lists?

- If it's a degree program, what percentage of students finish their degrees?

- If it's a vocational training program, what kind of assistance is offered in getting a job and what kinds of jobs are graduates getting?

- If you're working toward a degree or certificate and you feel you have courses from another school—or work experience—that may count toward your credential, be sure to ask about that.

- Consider asking what kinds of tuition increases the school has imposed recently and what can you expect if you enroll in a multi-year program. If these numbers sound high, that's a warning that the school may be putting profits ahead of preparing students.

When Pamela Harris was deciding whether to apply to a master's program in library science, she called the director of the program and peppered her with questions: "Could I get in?" "How would someone my age do in the program?" "Will I be able to get a job when I get out?" Not everyone is as assertive as Harris, but I've heard enough stories like hers to see a pattern here: With age and experience come the ability to figure out what's right for you and go after what you want.

How to Prepare; What to Expect

If you haven't taken classes in the past decade or more, going back to school may be very different than what you remember. Gone are the days of "this is how we learn—take it or leave it." Schools now treat students like consumers, and they should because there is lots of competition out there. And

Getting Credit for Experience

Many academic institutions and certificate programs will give you credit for prior work that you've done.

Work you did as part of your military service, professional development or trainings at work, an open-source study, or even working as a volunteer could qualify. This is called *assessment of prior learning*, which means any learning done outside of a typical academic environment.

Check out the Council for Adult and Experiential Learning (CAEL) site LearningCounts.org and the American Council on Education's adult learner services page (acenet.edu/AM/Template .cfm?Section=Learners) to learn about the kinds of prior learning that could earn you academic credit and how to go about getting that credit through testing or preparing a portfolio to show what you know.

Learning Counts is run by CAEL, a nonprofit that focuses on helping adult learners gain the skills needed to succeed in meaningful work. The site offers free contact with advisers who can answer questions about your specific situation.

many of them have lots of resources available to make sure that students get the support they need.

"Don't just be a person who comes to class," advises Ami Dorn, who returned to Anne Arundel Community College in Maryland to become a medical assistant. "Take advantage of everything the college can give you— tutors, instructors' office hours, library services, counseling."

Still it's common to feel nervous. Even though she had taken courses on and off all her adult life, when Julie Weiss returned after fifty to the University of New England to begin a master's program in social work, she said it was like being in first grade all over again. "What if no one wants to sit next to me?" she wondered. As it turns out, she had no reason to be nervous. She has always loved being a student and she immediately fell right back into the routine of going full time. And she jokes that she finally knows what it's like to be the cool kid. "Lots of people want to work with me on group projects," she said. "I've waited all my life for people to want me on their team." There are several people her age in their program, and they've developed a bit of a clique. "The classrooms are completely overheated so all the women over fifty sit together near the window," she said, adding, "It's a menopause thing."

Priscilla Santiago was completely frightened when she went back to school decades after dropping out of high school. She felt most out of place while going for her GED, but by the time she got to campus for her associate's degree, and eventually her bachelor's, she became increasingly comfortable. "I got encouragement from the other students, from teachers, and from advisers," she said. And from her mother, husband, sister, kids, and grandchildren, all of whom were impressed by what she was doing. "The thing that kept me going was keeping my eye on the goal—getting that degree," she said.

You'll need to prepare by setting up your life to accommodate being in school. Have you carved out time and a physical location where you'll be able to do your work? Do you need to adjust your work schedule or manage any other logistics, like child care or eldercare? Are you familiar with the technology needed to participate?

Often a program will suggest or offer refresher courses to help returning students—math and English are common ones, as are courses on technology and library research. If there is a particular technology platform being used in the program, you'll have adequate opportunities to learn how to use it, but make sure to do any suggested tutorials before the course begins. If there is something you are particularly concerned about, talk about it with someone who works at the school.

Your course of study will dictate any additional requirements. Some programs that involve field placements will require that you have a background check, fingerprinting, or certain health tests before you can do the work. Be sure you know in advance what those requirements are and get started early to take care of them.

If you want credit for prior education or training, you will have to dig up old transcripts or provide proof of graduation. If you're working on a college degree and hope to get credit for some work experience or training, gather up any relevant samples of your work product. If you're applying to a competitive program, you might need to take graduate admissions exams or write extensive application essays.

Most important, ask for some support from close friends or family so that they understand you may not be as available as you'd like to be. Going back to school can feel challenging at any time in life, and it can't hurt to have a couple of cheerleaders nearby.

Fast-Tracked, Accelerated, and Compressed

To help mid- and late-career people get the credentialing they need more quickly, schools often create different kinds of programs that offer ways to bypass the traditional way training is delivered. As you look into programs, you'll notice terms like *fast-tracked, compressed, accelerated,* and *alternative* in these descriptions.

According to Mary Beth Lakin of the American Council on Education, there aren't uniform definitions of these terms, so there is a lot of overlap. But here are some general guidelines to help you understand program descriptions you may encounter.

Compressed means that the program is fitting more material into a shorter amount of time. So if the course is usually completed over fifteen weeks, with a once-a-week meeting, instead it may be offered in a compressed version over the course of three long weekends.

Accelerated, which is often interchangeable with *fast-tracked,* means that you actually speed up your study. If you've been out of school for a while and need to take a computer or math refresher course, for example, you may be able to take refresher classes at the same time you start work in the program that's training you for the work you want to do.

Alternative credentialing refers to different ways for people to meet necessary licensing or certification requirements. Teaching programs that cater to sector-switchers or Troops to Teachers, which helps veterans transition to teaching, are examples of this.

As you consider different programs, rather than focus on the terms used to describe it, look at the following elements instead:

- What's the schedule and is the course offered at different times?

- Are there any options that would allow you to complete the program requirements more quickly?

- How much content are you tackling over what period of time?

- If you need help with English, math, computers, or something else, is there a way to tackle those things at the same time?

Learning from and with Young People

Some people choose a course of study specifically *because* it will put them in touch with younger people. That's how it was for college professor Nicki Robb when she joined the first class at Sansori, an innovative program to help people get social purpose ventures off the ground. Robb had years of experience in developing educational programs focused on agriculture and farming. She was exploring a new project that would offer a farm-based animal therapy program for special needs children. She had solid skills in many areas—budgeting, managing on-the-ground operations, and working with animals and materials like soil and compost to create sustainable farm systems. "I know what it's like to be a foot soldier on the ground," she said.

Robb hoped that Sansori would help her get a sense of how people spread ideas today. "I've been promoting ideas since I was twenty-one," Robb, now fifty-six, explained. "But there's been a change in how we communicate, and I realize that I'm of a different generation, so I recognize my limitations. I also look at young people today, and I see that they have learned how to work smarter and more efficiently. I want to learn from them."

After only a few months in the program, Robb already saw a lot of potential for cross-mentoring. A fellow student helped her to set up a profile on Google Plus, an online tool the class is using to communicate virtually. In return, Robb teaches her younger students at Amherst College—"a whole new generation of students who are passionate about agriculture"—what she has learned over decades.

Don't assume you'll be the only student your age. You may be in a program specifically designed for mid-career or encore students. Community colleges and continuing education programs are magnets for older and other nontraditional students.

Regardless of the type of program you choose, your instructors may be considerably younger than you. Learning from someone who has less life experience than you do may take some getting used to. But consider it great preparation for working alongside younger colleagues and even a younger boss. (For more on working with younger people, see page 151.)

Is It Worth It?

Going back to school has costs. In addition to the financial costs of any program, there's also the cost of your time, which you could be using to earn an income—or even to learn in some other way, such as interning or taking a paid job. On the flip side, going back to school could be a way to give yourself a credential that will boost your earnings over the long term.

So as you make a decision about going back to school, you'll have to weigh several factors—how long it will take to get the training you need to do what you want to do, how much it will cost, how much you will be able to earn with your new credentials, and how long you plan to work in your new field. Of course, there's no way to predict whether you will be physically able to work as long as you would like to or whether you'll be able to earn the income you expect in a new field. But this process should help you make as informed a decision as possible.

I did this kind of analysis when I left my corporate career ten years ago and decided to train to become a journalist. I weighed the cost of returning to school for a master's in journalism (close to $50,000), plus the loss of income for a year or more against the likely income I'd earn upon graduation (probably less than $50,000 a year to start). More important, I looked at whether the degree would help me to have the kind of career I sought and whether there were other, less expensive, and equally good ways to build the skills I wanted. When I researched the jobs that recent journalism school grads were getting, few of those even appealed to me. So I took several classes for a few hundred dollars in continuing education programs, while building up my writing skills and my portfolio. I attended several key conferences that had helpful workshops. I also found a few mentors who introduced me to editors and hastened the process, something that's easier to do when you have a strong network.

Peter Johnson, a longtime technology entrepreneur, went through a similar process when considering how to become a professor. The question: Should he get a Ph.D. in marketing? Johnson was fifty-six and teaching as an adjunct professor while still working days in his business. He expected the degree would take four years, but planned on working at least ten years beyond graduation. After doing some research, which showed that professors in business schools would be in demand, he decided it was worth it to go for the degree. It was a calculated risk and it paid off. By the time Johnson completed his coursework for the Ph.D., he got a full-time tenure track position at Fordham University.

Financing Your Education

An encore education doesn't have to be expensive. Community college programs are designed to be affordable, as are many certificate or online courses. But don't give up if you find a program that interests you, and you're daunted by the price tag. If you need or want some kind of financial assistance, the best place to start is the administrative or financial aid office at the college you're considering. (If it's a small program, you'll likely only have one point of contact for everything and that person should be able to help you.) Some programs reserve a number of slots for students who get discounted tuition or are on full scholarships. It may even be possible to volunteer in a way that could reduce your tuition.

If you are working in a corporate environment, check if your employer has a tuition assistance program. Often companies have programs that they don't publicize, so it pays to ask your human resources department.

Explore scholarships and grants. Most scholarships and grants are silent about age but some specifically focus on older adults, with several options for women returning to the workplace or improving their job skills. AARP Women's Foundation, for example, offers scholarships between $500 and $5,000 for low-income women over the age of forty needing new job skills. The American Association of University Women (AAUW) also offers scholarships between $2,000 and $12,000 for women who hold bachelor's degrees and are preparing to advance their careers.

Also consider federal grants and loans. Pell Grants are federal grants of up to $5,550 a year for those with financial need. Unlike a loan, these do not have to be repaid. The amount available is based on financial need and whether you go to school full or part time. Most recipients of Pell Grants earn less than $50,000 a year. Pell Grants are restricted to a first bachelor's degree, but in some cases they can also be used toward a post-baccalaureate teacher certification program. If you've been laid off or are leaving a job to return to school, there is a procedure to have your income adjusted to reflect your current circumstances. (Keep in mind that any severance or unemployment will be considered.)

Stafford Loans, the main federal loans for students, have a very low interest rate and don't require repayment as long as you meet certain income requirements and you're in school at least part time.

If you're considering taking out a loan to pay for your education, be careful. Many for-profit institutions have been criticized for helping their students get financial aid to pay for tuition but then graduating students with excessive debt and meager job prospects. Don't go into debt unless you are confident that you'll be able to find work at a pay rate that makes sense, given the burden you're taking on.

If you do take out a loan, the Education for Public Service Act reduces monthly payments on federal student loans for graduates who work in public safety, public health, education, social work, or the nonprofit sector. The law provides complete loan forgiveness for graduates who work full time for ten years in public service.

Even if you can't get your education paid for, you may be able to get some tax breaks. If you've got money put aside in a 529 college savings accounts for your kids, you can use that tax-free money for anyone's education, including your own. (For a discussion on other tax incentives for financing your education, see page 96.)

FAQs

How do I know if I'm a good candidate for an online program?

People who do well in online programs tend to have a lot of self-discipline, are comfortable working at their own pace, and have good time-management skills. They also have a certain comfort with technology or at least an interest in spending a fair bit of time on a computer. Online learning platforms often allow you to interact with your teacher and classmates, raise your "hand" to ask questions, or even watch a lecture via live streaming video.

Keep in mind that online or distance learning can mean a lot of different things. So again, it's important to ask lots of questions about how things work.

- Will you be using an online platform where people can interact with one another and with the teacher?
- Will you be watching video lectures?
- Will you be using a teleconference line to take part in a live lecture?
- How much time will you be spending online and what kind of participation is expected of you?

If you can, try out a course, a lecture, or a free online class. (See the box on page 199 for some ideas.) As good as an online program can be, it's important to realize that you may just be one of the people who yearns for the experience of meeting people face-to-face. You also may find an exclusively online program daunting if you have a slow Internet connection that makes it difficult to watch videos and download large files.

You can get hints about how you would perform in different settings by thinking about what kind of learner you are. Do you enjoy watching videos on the computer, or would you prefer to sit in a classroom? How is your retention for things that you listen to? Do you need to see things in print to understand them? Some of the most popular programs combine in-person and online instruction.

Should I be wary of for-profit schools?

For-profit schools are on the rise, both for college degrees and for other kinds of learning. It's been hard to miss the ubiquitous advertisements for degrees or vocational classes. And the for-profit market is expected to rise dramatically in the coming years.

Some for-profit schools have been targeted by the Department of Education and others for allegedly preying on out-of-work individuals, helping them to secure large student loans that end up being difficult to repay when a course of study doesn't lead to the desired job. Not all for-profit schools were involved, of course. And since the charges, new regulations have been put in place, tightening the rules for schools that offer programs leading to paying jobs.

Still, the questions to ask of a for-profit institution are the same ones you'd ask of any school, with a little more emphasis on the school's track record in helping people find jobs. (For the list of questions, see page 200.)

If you're not familiar with the school or have some doubts, go further. Don't just rely on marketing materials. Try to figure out who is behind the program and pay close attention to the qualifications of the instructors teaching classes. Poke around online. Find alumni and talk to them.

Caveats aside, expect to see lots of innovative models for delivering education to huge numbers of people, something that may best be done by a business with the ability to make large investments and grow quickly to meet demand. Keep an eye out for public-private partnerships like Empowered UCLA Extension, the encore-focused partnership between UCLA's extension school and a private group of investors, which started offering online certificate programs specifically tailored to the encore market in 2012.

How do I deal with an instructor I don't think is competent?

Ellen Schall, dean of NYU's Wagner School of Public Service, offers this advice: "The first thing to do is check other people's opinions. If the other people in your study group think this person is no good, then you've got a real concern. If they all love him, then maybe it's you."

After you've validated your concerns, go through the proper channels. Almost all schools have a process for registering complaints against an instructor. Keep in mind that you can also do some research before taking a class. Many schools make evaluations of instructors available to people registering for a class. Your teacher is often just as important as the subject matter so, to maximize your chances of a good fit, choose classes after doing some research.

How do I know if it's necessary to go back to school for what I want to do?

Before plunging into any academic program, do some research! This always starts with talking to people in the field you're interested in, as well as people at the academic institutions that you're considering. Try to find people doing the work you want to do and ask them what kind of training they think is necessary to break into the field now—not what they did twenty or thirty years ago when they first got started. Ask them what kind of training they would do if they went back to school. Finally, make sure to look at the financial considerations and weigh whether or not it makes sense to invest years and money into a course of study given the opportunities you'll have at the end.

CHAPTER 10

Become
an Encore
Entrepreneur

**"I was old enough to understand the injustice I saw and
experienced enough to do something about it."**

—ROBERT CHAMBERS, ENCORE ENTREPRENEUR

O ut on the street as the result of restructuring (for the fourth time),
Milton Roye, a veteran corporate executive, decided it was time to
venture out on his own. Through his network, Roye, then in his early
fifties, learned of a new technology for a cleaner, more efficient ignition
system. The idea appealed to his urge to bring manufacturing back to the
United States and to do something helpful for the environment. He took the
reins and went out seeking investors.

Roye's company, ENRG Power Systems, was making some headway
signing up initial customers. But he soon realized he had a lot to learn about
running a start-up. "When you're working for Delphi or GM, life doesn't change
that quickly. It's pretty predictable," he explained. "I had the skills, but I didn't
understand what a business plan was in the context of what an investor would
need. In corporate America, we're used to two- to three-inch binders. For an
entrepreneur, it's never more than ten pages, with three pages of financials."

Roye's wife, who had been helping with the business, suggested he get involved in TechTown, a business incubator affiliated with Wayne State University and dedicated to helping revive Detroit.

Roye enrolled in TechTown's THRIVE program, enticed by the promise that he would leave with an investor-ready business plan and presentation, exactly what he was looking for. When in the program, Roye learned from experienced businesspeople who mostly volunteer their time to mentor first-time entrepreneurs. He was impressed with the passion and social consciousness of everyone involved. "They were doing it because they recognized that Detroit had been based on the automotive economy, and it would never come back the way it was before," he told me. "To succeed, it needed to tap into the expertise of a whole bunch of people who had never been out on their own."

Roye's story reflects two converging trends. Studies have shown increases in entrepreneurial activity in those over fifty. There are several reasons for this. Americans are living longer, healthier lives. At midlife, people have a wealth of experience, confidence in their abilities, and the itch to work for themselves. Then there are those who hatch their own businesses because it can be hard to get a job after a certain age.

The second trend is that midlife pull toward generativity—the impulse to build and create something lasting, something that will connect you to future generations. So it's not surprising that a lot of people interested in encore careers are drawn to starting entities that seek to solve some kind of social problem or help their communities. According to a MetLife/Encore .org 2011 survey, one in four Americans between the ages of forty-four and seventy is interested in starting a business or nonprofit venture in the next five to ten years, and half of them are interested in creating businesses or nonprofits that will help meet community needs.

Definitions, Please

Encore entrepreneurs are later-in-life entrepreneurs who don't follow the old-school profit-first or profit-only motives for starting a venture. Instead, they identify with the very of-the-moment idea of using business savvy to solve social problems and fix the world, while also generating income. Just like people in encore careers are a subset of people in second and third acts, encore entrepreneurs are a subset of older entrepreneurs—social entrepreneurs with some life experience behind them.

So, what's *social entrepreneurship*? Loosely defined, it's when entrepreneurial techniques are used to achieve social change. Social entrepreneurship is a big tent, covering those working on global issues, those starting organizations to solve community problems, and lots in between. It includes for-profit businesses with a social mission; innovative nonprofits that use ideas from business to have bigger impact; and those adopting new business structures to create hybrids that combine aspects of both nonprofit and for-profit organizations. Social entrepreneurship also goes by a lot of names—*social enterprise, social innovation, social business, social venture, sustainable business, double bottom line, low-profit, public-benefit corporations,* and more.

Serial social entrepreneur Daniel Lubetzky uses the term *not-only-for profit* to describe companies he has founded that infuse business with a social mission, like PeaceWorks, a gourmet food company employing Arabs and Israelis in neighborhood cooperatives in the Middle East. Amy Pearl of Springboard Innovation, a Portland, Oregon, nonprofit that helps people launch social ventures, likes the term *multiple return enterprise,* meaning a venture with more than a financial return.

Whatever you call it, this is big business. According to Social Edge, an international online community for social entrepreneurs sponsored by the Skoll Foundation, "U.S. consumers are estimated to spend over $220 billion annually on goods and services related to health, the environment, social justice, and sustainable living." Why so much and why now? People are starting to demand more from business—witness the attention on the labor practices of factory workers in China where iPads and iPhones are made. Caring for the environment, treating workers fairly, and social responsibility are ideas that are gaining traction in all kinds of ways. So it's a very friendly moment for ventures that think *socially* in one way or another.

Gifford and Libba Pinchot, founders of Bainbridge Graduate Institute (BGI), one of the first business schools completely dedicated to sustainable businesses, believe that all business will move in this direction, as consumers increasingly demand accountability from the businesses they support and young people are increasingly interested in employers that can demonstrate socially responsible behavior. "People are not going to stop eating food

Do You Have What It Takes?

Take a look at the following questions. The more times you answer yes, the more likely it is that you have the personality type and attitude to be an encore entrepreneur.

- Is there a social problem you feel so strongly about that you want to immerse yourself in fixing it?

- Do you have an idea or innovation that could have a serious impact on that social problem or issue?

- Do you have access to a network and a willingness to tap it for favors?

- Can you enlist a team of supporters and volunteers?

- Are you comfortable facing rejection?

- Are you willing to play many different roles in an organization, even if some of those roles feel menial or not exactly suited to your talents?

- Would you be comfortable explaining your vision repeatedly in different contexts and to different audiences (e.g., potential funders, the media, and people you want to work for you)?

- Do you have a high tolerance for risk?

Answering no to this last question doesn't mean that you're not cut out for encore entrepreneurship. But it does mean that you'll want to spend some time figuring out some ways to minimize the risk in any venture you launch. You may even be more suited to applying your entrepreneurial skills to an existing venture rather than starting one of your own.

or buying cars or traveling or living in buildings," Gifford told me. "Those things will go on. But they will be done in a more socially responsible way." Through the efforts of pioneers such as the Pinchots (who created BGI in their encore careers!), many business schools around the country now have MBA programs that focus on sustainability.

Some people believe that profits and social mission can coexist peacefully. Others take a stricter view, believing that the social mission always needs to come first. Encore entrepreneurs fall all along this spectrum of activity, whether they lead organizations with a social mission or their work brings a level of social accountability to an existing organization.

Most encore entrepreneurs don't expect to make big bucks from their ventures. Research shows that most would be satisfied with ventures that generate less than $60,000 per year. They're also not generally looking to run big operations—most are drawn to creating small, local organizations employing up to ten people. Some hope to do their work completely on their own as consultants or one-person operations (often called *micropreneurs* or *solopreneurs*). Others will join up with existing organizations, working as *intrapreneurs* innovating from the inside. Still others will use their business experience to mentor and guide people who are starting their own ventures.

Defining Traits

Encore entrepreneurs tend to share some common traits, including some that set them apart from younger social entrepreneurs.

For one, they feel the pull of time. By the time middle age arrives, there is a sense of urgency for many, and the stakes can feel high. "When you're young, if you screw up, there's plenty of time to fix it," said Gifford Pinchot. "When you're older, if you mess up, you could end up without any retirement funds, which is what many people are facing today." That sense of urgency is what drives the encore entrepreneur, much like a sense of *nothing to lose* is what often brings young people to social ventures.

But encore entrepreneurs also size up risk differently. "When you're older, risk is more existential," said David Bornstein, a journalist who has written extensively on social innovation. "When you're young, you think about risks in terms of health, safety, or financial aspects. As you age, you realize that the biggest risk is dying without having really expressed who you are."

For the encore entrepreneur, their venture is part of a bigger life picture. Like all encore careers, a leap into encore entrepreneurship is as much about life circumstances as it is about career change. Nearly every encore start-up story involves another story—a marital shift, a health scare, a deep sense of unfinished business.

Like most people at midlife, encore entrepreneurs think about their legacy and about the future. They are often motivated by a desire to improve the world for their children, their grandchildren, or future generations. They also pay attention to succession planning. "Who's going to do this work when I'm gone?" is a question that comes up even in the start-up period. (The opposite can be true, too. Some people start short-term ventures designed to end when they are no longer in a position to lead.)

Encore entrepreneurs are weavers, bringing together various skills, talents, and experiences. As Pinchot told me, "Older social entrepreneurs have the advantage of more threads to combine." They've also lived long enough to know that failures and detours are inevitable. They know they will experience many ups and downs. Even in ventures that begin with a sense of mission, conflicts arise and bad days happen.

Encore entrepreneurs have resources beyond the financial kind. Although the recession has wounded many a retirement account, older people still tend to have more savings, houses they can borrow against, and longer credit histories, which bodes well for securing loans. They understand and embody practical idealism and realize that there are trade-offs in every venture, that doing good isn't always easy, and that perfection is rarely the right objective.

Starting Social Ventures

The steps to becoming an encore entrepreneur aren't all that different from the process of embarking on any encore career. And the pieces have analogs that mirror those you've read about in the earlier chapters. You'll likely begin with moments of discovery, then move into exploration, research, and preparation. Along the way you'll craft experiments to get you closer to what you want to do. Bear in mind that all this might happen completely out of order!

Before we jump in, let me offer one caveat. Starting a social venture is way too big a topic to cover in any depth in one chapter of a book. And there are several excellent guides I'd recommend for detailed advice, like David Bornstein's two books *How to Change the World* and *Social Entrepreneurship: What Everyone Needs to Know*. (There are others listed on page 303.) Instead this section covers what's unique to *encore* entrepreneurship—and how you can leverage the experience of your life stage to have both the impact and lifestyle you want.

Seize the Moment of Discovery

As with all encores, many people find their way to entrepreneurship after passing through a period of upheaval. Sue Crolick had been the first female art director at two different design firms and won several awards in her nearly thirty years in the business. But she hit her professional stride when arts professionals worked with drawing boards and colored chalk or pastels. "In our field, they call people my age *designosaurs*," she quipped. By the time she was in her late forties, Crolick had a stark choice to make: Either learn new skills and invest thousands of dollars in new equipment, or change tracks and focus on doing something else. At the same time, she faced a harrowing health ordeal: During surgery to remove a benign tumor, her vocal cord was severed. For a while, she feared she would never be able to speak again.

> **"I saw how the elderly were living and didn't like it. And it didn't seem all that complicated to do something about it."**
>
> –Elaine Santore, nonprofit cofounder and executive director

After she partially recovered her voice, Crolick became determined to use her creative energy to help others going through hard times. And she wanted to volunteer in a way that would connect her to other creative people. So she organized a fund-raising event enlisting scores of volunteers from the design field to decorate cardboard boxes and fill them with food to be delivered to kids living in shelters. After the event, she was talking with her sister, a corporate attorney, about how she wished she could make a living doing similar events. Her sister responded, "Of course you could make a living. Open a nonprofit and get some funding." Before that moment Crolick had never even considered starting her own organization. Since 1995, she has been running Creatives for Causes full time, drawing a salary that sustains her.

Some people come to their encore venture by working in a field for years, noticing a need that is not being filled and deciding to fill it. As the secretary for Aging and Adult Services for the state of Florida, Conchy Bretos was distressed by the lack of services available to low-income elders and disabled adults. And when she found herself out of a job in her late forties she put her energy toward doing something to help. Beginning with a small consulting contract from the agency where she used to work, she started what is now MIA Consulting, a for-profit (and very profitable) company providing assisted living services that allow low-income residents to stay in their homes rather than move into nursing homes. The innovation at the core of Bretos's idea was that it was cheaper to provide assisted living services in public housing than to send people to nursing homes at the government's expense.

Often the motivation for an encore venture comes from a desire to work on an issue that no one is focusing on or talking about. That was the driving force for Kathy Hull, a clinical psychologist, and Barbara Beach, a pediatric oncologist, when they founded George Mark Children's House, a new model of long-term care for terminally ill children, which has helped more than 300 families since it opened in 2004. "No one wants to talk about dying children," said Hull. When they opened their first facility—a lively, homey, pediatric palliative care center for children and their parents in San Leandro, California—it was the first such effort anywhere in the United States.

Though many encore entrepreneurs get started because they are consumed with a particular problem they want to solve, it's also possible to start with an itch to go out on your own but not much of an idea of what you want to do. The best way to start is by looking at what troubles you, what keeps you up at night, what problems you want to solve. (Look back at Exercise 5 on page 49). Then start exploring where you see needs or opportunities. At the same time immerse yourself in areas where the vibrant and ongoing conversation around social entrepreneurship is taking place. Get acclimated to this world. Spend time on websites like Dowser.org, EchoingGreen.org, and SocialEdge.org. Sign up for newsletters like the one published by Stanford University's Center for Social Innovation. Attend a panel discussion, conference, or other gathering for aspiring social entrepreneurs. (Have a look at the resources section on page 293 for more ideas.)

Be Your Own Boss? Really?

You may be drawn to starting your own venture for autonomy and flexibility, but any entrepreneur will tell you that being your own boss is generally harder than working for someone else. Sure, you can take as much vacation time as you want. But will you take the time when it means walking away from a new venture? And that "no boss" idea can be a bit of a misnomer—customers, board members, investors, or funders can all exert a lot of control over your life. Going out on your own is generally not a recipe for lowering stress levels.

As the executive director of BOOM! The New Economy, Randal Charlton, seventy-three, is both an encore entrepreneur and adviser to other encore entrepreneurs. One of the first things he tells anyone thinking about launching a business at this life stage is to keep an eye on your health. "What you're about to take on will be hard and demanding, and unless you are physically fit, you won't be able to perform at your best."

That's why it's important to think about how much responsibility you want to take on. One reason that Charlton moved to his current role is that he wanted to pull back a little from the pace he was keeping in his last position as executive director of TechTown, the Wayne State business incubator where Milton Roye took his course. At TechTown, Charlton routinely worked long hours and rarely took a day off. With three adult daughters living overseas, he wanted to move into a role where he would still have significant impact, but where he could take more time off with a clean conscience and work virtually when he wanted to.

But Charlton's move to a smaller start-up with scant resources had its own challenges. When I last spoke to him, he was in the midst of the frustrations of finding office space and becoming his own IT department. He also said he missed the discipline of a structured work environment. Once again, it's all about trade-offs.

Your own challenges may lead you to the problem you want to solve for others. Rosalind Joffe, a multimedia producer, professor, and, later, a mediator, decided to start a chronic-illness coaching and consulting practice after years of dealing with her own health issues. Finally, she came up with a career choice that accommodated her own health conditions while helping others overcome theirs. Today, much of her work—writing and working with clients by phone—can be done from home, and if she has to cancel appointments, she can do that.

If keeping your venture manageable is important to you, think about starting something close to home, with low overhead. Elaine Santore's business, Umbrella of the Capital District, fits this model. Santore was sixteen when her father died and her mother had to sell their family home because she couldn't take care of it on her own. Later in her life, Santore cared for an aging aunt facing the same quandary. She credits these two experiences with her decision to start a nonprofit agency in Schenectady, New York, that matches handy people with aging adults or others who are homebound.

Santore started in a home office, working with a partner, Ron Byrne, who was also motivated by the difficulties his family members had experienced aging in their homes. Start-up costs were next to nothing, and her husband had a solid income she could rely on until the venture got off the ground. As the business has grown, Santore has secured grants from community foundations and banks.

Santore and Byrne each earn a modest salary—about $40,000 per year—and they keep to a fairly standard forty-hour-a-week schedule. Their skills complement each other well; Byrne enrolls people in the program, and Santore focuses on writing grants. They aren't looking to increase profits. "If we started charging more for the services, people wouldn't be able to afford the program," she explained. "And the idea is to provide a safe, economical way to keep people in their homes."

Another option if you want to manage both your risk and have some control over your time is to use your entrepreneurial talents to help an existing venture or a start-up advance its goals—on your terms.

Be an Explorer

The best way to dig in is to network, research, and start doing things. When you have some hunches or areas that interest you, narrow down your ideas using the same processes outlined in the earlier chapters.

As you do your research and interviews, try to get answers to the following questions:

- What have other people tried to do in this area? What's succeeded, what's failed, and why?

- What are the current trends in the field you're investigating?

- Who are the important players in the field? And who might be potential collaborators and competitors?

- What kinds of needs aren't currently being met in the marketplace you're exploring (and why—have others tried and failed)?

- How have people raised money to do the kinds of things you're considering and how have they structured their ventures?

If you're interested in starting a nonprofit, perhaps the most important question to answer is whether you can have more impact by starting a new organization or by helping an existing one. The United States has well over 1.5 million nonprofits, many of which compete for foundation grants to do similar work. Before you decide that your idea needs an organization of its own, make sure that you're actually filling a void or meeting an unmet need.

You'll be able to learn a lot from research and interviews. But ultimately you may want to test out your ideas. As you saw in Chapter 8, your tests can be "little bets."

When Sue Crolick acted on her idea to organize creative professionals around causes, she wanted to find a way to both do good in the community and create a fun, gratifying experience for volunteers. She learned a lot by volunteering with other organizations and placing some little bets.

Her first event, where the creative volunteers decorated boxes to house food and toys, was successful. But she wanted to do something that would have an ongoing impact. Eventually she created Art Buddies, a mentoring program that brings together low-income children with graphic designers, art directors, writers, illustrators, and architects. She had volunteered as a Big Sister, and one of her frustrations was that she often felt lonely—driving long distances to another part of town to meet with her mentee. In the Art Buddy model, mentors and mentees get some concentrated time together, but they also get to be part of a larger group setting. "We're all together in a giant room with wild art supplies—making journals, costumes, jewelry, and stuff with fake fur, fabric, and glue guns," she explained. "Creative people are on their computers all day, and they don't get to work with their hands. This is so tactile. There is still a longing for it."

Crolick learned a lot from hands-on volunteering. But if you're thinking of starting a nonprofit, also consider joining a nonprofit board. Laura Gassner Otting, the nonprofit recruiter, suggests finding an organization doing work of similar scale and complexity in an area unrelated to your interests. "It's also a good idea to find a nonprofit that's established and growing—so you can see how they are handling issues such as staffing, managing consultants, and deepening impact," she said. "While you're at it, get to know the executive director to see if you like the life—lots of breakfasts, lunches, and off-hours schmoozing. In the end, you may decide you're not suited to it at all." (For more information on joining boards, see page 168.)

Just like the entrepreneurs they now teach, Gifford and Libba Pinchot, the founders of Bainbridge Graduate Institute, came to their idea for their business school only after an earlier idea failed. Libba Pinchot invested a year of her time and $30,000 trying to get a program started that would teach social enterprise to public high school students. After seeing that they could not effectively introduce their program in large numbers of public high schools, they concluded that they could make more of an impact in adult education.

Build a Team

Though working for yourself is often a big motivator for encore entrepreneurs, very few are able to accomplish anything without a whole lot of support and collaboration.

This is where your age can be a real asset. Encore entrepreneurs tend to have well-established networks and are savvy about how to use them to help their ventures get off the ground. They are accustomed to collaborating and are prepared to ask others for help, favors, and resources. Often they tap their friends, family members, or life partners for support of various kinds—from financial assistance to marketing or legal help. "Older people are adept at repurposing their assets," observed David Bornstein. "Friends become volunteers. Professional contacts become advisers. You realize that you've built up a lot of equity even if it's not all financial." Knowing how to tap "human capital" is a great asset.

As you assemble your team, remember that if you share your passion you'll likely be able to pass that spark along to others. But also find creative ways to show your appreciation. Take a lesson from organizations that know how to treat their volunteers well. Every year around the holiday season, I get a gift from a venture I've been advising. It's always just a token, but a thoughtful one that comes with a handwritten note. Gestures like that go a long way toward keeping people invested.

Include a lawyer, accountant, and/or financial adviser on your team. This is one area where it doesn't pay to go at it alone or rely on self-help books.

Consider getting peer and mentor support. If you think you'd benefit from being surrounded by other would-be entrepreneurs, investigate business incubators and coworking spaces near where you live. Look into places that offer support to first-time entrepreneurs. Molly McDonald who started the breast cancer charity, the Pink Fund (see page 94), got help in writing a business plan from one of the mentors at TechTown in Detroit.

> "It's critical to surround yourself with good advisers who have permission to tell you you're crazy."
>
> —Art Ammann, nonprofit founder and president

You can find that kind of help, plus live workshops and mentoring, at organizations like SCORE (score.org).

Family members can be valuable team players. In my interviews, I often heard about the son who handles fund-raising, the niece who manages the Facebook page. If the old family business model was to pass a business down to the children, one of the new models is to launch a business with a child, or even a grandchild.

Nancy Burkhart and her daughter Jessica Arellano run a business together. Having run several arts and crafts product-manufacturing companies, Burkhart knew firsthand just how toxic paints, varnishes, and other art supplies can be. Her own hands were dry and cracked from years of handling these products. When Jessica graduated from the College of Natural Resources at the University of California, Berkeley, the two developed a new business to create and market a line of completely safe and toxin-free art supplies. The company runs lean. Operating out of her garage, Burkhart developed the formulas for the product line with the part-time help of a chemist, also in his encore career. Burkhart and Arellano hand-make, -mix, and -bottle the products themselves using recycled containers. The mother-daughter team toggle between business and family life, working around school schedules. Four grandchildren and some of their friends make up the Green Musketeers, educating children about art and the environment.

Here's an example of three generations at work. Dr. Samuel Lupin had practiced medicine in the same Brooklyn, New York, neighborhood for more than forty years and as he approached seventy, he started thinking about retiring. Always devoted to his patients, Lupin increasingly found that his work involved visiting patients, aging and often homebound. Around the same time, Lupin's grandson, Daniel Stokar, was graduating from college and trying to figure out what to do next. An accounting major, Daniel had an offer from KPMG, but his goal was to work in health care, helping the aged. As family discussions centered on Lupin's housecall practice and Daniel's desire to work with the elderly, an idea emerged for a redesigned medical practice. Brooklyn Housecalls, a housecalls-only medical practice, was born.

In business for four years, Brooklyn Housecalls now employs nine physicians. With Daniel's head for business, his father Avi's IT and engineering background, and Lupin's knowledge of the needs of their patient base, the three refined a business model that is delivering high-quality, low-cost health care to a group of patients who would otherwise be calling 911 and visiting emergency rooms on a regular basis.

Daniel feels "privileged" to work with his father and grandfather in this way. "If you did a Venn diagram with each of our personalities, expertise, and abilities overlapping in just the right way, this would be it," he told me. "It's really a perfect calling for all of us."

Study Up

Encore entrepreneurs often move into their work without any particular training. It's no surprise that people with the gumption to start their own ventures tend to have a learn-as-you-go spirit. It happens to be an especially good time for self-directed learning. As you start your research, you'll no doubt find that your inbox, like mine, is flooded with emails offering webinars and courses on social media, fund-raising, business plans, or just about any challenge you're facing.

Milton Roye's experience in the THRIVE program at TechTown in Detroit served a few purposes. For a relatively small investment ($2,000 tuition, deferred until after the program is completed), he was able to develop his business plan, have access to mentors, and be a part of a community of other entrepreneurs. Programs like this one are becoming increasingly common. Nicki Robb was looking for the same things when she joined the first class at Sansori.org, a new hybrid online and in-person program that helps would-be social entrepreneurs get their ventures started. Jeff Williams, a coach in the Chicago area, offers online workshops, personal coaching, and workbooks for entrepreneurs over fifty through a company called

BizStarters.com. Expect to see more offerings like this as the market responds to the growing interest in midlife entrepreneurship.

You may find that you need to learn something vital to the specifics of your business rather than something relating to entrepreneurship. That's how it was for Gary Bates. In thirty-seven years as a pilot for American Airlines and TWA, Bates saw the difficulties faced by older travelers who can't manage on their own or are frustrated by the new realities of flying, such as dealing with the complicated security rules and baggage requirements. When he retired from flying, he and his wife, Beth, decided to start Care-to-Go, a business providing traveling companions for aged or otherwise physically challenged people. Gary and Beth, who had years of caregiving experience but no formal training, wanted to familiarize themselves with certain elements of caregiving as well as pick up some needed credentials. They were able to do both through a one-week course at GateWay Community College in Phoenix. "The course was one-stop shopping," Bates explained, teaching them about things like first aid, CPR, how to move people from wheelchairs, and how to pick them up when they've fallen down.

Once you've identified what you need to learn, go on a quest to find the best places to do that. Follow the processes outlined in Chapter 9 to figure out what would work best for your learning style and your needs.

> **"Arts nonprofits begin from a romantic idea with great passion. Then you realize you need an IRS certification and an accountant who knows nonprofits. Right now I know more about databases than I'd ever wanted to know."**
>
> —Sue Crolick, art director-turned-nonprofit-founder-and-president

Sketch Out a Business Plan

After you've zeroed in on your idea and perhaps done some research and experiments, you should be ready to create a business plan. A business plan is basically a sales document, and in it you will be selling the idea of your venture.

Business plans take many forms and generally run anywhere from fifteen to sixty pages. To write a business plan, keep many different kinds of readers in mind—potential funders, partners, board members, even key employees. Writing a business plan will force you to answer the most important questions about your idea—what it will accomplish, how it will be funded, what kind of revenue model it will have, and perhaps most of all, what you and the rest of your team will bring to it. Writing a business plan is usually an ongoing process, and it's common for the document to be a work in progress even after the venture is up and running. It's also possible that you'll write your business plan and never show it to anyone! It will help you to organize your thoughts on why your idea is worth pursuing.

Business plans are useful even for the smallest ventures. I've talked to solo workers and consultants who found the process of creating and revisiting a business plan useful. Rosalind Joffe, the chronic-illness coach, told me that every September she rewrites her business plan, reminding herself of what she's looking for, noting the changes she wants to make, and keeping an eye on how much money she's had to invest. She said that reviewing the plan from year to year helps her realize that she's in it for the long haul.

You can find advice and models for writing business plans on the Small Business Administration's website (sba.org) and at Score.org. REDF, a San Francisco–based nonprofit, has a sample social enterprise business plan in its "REDF Tools" section on its website, redf.org. I've also provided an outline for crafting a business plan specifically for an encore-led venture (see page 283). Of course, you may find that you have a more effective vision for presenting your idea than any of these suggested templates. If that's the case, and you feel you're conveying the necessary information, go with it.

You may also want to consider doing what's called a SWOT analysis, assessing your venture's **S**trengths, **W**eaknesses, **O**pportunities, and **T**hreats. As part of that, you'll look at what kinds of skills you possess and what you will need to bring in with volunteers or employees.

Both of these exercises will help you think about your *elevator pitch*—a short, simple statement explaining your venture that you can say in the time it takes an elevator going from the lobby to the sixth floor. Like the stories you tell about yourself, you'll want to think about refining your pitch for different kinds of people: your competition, potential staff or board members, partners, funders, or investors. Remember two things: People relate to stories, and they want to know why your product or service is needed. So rope them in with both elements. "In the end, it's stories that compel us to open our wallets," said Laura Gassner Otting. "It's about little Jimmy who left the gang and didn't want another brother shot and brought his mom to learn English and now he's the first in his family to graduate."

Gary Bates, from Care-to-Go, has a great elevator speech. "As people age, life closes in on them. Most of our calls are to help make sure that people can make it to family reunions or get Grandma to that wedding or graduation." That's all he needed to say, and I instantly understood what they do and why their service is needed. And when I learned that he'd been a pilot for thirty-seven years and his wife had experience in home health care, I thought, "Wow, they are the right people for this work." That's what you're looking for in an elevator pitch.

Figure Out the Financials

When you sit down to think about the financial side of your entrepreneurial venture, try to answer three questions: How will you fund your transition? How will you fund the launch of your venture? And what kind of income will you be able to generate while running it?

Entrepreneurs fund their transitions in many of the same ways encore civilians do. They use severance packages or inheritances, hang on to jobs, find new stopgap jobs, rely on the earnings of a partner, and raid their retirement funds. And because it can be hard to predict when the money will start flowing—either through revenues or a salary you pay yourself—it's best to assume you won't earn an income from your venture for the first six months or even longer.

As you immerse in your field and refine your idea, you will learn about the funding sources that make sense for the kind of venture you're going to launch. That will look very different if you're thinking of starting a small nonprofit on the side—where you might fund-raise through donations from friends and family—or a larger for-profit business that would be funded by private investors or a bank loan. It's also possible that you'll create a small-scale business where revenues will cover your expenses almost from the start.

After you have your idea in place, put together a budget for what it will cost to launch and operate, and include it in your business plan. As you do that, here are a few things to consider: If you're building a for-profit

(continued on page 230)

When You Are Your Business

Your business model may not involve other employees; freelancers, consultants, and solopreneurs are also entrepreneurs. Whether you're looking at self-employment by choice or because it's your only choice, consider the following:

- **Build up a cash cushion.** When you work for yourself, paydays aren't predictable. Unless you have another stable source of income, you'll want to sock away enough savings to cover your basic expenses until you start generating a more reliable income. One way to do this is to start freelancing or consulting on the side while you still have a job. Before you walk away from another source of income, try to line up one or two anchor clients willing to give you a good contract. The Freelancers Union offers disability and retirement insurance, as well as health insurance in a growing number of states. Also check out the National Association for the Self-Employed (NASE).

- **Work for free for a little while.** If you're just starting out and you don't have many clients, consider doing a few projects for free. (Notice the words "a few" here.) Obviously, there are plenty of nonmonetary benefits to helping out an organization you care about, and it's possible that your encore may not involve any income-producing activities. But if your plan is to create a consulting or freelance life that can support you, it's wise to ask for something in exchange, even if

you're not getting paid. At minimum, if the client is satisfied with your work, ask for a testimonial for your marketing materials or a recommendation on LinkedIn.

Michelle Goodman, a veteran freelancer and the author of *My So-Called Freelance Life*, calls this "PIE" or getting "paid in exposure." And she cautions against too much of it (just like real pie). You don't want to muddy the waters between your volunteering and the business you are legitimately trying to build. Remember, there is nothing unseemly about expecting payment even if your clients are mission-focused organizations.

- **Follow the money and take your payment seriously.** Get savvy about working with clients who can pay the rate you need to earn. Though you should never deny yourself the chance to do work that matters to you, if that work can't generate the income you need, budget for that as your pro bono activity—and then target better-funded nonprofits or mission-focused businesses for your paying gigs. Professional associations often poll members and share general information on pay rates. The International Freelancers Academy publishes an annual Freelance Industry Report, for example. But by far the best way to learn about pay rates is to trade current information with a group of peers who are working in the same market.

- **Don't ignore the business parts.** The nuts and bolts of running your business can consume as much as half your time. If you aren't adept in these things, find someone to help you, consider taking on a partner with complementary skills, or learn what you don't know. There are plenty of resources you can turn to for help. The Freelancers Union offers template contracts and a client scorecard where members rate clients based on how they treat freelancers. Service Corps of Retired Executives (SCORE, score.org) can match you up with an experienced business mentor. SCORE also has a section of its website devoted to 50+ entrepreneurs. Online communities, such as the International Freelancers Academy, StartupNation.com, and FreelanceSwitch .com, offer ways to network with other independent workers and learn through blogs, articles, and low-cost webinars. The Small Business Administration (Sba .gov) website is another rich resource; pay attention to special programs for women- and minority-owned businesses and the counseling services offered in local areas.

- Figure out your workspace and time management systems. Take the time to think about logistics like where you are going to work, what kind of technology you need, and how you're going to structure your day. Goodman argued that the downfall of many indie workers is the failure to keep a schedule and advance the ball. "If you're a time management mess, you need to get over

that," she said. "Recognize that you can't accomplish more than two or three big things in a day, and set yourself up to do those." You may enjoy the solitude of home, but if you are craving company, consider coworking (working in a communal setting with other independent workers), finding an office space, or spending part of your day working in a café.

- Get comfortable with selling yourself. This is true for everyone, but even more critical if you're self-employed. "You need to get over the idea that selling yourself is about putting on a suit and going door to door doing something nasty," explained Goodman. "It's letting people know what you do and finding out if they have a need." Initially you may have to do some big pushes—an email blast or other announcement to your network. But after you build a name for yourself, clients will start to find you.

- Start where you have some connections. One of the secrets of successful freelancers is that work comes from well-oiled networks. That was confirmed for me when I spoke to Sara Horowitz, founder of the Freelancers Union: "If freelancing is your way of life, you have to be a good citizen because that's the give and take of how your network works, and the minute you are short-sighted, your network will dry up."

(continued from page 227)

venture, how will you finance it? Are you willing to use credit cards or personal loans? Are you going to seek outside funding? If so, start researching who would be interested in your issue and who has invested in or funded similar ventures. When you raise the initial money to get started, will the venture be able to generate revenues sufficient to keep it going—and provide you the income you need? Or will you need to find continued sources of funding?

If you're considering a nonprofit, you'll likely be looking at applying for grants from foundations or other sources. Educate yourself on what kinds of grants are available for the work you want to do. Start by examining how similar organizations are funded. The Foundation Center (foundationcenter .org) is a phenomenal resource that can help you identify which foundations support the issue you're working on. Also look at local community foundations (search "your town/city" and "community foundation").

Here's how some encore entrepreneurs initially funded their ventures (note: As these ventures matured, the financing models evolved):

- Conchy Bretos got a sizable contract from the state of Florida to deliver services to a housing complex where she piloted her idea.

- Elaine Santore started Umbrella of the Capital District out of her garage, with few expenses other than $500 for a lawyer to register her venture as a 501(c)(3) nonprofit (the common legal entity used by nonprofits).

- Catalino Tapia started the Bay Area Gardeners Foundation, a nonprofit to provide scholarships to low-income students by seeking donations from his clients and those of other gardeners in the area. He runs the foundation on the side while continuing to work at his day job and has never taken a salary from the nonprofit.

- Sue Crolick found her start-up funding almost by accident. While still working as an art director, Crolick gave a talk at a design conference in which she talked about the fund-raising events she organized and mentioned that she hoped to move into that work full time one

Invest for Impact

Social entrepreneurs seeking start-up capital for a venture poised for high growth can now look to a growing niche of funders who incorporate aspects of both philanthropy and venture capitalism. They call what they do impact investing.

Some of these investors are "financial first," meaning they want to see market-level financial returns; any social impact is gravy. Others are "mission first," meaning their highest priority is social impact; they might be happy just to get their capital back, perhaps with a small premium.

The key to reaching impact investors is to be able to describe both your venture's financial model and its social impact in measurable ways. If you're keeping formerly incarcerated people from returning to prison, calculate those projected savings. If you're helping to raise high school graduation rates, project your students' higher future earnings. Visit SocialVenturePartners.org to learn more about finding investors.

day. After the talk, a woman affiliated with a foundation approached her, eventually helping Crolick get backing from Nordstrom's that allowed her to lead art events all over the country.

• Nancy Burkhart financed Earth Safe Finishes with Social Security checks, a home refinance, and a part-time job at a nonprofit.

Moving On

Barry Childs created Africa Bridge in 2002 to help improve the quality of life in Tanzania, where he spent his childhood. In his mid-sixties, after running Africa Bridge for about eight years, he started to wonder whether the organization could survive without him or whether "it was dependent on some old guy who had this vision." He also acknowledged that he was "getting pretty damned tired, working harder than I had when I'd gotten paid, and I hadn't had a holiday for years."

Childs convened his board of directors to make a decision on whether the model was sustainable and, if so, how to keep it moving forward without him. When all agreed the organization could and should continue, Childs made it a priority to raise double the money Africa Bridge would normally need in a year to give a new executive director and staff some cushion. He then found and trained an executive director and, instead of walking away, transitioned to more of an advisory role, joining the board. These days he's "an ambassador for the organization, doing PR, spending time with major donors, and trying to be the voice of Tanzania and Tanzanians here in the United States."

Letting go and giving up control have not been easy. "Despite my best intentions, I do get angry when things aren't handled the way I would handle them," Childs said. Still, he knows that the time is right to make this change. "My children and extended family are just delighted that I'll have more time with them. Everyone was concerned I was working too hard, and even I know it's what I need."

Pass the baton, exit the stage, hand over the reins—the metaphors for stepping down from a founder or executive director role abound. Unlike younger entrepreneurs, those who are starting up in their encore years need to have a plan for winding down, whether or not they develop it from the outset or develop it along the way.

Nicki Robb thought about this issue from the start and is baking it into the business model for the animal therapy program she's developing. "I'm in my mid-fifties," she explained. "And I couldn't put out the level of energy that I'd put into the previous work I've done." A professor at Hampshire College in Massachusetts, Robb has already identified some students who could continue the work she sets in motion. "If I get hit by a bus or have a heart attack tomorrow," she told me, "they will be able to sustain what has been launched."

Mark and Arlene Goldsmith, both in their mid-seventies, have taken a different approach. Arlene is executive director of New Alternatives for Children, a New York–based organization that provides an array of services to chronically ill children. Mark founded Getting Out & Staying Out, which helps inmates and ex-offenders build new lives and stay out of prison. They jokingly call themselves the "nonprofit power couple," because of the pace they maintain. Both routinely work more than forty hours a week, and Mark works every Saturday.

The Goldsmiths didn't address the issue of succession until it started to come up in discussions with funders and their boards. At that point, Mark began to groom a successor. "My plan is to work another five years full time, and even then I'll stay involved. I'll probably focus more on the mentoring, less on the fund-raising," he told me. "But it's not about more leisure. Whatever I do, this is going to be my life's work."

Arlene said she was also thinking of succession issues, but she hadn't yet found anyone who was exactly right for the job. And the notion of retiring scared her. "I saw what happened to our fathers when they retired. Both died soon after. So I'm not sure I'll retire at eighty," she said. "This organization is like a baby. We started with nothing and now we have a $20 million budget. This agency is a passion in my heart."

FAQs

Can I make a living as a social entrepreneur?

Definitely. Salaries vary greatly depending on the kind of work being done, the stage of a venture's development, the role the founder plays, and whether it is a for-profit or nonprofit. Often founders start without receiving any salary. And often they start their ventures while continuing to work full time at something else. But established social ventures and nonprofits pay their executives' and staff's salaries. And if you're hired into an existing organization, you'll be recruited and interviewed just as you would be for any other kind of job. For-profit social ventures tend to pay better than nonprofits, but well-funded nonprofits pay competitively as well.

How do I measure the effectiveness of a venture with a social mission and why does it matter?

When you start a business whose only mission is profit, it's easy to know if you're succeeding: Are you hitting your numbers? But when your organization is trying to solve a social problem, you need to think about how you will measure success. How will you know you've succeeded? Or, as they say in the nonprofit world, what are your metrics?

If you are running a job placement program, make sure you count the number of people who are successfully placed. If you are fighting a social or health-related problem, consider doing a survey to track outcomes. If you are offering a service, how many people are using it? Being able to show the efficacy of a venture is critical for attracting funding, media attention, and the right kind of staff and volunteers. Smart organizations build in ways to track and report on these kinds of successes from the outset.

Numbers also have their limitations, warns David Bornstein. "When counting you need to think about outcomes versus inputs. For example, if you're running an after-school program, the inputs are how many students attend and how long they stay. Outcomes would be whether their math or reading skills have improved. Historically, many organizations have measured inputs, boasting about attendance. Today, the movement is toward outcomes. That said, in many types of social-change work, outcomes are very difficult to quantify. Say you help disabled people live more independent lives. The challenge is trying to find a way to reflect your success in numbers."

What if I want to support or work for a social enterprise, but I'm not interested in starting something of my own?

Social businesses need all kinds of help and, like nonprofits, they need both volunteers and employees. So after you identify some organizations that appeal to you, contact them and figure out ways to get to know them and get involved. Start-ups generally may not have a budget to hire, but they need help on everything from legal and business issues to office management, technology assistance, public relations, and fund-raising. Like nonprofits, social businesses will care about both your skills and your interest in the cause or issue involved in the work, so be prepared to demonstrate your passion.

What if I have a great idea for a new venture and want to be involved but have no interest in running it on a day-to-day basis at this stage of my life?

This is not an unusual scenario. In fact I've had conversations about this with many people who are passionate about an issue but are concerned about finding a contained way to work on it.

When Ellen Goodman, the Pulitzer Prize–winning newspaper columnist, gave up her column in 2010, she became engaged with the idea that so many people were dying in ways they wouldn't have chosen if their end-of-life wishes were known. She told me we have a long way to go to "do death" better. So she started the Conversation Project, which seeks to raise awareness in a way that make these kinds of talks easier.

When Goodman started out, she was hardly looking for a full-time commitment as she'd finally escaped the pressure of weekly deadlines. But as a founder, she couldn't easily let go and in the early stages she was traveling, fund-raising, and speaking way more than she expected. When I last spoke to her about this, she was preparing for a big campaign. "I'm fully committed, but my goal is that after the launch I'll be able to do this in a way that isn't quite as consuming," she said. "I haven't yet found the balance, but some of that may just be me."

Goodman may eventually find the balance she is seeking. But if you're seeking to avoid overload you may want to start out by finding a role within an existing organization doing work you admire.

As is true with all of these encore choices, there's no one right way.

Why do social ventures stumble or fail?

According to Gifford Pinchot, social ventures have particular challenges. "Failing to manage people problems is a big one. When you have idealistic people, they tend to use inspiration in place of pay (or some of it) and they tend to work people very hard. You burn people out. And that can lead to failure. They also fail to recognize how hard it is to break into a market." As Pinchot said, "Idealism can also get you into trouble if it isn't matched with self-awareness. People want to go into alternative energy but don't understand the physics of energy. Or they want to go into food distribution but don't understand how the game is played." Some ventures fail because they simply can't raise the money to support the work over time. And let's not forget the infamous "founder's syndrome," in which the person who created the organization just isn't the best person to lead it on a long-term basis but doesn't see it that way.

How can I avoid being one of the failed ones?

Count on mentors and choose areas to go into that correspond with your strengths. "There are very few new ideas," said David Bornstein. "Almost every new social venture is a modification of an idea that failed before.

Regardless of the issue you're working on, it's important to answer a few questions and apprentice yourself to the field. What are the three most common mistakes people make vis-à-vis this particular challenge? Also, know the three most innovative things going on in the sector today. In order to answer these questions, you have to have fifty conversations with the right people, asking them over and over. It is all part of the honing process," Bornstein said. "When social enterprises fail, it is usually because its leaders were unaware of well-known steps they could have taken."

I like the idea of working for myself, but entrepreneurship sounds intimidating. What if I want the autonomy of running my own venture, but want to do something on a smaller scale, without having employees or taking on any risk?

Encore entrepreneurship is a big tent that includes those who want to start ventures with sizable budgets and staff as well as those who want to make an impact on a smaller scale and with less overhead. The quiz on page 214 can give you a sense of whether or not you're well suited to starting an organization bigger than you. If you feel daunted by the idea of starting something from scratch, it's still possible that you might be drawn to working independently as a consultant or freelancer. The box on page 228 ("When You Are Your Business") is meant to get you thinking about the kinds of things you'll need to consider in one of those models.

CHAPTER 11

I'm in My Encore, Now What?

**"America has never been a retirement party.
It's a constant effort to suit up and play again."**

—BILL CLINTON

U p until now, this book has focused exclusively on crafting your encore role. But people who've started encore careers have nearly as many questions as they had before they started. The questions are just different ones: How can I keep myself going? Will I want to keep doing what I'm doing or find a new challenge? When will I want (or need) to slow down? Is my spouse or partner on the same page? What about my kids? Is the stress worth it? Do I have time to take care of my health? What about planning for the next stage? Do I want to eventually find my way to something that looks like old-school retirement?

It shouldn't be surprising that there's a new onslaught of questions. After all, this is a new stage of life, with new promise and more challenges. The encore years present not just one big shift but a series of smaller adjustments to living and working in new ways and to new ends.

Here's how some trailblazers are finding answers.

Managing the Learning Curve

Finding an encore career is one thing, and we know that's not easy. Fully immersing into a new kind of work and culture is another. Let's just state for the record: It's not easy either.

For example, it can take years for new teachers (of any age!) to get comfortable in their role and even more time to hit their stride. John Kostibas, the telecommunications-executive-turned-math-teacher (see page 195), said that his training only skimmed the surface of what he needed to learn, leading to many mistakes as a student teacher. In time, he said he learned some ways to get students to pay attention. "Embarrassing them doesn't work," he explained. "So you learn that you don't say anything negative out in the open. You also have to learn how to communicate with today's youth." For Kostibas, the key to communications has been technology. He's gotten kids excited about calculators by showing how equations can make things happen, like a monkey jumping on a favorite video game. He's also realized that he'll get more response showing a video from Kahn Academy than assigning a book to read.

Discussion Prompts
Where are you in your encore transition? • Have you taken any steps or are you still at the thinking stage? • How has your thinking changed since you picked up this book? • What's making you feel inspired, and challenged?

Still, Kostibas said he's far from what he would call a master teacher, "someone who'd really know how to deal with the most difficult students." But he's working at it, taking advantage of every opportunity for training and mentoring offered by his school district. He's worked hard at forming relationships with students who were acting out in class by getting to know what's going on at home. "The content is the easiest part of the job," he explained. "The tough part is connecting with teenagers, especially the ones with difficult lives."

Teaching has required other adjustments for Kostibas. Salaries are public information. And even communicating with colleagues is different. "In business, when you meet someone, whether it's an engineer or the CEO, you are on a first-name basis after the first handshake," he said. "In academia, you stay with Mr. and Mrs. practically forever." Kostibas learned this lesson on the first day of teacher training when he stood up in front of a classroom and said his name was John Kostibas. "My mentor-teacher practically fell to the ground," he said. "She pulled me aside later to say that I should never ever introduce myself with my first name."

Building a business or practice has a steep learning curve of its own. Marcy Gray Rubin, the television-writer-turned-therapist (see page 8), quickly discovered that being a psychologist wasn't just about helping people with their problems. "I came into therapy in an era when therapists have to market themselves," she told me. When I last spoke with Rubin, she was trying to figure out when it would be appropriate (and good marketing) for a therapist to blog and Tweet.

> **"This is why I was educated, to give back. If not me, who else?"**
> —Wanjiru Kamau, nonprofit founder and executive director

Diana Meinhold (see page 43) recounted a similar experience. After she got credentials as a fiduciary and case manager for people who could no longer take care of themselves, she realized that to do her work she would either need to be hired by the family of an aging parent or appointed by a court. So she set out to find ways to connect with people who could make those kinds of referrals. She networked at events sponsored by the Council on Aging, and she got involved in local bar association sections relating to elder law, trusts, and estates. (To her surprise, being a lawyer wasn't a requirement to join.) "In this field, people have to feel some sort of relationship with you because it's about entrusting someone's life to you," she explained. "Face-to-face networking has been invaluable." But it didn't happen overnight. Even with thirty-eight years of business experience, she felt like she was starting at the bottom in her new field. "I put on my best executive demeanor, dressed like the attorneys dress, had my business cards, and always followed up with thank-you notes acknowledging someone who could refer business to me," she explained. "Still, I was astounded to find that the referrals started to happen."

Redefining Ambition

Many people doing encore work have told me that they feel they have less to prove than in earlier life stages. As a result, they say they're able to focus more on the impact of their work than on climbing the ladder, and they're fueled less by ego than by knowing their work has meaning.

This adjustment doesn't always come naturally. Wendy Bay Lewis, a lawyer-turned-nonprofit-leader, decided that her encore would be as a coach helping others find their encores while also continuing her work promoting economic development in Bozeman, Montana. One of the challenges for her is letting go of her orientation toward "accomplishing" or "winning"— which was borne out by her choices of work, first as a lawyer and then as a fund-raiser. In both cases, she said, "There are lots of hard measurements and colleagues who use the same measuring sticks." These days, particularly as she recovers from a breast cancer recurrence, she said she is much more oriented toward finding colleagues who focus on helping people. She said it's still a work in progress. For example, she was having doubts about whether she could call herself a success if a client hasn't landed a job. Her mentor convinced her that she could be making an impact even if she was the catalyst for a client taking the next step, or becoming aware of possibilities. She said she continually has to remind herself that personal growth and fulfillment may be the most important measuring sticks for this time of life.

Finding Balance, Staying Engaged

When Randal Charlton (see page 218) was executive director of TechTown, his three daughters staged what he calls an "intervention," asking him to make more time for them.

The lesson here: Your encore isn't just about you. The people around you will likely have opinions about what you choose to do and how much time it takes. It's not easy for most of us to ignore requests like this from people we love. In fact, I've spoken to many people who shaped their encores to accommodate someone else's needs or wishes, most commonly partners and grown children.

For couples, decisions about how intensely to pursue an encore are rooted in the classic marital tensions around retirement. Do you and your partner have the same goals for this stage of your life? If not, can you come to some good compromises that let each of you do what you want to do while also honoring the relationship? Time is often the challenge; one person may have thought there would be time for more leisure or travel, and the other is still so engaged with work that she or he doesn't need the same level of play.

I spoke to Dorian Mintzer and Roberta Taylor, relationship therapists who coauthored *The Couples Retirement Puzzle*, to get their perspective on this. Mintzer and Taylor confirmed that plenty of marriages break up around retirement age—with kids out of the house, long-term couples often find themselves on their own again. With so many dynamics at play, it's hard to say whether tension over what partners want to do with their time and their lives is at the root. And, even in newer relationships, negotiations around how to spend time are often trouble spots.

When couples have what Mintzer and Taylor refer to as a "win-win dynamic," it's usually because they are excelling at communication and compromise. And to be successful on those two fronts, there has to be an underlying awareness that talking about the next chapter of life is important. I've heard numerous examples of this from people who were nurturing both an encore career and a successful life partnership.

> "I don't know that I can fix the system, but I don't know that I can't. In my golden years, I plan to perfect my skills as a troublemaker, which is much more fun than being nice."
>
> —Toni Heineman, nonprofit founder and executive director

Before John Kostibas became a teacher, he toyed with the idea of joining the Peace Corps, which would have meant going overseas for two years to an assigned location he couldn't choose. Because his wife wasn't at a point in her life where she could have joined him, Kostibas decided to focus on his other idea—teaching—which would allow him to have an impact closer to home.

Some couples find that their encores are not just compatible but mutually reinforcing. Arlene and Mark Goldsmith (see page 232) fall into that category. When Mark left a long career in cosmetics marketing, it was Arlene, already a veteran nonprofit leader, who pushed him to try Principal for a Day, the program that unlocked his desire to work with men in and just getting out of prison.

Mark refers to Arlene as his mentor because she guided him into nonprofit life and showed him the ropes. (Her organization is much larger than his, with a staff and budget nearly twenty times the size of his.) The two are almost competitive in their zeal. Both routinely work more than forty hours a week and, in their mid-seventies, don't show many signs of slowing down—although they do make time for travel, culture, and socializing with friends and families. They also appreciate that they are still earning an income in these years.

Still, even work that contributes to the greater good will have imperfections. Bad management, difficult colleagues, and workplace blahs exist just about everywhere. And socially minded work has added challenges—tight budgets, limited resources, and the morale issues that come with working on intractable problems where you may not see quick results. In the end you'll have to decide if the trade-offs are worth it. Now is the time to ask yourself some important questions.

Are you feeling like you are able to have an impact doing what you're doing? Do your feelings of frustration outweigh your feelings of satisfaction? Do you spend a lot of your time fantasizing about what else you could be doing with your days? Even if you've answered yes to these questions, before you decide to move on, ask yourself whether you can use your experience to solve any of the problems you see, and whether the satisfaction you are getting outweighs the annoyances or frustrations. If the answer to those two questions are no, it's probably time to explore other options.

John Kostibas isn't blind to the problems in our education system, and after years of working in business where pay is tied to performance, he said he is still not used to the fact that earnings are based on years of service rather than ability. But on balance, he said that teaching is "the best encore I could have imagined," and he plans to stick it out.

Taking Care of Yourself

While we all seem to feel younger than we are, how we age and how we feel as we age varies wildly. One person can feel spry and energetic at eighty, whereas another battered and beaten down at seventy. Some of this has to do with good (or bad) genes, but we have some control over it, too.

When I asked Laura Carstensen, founder of the Stanford Center of Longevity, if there is an age at which people start to identify themselves as old or slowing down, she told me, "There's nothing magical about any number. Aging is a pretty steady process and happens from the day we are born. It's not that one day you suddenly become different. Aging itself isn't what does people in. It's the interaction of aging with other factors that leads to problems for most people. Lifestyle makes a huge difference."

Which is probably why so many people thriving in their encores like to tell me about what they do to take care of themselves. It's usually some variation on the basics—regular exercise, a good diet, social connections, and continuing to learn. A new study from the Sloan Center on Aging and Work at Boston College shows that engagement in paid work, volunteering, and education is key to well-being as we age. Jan Hively, a leader in the positive aging movement, said that maintaining intergenerational connections is another.

Still it's naïve to think that you'll never change and that your energy level at seventy-eight will be what it was at sixty or fifty-five. But your attitude may be stable, or even improve. Study after study shows that one of the benefits of aging is that stress, worry, and anger seem to diminish with age. Sure, lots of bad stuff happens, but we seem to be more equipped to handle it and focus on the positive. As Carstensen explained, "It's too simplistic to say that older people are happier, but they are likelier to experience mixed emotions and engage with sadness more comfortably."

Randal Charlton said that remaining physically fit has been crucial to keeping pace. "As you become older, you become less immune to your own bad behavior," he explained. "Now I'll have a drink on Friday night and maybe on Saturday, but never on Sunday. You may be in a wheelchair, but you have to be as fit as you can be. My thirty-year-old self would laugh at me, but during the week I'm in bed by ten. I've got to compete with twenty-five- to forty-year-olds and give myself the best chance of doing that."

For people whose encore work is emotionally taxing, there is an extra layer of self-care to consider. One of the benefits of maturity is that you know yourself well enough to know what keeps you going and helps you to feel centered. But new work can bring on new needs for dealing with the stress caused by disturbing or emotionally difficult situations.

Nancy Morrow-Howell, a professor of social work at Washington University, said that it's crucial for people who are entering potentially stressful situations to know what they're getting into and how to take care of themselves. Training programs in social work and therapy, for example, teach how to set boundaries and avoid burnout. If you aren't getting trained through a formal program that will provide this kind of support, find ways to get what you need, either through the organization you're working with or through some other channel. "Find people you can talk to and who can supervise you—ideally someone who's been around the block and can give you professional advice," said Morrow-Howell.

Ed Speedling, who has been working in various roles related to homelessness for nearly ten years, said that having a quiet meditative start to his days has been incredibly helpful as he ventures out onto the streets. "If you're not ready for the day, if you haven't slept well or partied too much the night before, you cannot do this work," he told me. Although he braced himself initially for what he thought would be difficult encounters—engaging with people who are mentally ill, living in "god-awful places"—he counts some of those contacts as the most authentic experiences in his life.

"I've had so many joyful moments," he said. "Homeless people take nothing for granted. Every day is a day they have to survive. When something good happens, like getting a bologna sandwich, they recognize it. In all the years I worked as an administrator in medical centers, I didn't put my hands on too many people, didn't laugh or cry much. In this business, you hug, you get close to people, you laugh, and you cry. It's so life-giving. I'd never go back to anything full time that didn't have this element to it."

In the first year of her new role as a case manager and fiduciary, Diana Meinhold experienced the death of her first client. "It was very hard," she wrote to me, "but as long as I tell myself I am improving the quality of their lives for whatever time they have left, I can deal with the loss. What I do have to do better is find more time for fun in my own life, as this can certainly become all-consuming."

When Life Gets in the Way

You can plan all you like, but life has a way of getting in the way. Sometimes, health issues, such as a diagnosis or a scare that reinforces your own mortality, can be the reason to move to a career with more meaning. Just as often, personal or family crises show up and affect the course of an encore.

As I reached out to people to interview for this book, many times an email would go unanswered and then, months later, I would get a reply indicating that a stretch of time devoted to caregiving, or a bout with some health problem that eclipsed everything else for a time, had just ended. These aren't things we can plan for, but the inevitability of these life events explained why so many people prize a certain amount of flexibility in the encore years.

My Encore.org colleague Judy Goggin was going full tilt in her encore when she found out her first grandchild would be born with a life-threatening heart condition. Over the course of her first few years, the baby would require three surgeries to repair her heart—the first right away, the second within three to six months, and the third when she reached two years old. Judy, then sixty-four, knew that she wanted to be there for her daughter and son-in-law as they managed the crisis. Despite the advance warning, she didn't have a long-term plan. She just followed her instincts doing, as she said, "what anyone else would do."

Judy managed by modifying her work schedule several times and continuing to tweak and adjust it. She took off a few blocks of time, for the birth and the surgeries. And when she did go back to work, she adjusted her schedule month by month, responding to the family's needs. Her husband and she moved into their daughter's home for months at a time, creating shifts of caregiving. For a time, Judy covered the night shift, from 3 a.m. to 9 a.m., went to work for a full day, and then went to sleep right after dinner to do it all over again.

Being at a stage of life where she had some flexibility and financial options helped. Judy was eligible for Social Security and Medicare, which eased the financial burden somewhat. At work, she set up weekly planning meetings with her boss and the others covering for her to make sure that her workload was effectively managed without raising costs to the organization. "I took on the responsibility for coming up with the plan, the ideas, and the resources to get the work done," she told me. As this book went to press, Judy was working half time and helping with her granddaughter and a new grandson.

As for what's next, Judy hasn't gotten there yet. "I look at this two-year slice of life as a time my family desperately needs me," she said. "It could end up being longer. And for now, I've put off thinking about how much I'll want to work once this piece isn't in the mix."

John Fanselow's caregiving decisions defy the stereotypes—he's taking care of his mother-in-law in Japan. After retiring from a tenured faculty role at Columbia University's School of Education, Fanselow found a host of new ways to stay involved in the English as a Second Language field, more because he enjoyed the work than because he needed the income. He continued to write, teach as an adjunct, and consult with colleges in New York, Japan, and New Zealand.

More recently, Fanselow has been collaborating with a group of entrepreneurs on a start-up venture that would deliver lesson plans via mobile technology to teachers in remote parts of the world. It fits him well, considering his Peace Corps experience in Somalia nearly fifty years ago and the years as a teacher that followed.

Fanselow and his wife, also a professor, now live in Japan, just blocks away from his mother-in-law, who is in her nineties and needs a good deal of support. Because his wife still works full time as a professor, Fanselow has become his mother-in-law's primary caretaker, an arrangement that seems to work for everyone involved. "I prepare meals, run errands, and do a whole lot of house-husbanding," he told me. "It's really gratifying, relaxing, and refreshing." Having work that he can do flexibly at any hour and in any place is a critical part of the mix.

There is nothing like a health scare to make you realize that time is precious and that you may want to think differently about how you'll spend it. For Wendy Bay Lewis, her cancer recurrence and treatment caused her to set some new boundaries around work. Lewis has worked hard to create a life with less stress, fewer hours, less responsibility, and less exposure to environments that are liable to result in conflict or contentiousness. She's also decided that she wants her work to be much more about one-on-one mentoring experiences and less done through organizations. "I wanted to work in a setting with less stress, fewer meetings, fewer hours, less responsibility, and less conflict," she explained, adding that she specifically removed herself from work she knew had the tendency to be contentious. Finally, she's making time to write—something that I heard from enough people to know that it's a desire many share.

Chronic-illness coach Rosalind Joffe (see page 219) knows firsthand what it's like to continue to work despite debilitating health problems, and she now makes her living by helping others. She said that immersing herself in work that helps others is not at all uncommon among those suffering themselves. "Those who mention a shift in their thinking about work talk

Managing Health Concerns

Meaningful work can be a huge boon to your health and well-being, but only if you can find ways to work that match up with your energy and physical capabilities. Joffe, who had previously worked as a multimedia producer and a college professor, had to reassess her career after developing ulcerative colitis and MS. For long periods she was unable to work, and her health conditions made it hard to have jobs where she had to be available on a schedule she couldn't control. When her conditions stabilized enough for her to work, she was determined to craft a way of working that suited her. After years of working through a transition, Joffe became a chronic-illness coach and now focuses on helping others adjust their working lives to accommodate their health needs. She has built a reputation as an expert, coach, and advocate on managing chronic illness in the workplace. I spoke to Joffe about how to think about an encore if you are facing a health issue, and she gave these tips (some of which will be easier to apply when you know what kind of work you want to be doing):

- Assess your mental and physical capacity. Write it down and graph it over a week or even a few months. What are your symptoms? What is your energy level? What mental or emotional things are you dealing with? Are you often feeling depressed or tired?

- Make a list of the kinds of tasks you do or would need to do in the work you want to do—and consider how your symptoms would affect your ability to do these tasks.

- Think of ways you can work around the problem areas. Could you delegate some parts of the job to someone else? Could you work as part of a team so that when you can't be available someone else can? Could you create a flexible schedule that accommodates your needs for rest or your energy levels?

- Consider how you want to talk about this with other people and be thoughtful and strategic. Find ways to manage your emotional distress and get support for it outside of your workplace so that you don't have to bring that to the job.

- If you're negotiating for a position, anticipate and address your needs before they arise. That will be more effective than dealing with them after you realize that you're underperforming.

about doing work that is useful to others rather than retreating more inward and only worrying about themselves," she wrote to me. "It's not just that it takes attention away from you, but also that you feel valuable and useful," she added.

Pacing Yourself

When you start a career at midlife or later, there are the obvious questions of how long you'll do it, how intensely you'll do it, and how you'll move to the next stage. You'll probably make your decision based on what else is calling to you in this period.

Helen Karr wanted to control the amount of time she gave to her encore from the start. After a first career as a flight attendant and a second running a chain of hair salons at hotels, Karr went back to law school in her fifties to figure out a way to do something about elder financial abuse, a problem she learned about through the stories of clients in her salon. "You learn a lot as a hairdresser," she said. "And these ugly stories would filter back to me about caretakers or children taking advantage of older adults by taking money from them, often spending it on drugs."

While at law school, Karr took classes and worked part time, leaving little time for her husband and a social life. When she graduated, she volunteered her way into a paying job with the San Francisco district attorney's office helping to set up an elder abuse unit. From the start, she was committed to working less than full time. "At this stage of life, it doesn't have to be whole-hog," Karr explained. "My husband was older and he'd been supportive through four years of law school. When I was out, I wanted more time with him."

Later, after her husband died, Karr allowed herself to be recruited back to the DA's office. Then in her mid-seventies, she accepted a two-day-a-week contract position, which left her time to continue volunteering for the California state bar association and the San Francisco museum bookstore. "I learned a long time ago that you need balance," she said.

> **"I have discovered qualities within myself that I never knew I had."**
>
> —Judith Broder,
> nonprofit founder

Continuing to find paid work as you age is definitely a challenge. And it will likely remain so during this transitional period when people are still getting used to seeing elders as a part of the fabric of work. That said, whenever I talk to someone who is continuing to find paid work opportunities, I notice a few common characteristics. First is a determination to remain engaged and plugged into a social network that continues to provide opportunities; second is a commitment to keep learning and building skills; and finally, and perhaps most important, is sheer persistence. George Wolf (see page 155), now eighty-four, found himself looking for paid work well into his eighties, a position he never thought he would be in when he ran a successful manufacturing business in his sixties. But after that business went bust, he found a part-time role as marketing director for the Blue Card, which aids destitute Holocaust survivors. He found that position through ReServe, which paired him in several nonprofits in fund-raising, marketing, and communications roles. The pay is low but gratifying. Last we spoke, he was considering an idea to teach grant writing to encore seekers.

Easing Back

Howard Johnson (see page 151), the fishing industry consultant who transitioned to a full-time job at a sustainable fishing nonprofit, was sixty-nine at the time of our interview. He told me he was logging 175,000 miles a year traveling for work. "I never thought I would be doing this at my age," he said. He promised his wife he would travel less once he hit seventy, and he said he planned to "semiretire" then. "They won't let me retire," he chuckled, "but my plan is to go on the board and do about 30 percent of what I'm doing now, which is probably about 140 percent of normal."

As Johnson's story reveals, it's not just the when, it's also a question of how and what next. After twenty-eight years as a parole officer in New York City, Fred Weinberg retired at fifty-five and went on to a series of mostly full-time encores over twenty years. Several of these positions built directly on his experience in law enforcement. At the Vera Institute for Justice, he worked on alternatives to incarceration. At fifty-eight, he went back to school to become certified as a police officer, then took an investigating position at the Brooklyn district attorney's office. At sixty-three, he started a five-year stint at a neighborhood drug crisis program where he earned more than he made in his years as a parole officer. He even taught a class, "Everything you always wanted to know about crime in New York," for the New School's Institute for Retired Professionals.

In his early seventies, Weinberg was ready for a change and wanted to explore an earlier interest in medicine, which he thought he could do in a part-time way as a volunteer. "I'm a frustrated doctor," he told me, "and I wanted to work with older people in a hospital setting."

How Will You Live Your Legacy?

As my colleague Marc Freedman likes to say, creating an encore career is a natural way to *live* your legacy rather than just *leave* one. We think of legacies as sums of money passed on to charities and names inscribed on buildings, but why not think about an encore career that creates a better world for future generations?

As you finish up this book, I hope you'll write a brief note about your legacy. How has your experience made a difference for others? What's the most meaningful thing you've done so far? What else would you like to accomplish?

If you feel comfortable sharing, please send your letter to me at ECH@encore.org with the subject line "My Encore Legacy." If you give your permission, I'd like to post some of these on Encore.org as a way to inspire people to choose work that leaves the world a better place than we found it. I look forward to hearing from you.

He networked around and ultimately stumbled into an ideal position—working along with a social worker in a hospital program that helped older, low-income, chronically ill people navigate the medical system. Though he was willing to volunteer, the job pays a modest stipend through an arrangement with ReServe.

At three days a week, the job allows Weinberg time for other things that have started to become more important to him—a day each week in New Jersey with his grandchildren, an immersion in a memoir-writing group. When we last spoke, he said the job was working well. "I'm going to be seventy-nine and I'm in good shape physically and cognitively. But if one day I wake up and say I can't do this anymore, I will walk in and say it's time for me to leave."

Weinberg embodies the spirit that Jan Hively, a leader in the positive aging movement (see page 114), calls "meaningful work—paid or unpaid—until the last breath." Hively, approaching eighty when I last spoke to her for this book, was in the midst of a transition to her new chapter of work and life.

"It's a very creative time in my life," Hively writes. "There is time to reflect. And to think about legacy, to make sure that the things that have counted most have at least been advanced—and ideally have been taken up by others."

In Hively's own life, this chapter involves a new love and a move from the Minneapolis area to Cape Cod to fulfill a lifelong dream of living near the beach. She is working on two projects related to positive aging, but the work has a new, slower rhythm. "My commitment with my partner, who is twelve years younger than I am, is to go to the beach every day." In the shorter days of winter, "we leave by 3 p.m., so I move whatever I thought I'd get done to the next day."

Leaving a Legacy

The word *legacy* comes up a lot in these next-stage conversations. Husband and wife Howard and Marika Stone have worked on their encore together, creating and running Too Young to Retire, a train-the-trainer program to bring their ideas about reframing retirement to social workers, coaches, and other professionals. They sold that business after running it for fourteen years and turned their attention to other passions, of which they both have several.

"Running that kind of business requires a lot of travel," Howard, now seventy-seven, told me, "and at this point in our lives, if we're traveling, it's to be with family." A lifelong musician, Howard now spends a lot of his time on music, entertaining, and performing at senior centers. Marika, seventy, teaches yoga to older adults near their home in Palm Beach Gardens, Florida. She's also taken up the guitar, and the two of them play in a Unitarian Universalist Church jazz band that has become a big part of their lives.

They're both brimming with ideas of new things they want to add to the mix. "When I look at music, there are infinite possibilities to grow and learn," said Howard. Marika, a writer, sees possibilities for a project to help people work on what she calls "living legacies," stories about their lives that can be shared with children, grandchildren, and great-grandchildren.

Hubert ("Hubie") Jones, a former professor of social work, has created, reformed, and transitioned out of many leadership roles in Boston nonprofits that work for social justice, better schools, and stronger communities. When I last spoke to him for this book, he was seventy-eight. "In earlier periods I wasted a lot of time in meetings and on boards where my presence wasn't making a difference," he said. "The key question for me is, 'Is my presence here making a difference in the work going on?' If the work can be completed without my input, then I shouldn't be there."

These days, as he is more in touch with his own mortality, Jones spends a lot of time mentoring and supporting new leaders. "I turn away most

"Everything I've done in my life has led to this job. Even my parenting skills are assets in this job. It's balderdash that older people can't teach. You can't keep me down in the classroom."

—Sandy Faison, actor/mom-turned-teacher

speech-making requests unless they are absolutely critical to something I want to achieve," he said. "There are a lot of younger voices that need to be heard."

Some people don't see a certain path for the next stage but have a sense of its contours. Ed Speedling, the hospital administrator who now works with the homeless, is in this group. When we last spoke, Speedling was approaching seventy. "At some point I'll transition to something with more witnessing, less doing. When older people show up at protests or marches, and when they join with other younger people, it energizes the situation. I may move into more unpaid roles down the line. Becoming a witness for what I believe. Showing up, holding a sign, lobbying, joining in advocacy. I don't know when, but I can see it."

Epilogue

About two years into our marriage, my husband and I were going through a particularly rough patch. I had been married before; he hadn't, so I often wondered if he doubted whether he'd made the right decision. One night we were walking side by side through Washington Square Park near our home in New York with a little too much silence between us, and I turned to him and asked, "Is marriage harder than you thought it would be?" "Probably," he replied. Then he quickly added, "But nothing worth having isn't hard." I often reflect on that sentiment when I think about encore careers.

As I wrap up this book, I think back with gratitude on the hundreds of people who opened themselves up and shared intimate aspects of their lives with me. These early adopters have taught me that encore transitions and encore careers are not quick and tidy. They are messy and hard. But for those who muddle through the mess and build something worth building, encore work has the potential to be a true capstone of life, worthy of the standing ovation image evoked by the term.

This book is packed with stories because I believe that sharing stories is an effective way to change expectations and because I believe that when you see enough people doing something, you're tempted to do the same. Author Tina Rosenberg calls that "positive peer pressure" and says it's one of the best ways to bring about social change. I hope so.

I've got a few other hopes, too. I hope this book has inspired you to share your story and to ask other people to share theirs. I hope it has given you a realistic look at what it takes to craft work that matters. Most important, I hope it has given you the tools to join the growing club of encore enthusiasts. I firmly believe the payoff—for yourself, for others, and for generations to come—will be enormous.

• • • • • •

Join the Conversation

You've heard about how others are crafting their encores and helping to create a movement for personal renewal and social good. Now it's your turn. As you start exploring and doing your encore work, here are a few things you can do.

• Join the encore movement. More details at Encore.org.

• Start talking about your goals for your encore with others.

• Start a discussion group or encore transition group using this book, *Encore*, and *The Big Shift* as your guides. (Group discussion tools are online at encore.org/handbook.)

• If you're already settled in an encore, pay it forward by mentoring others.

The Encore Hot List

The following is a list of promising encore jobs. Each of these has one or more of the qualities people tend to look for in an encore career: anticipated high need or demand in the coming years, opportunities for flexible or part-time work, and opportunities for self-employment. All of them are well suited to people with years of experience.

This list isn't exhaustive, but it should give you ideas for where to start if you're stumped. It helps to think creatively. If certain aspects of a role don't appeal to you but the field seems interesting, consider searching for other jobs in that industry. For example, if you like the idea of working in a hospital but would never consider nursing, start scanning job listings in hospitals. Or if you like the idea of working in a hospice but don't want to work directly with those who are seriously ill, consider working in a role where you deal with family members rather than patients. Even if none of these roles intrigue you, reading the descriptions may help you rule out certain fields of work and cause you to look deeper into others.

Salary data labeled as "average" comes from the U.S. Department of Labor Statistics unless otherwise noted.

Health Care

Nurse—Nursing offers a range of opportunities at various levels of experience and in many different settings, including schools, doctors' offices, hospitals, and private homes. Since nursing shifts run around the clock, hours can be flexible. Pay will depend on geographic location, work setting, years of education and experience, and other factors. Nursing is a job that benefits from maturity and experience in decision-making. For information about the nursing profession, including the nursing roles that are explored, check out discovernursing .com or vcn.org.

For jobs in health care, visit the Virtual Career Network—Healthcare (vcn.org/healthcare/), a newly launched site sponsored by the Department of Labor where you can learn volumes about eighty health care fields projected to be in demand during the coming years.

Nursing is an extremely popular encore choice, and many labor forecasters predict a strong demand for nurses in coming years. Despite the fact that nursing can be a highly physical, on-your-feet kind of work, that doesn't seem to deter people in their forties, fifties, and beyond from the field. Online message boards for nurses are loaded with personal stories of people reporting positive experiences resulting from launching nursing careers after fifty. In addition to nurses, other health care roles, like EMTs, physician assistants, physical and occupational therapists, and all kinds of lab technicians, are also suitable to shift work or part-time schedules, making them especially attractive to encore seekers.

To find nursing education training programs, including accelerated programs, go to allnursingschools.com.

Licensed practical nurse (LPN)—These nurses (also called licensed vocational nurses or LVNs) provide basic nursing care: recording vital signs, applying dressings, drawing blood, maintaining patient records, and providing emotional comfort. Training programs—usually in community colleges or vocational schools—require at least a high school diploma or equivalent, last a year or two, and can cost $2,000 and up. Experts predict that hospitals will move toward requiring all nurses to have bachelor degrees. That said, with the growth of facilities serving the aged, even nurses without degrees will likely find opportunities. *Average annual pay:* $42,040.

Registered nurse (RN)—Registered nurses supervise licensed practical nurses and have extensive training and increased responsibility. They perform physical exams, monitor patients' conditions, coordinate care with other health care professionals, and handle numerous aspects of patient care. This is a great job for those who enjoy one-on-one interaction—RNs often provide advice and emotional support to patients and their families. To become an RN, you need an associate's or possibly a bachelor's degree in nursing, or a nursing diploma (an option offered in some hospitals). There are accelerated nursing programs available for people who already have bachelor's degrees in other fields. *Average annual pay:* $69,110.

Nurse practitioner—If you're already a registered nurse and want to expand your skills and responsibilities, or if you want to start out in the nursing profession at a higher level, consider becoming a nurse practitioner. These nurses perform many duties often handled by doctors, including making diagnoses and prescribing medications. Most nurse practitioners work in hospitals, doctors' offices, and health clinics. Some have private practices. You'll need a master's degree for this work. There are programs available for registered nurses who have bachelor's degrees and for people who have bachelor's degrees in other fields. The length of education and training will vary based on the course work you've had so far. *Average annual pay:* $83,710.

Nurse instructor—Becoming a nurse instructor is a great way for nurses to pass on knowledge, mentor aspiring nurses, and stay connected to the field. Plus, teaching provides respite from the physical demands of a full-time nursing career. While smaller facilities may allow you to teach with a bachelor's degree, most schools and hospitals require at least a master's degree. There are college programs that offer nurse educator certificates, but you

The Occupational Outlook Handbook (bls.gov/ooh) is a useful resource maintained by the U.S. Department of Labor. For each listed occupation, you can see a description of the role—including information on expected hours, projected growth rate, national median salary, and similar occupations.

may be permitted to teach based on your education and work experience. *Average annual pay*: $67,810.

Physician assistant—The roles of physician assistant and nurse practitioner (see previous description) are similar. Though responsibilities overlap, training differs. Physician assistant training programs are typically two years long, but if you don't have a bachelor's degree, some programs allow you to earn both a bachelor's and master's degree in five years. Another key difference between the professions: Physician assistants work under the supervision of a physician, while nurse practitioners may practice solo. *Average annual pay*: $89,470. *Key resource*: American Academy of Physician Assistants (aapa.org).

Emergency medical technician (EMT)—If you are drawn to medicine but feel like it's too late to pursue a career as a doctor or nurse, working as an EMT is a chance to save lives. You need to be a quick thinker and have the ability to handle stressful and physically strenuous work. EMTs work for private ambulance firms, municipalities, or hospitals. The hours can be flexible. There are three levels of EMT: basic, intermediate, and paramedic. Training for the entry level requires 150 hours of course work. Paramedics train for 1,200 hours. You can find training programs at community colleges, technical schools, and hospitals. *Average annual pay*: $34,030. *Key resource*: National Registry of Emergency Medical Technicians (nremt.org; click on "Become an EMS Professional").

Home health aide (also called personal care aide)—With a growing aging population, home health aides are in great demand and will be for the foreseeable future. Home health aides assist people who are disabled, chronically ill, cognitively impaired, or frail. Aides help with such basic tasks as bathing, dressing, and going to the bathroom. They may do light housework and help with basic medical tasks, such as monitoring vital signs and administering medications. If you enjoy providing personal care, this might be a good fit, but the work can be grueling. Often employers will provide on-the-job training, but you can

The home health aide position can be a stepping-stone to a nursing role (see the "career pathway" map on the page for home health aide on vcn.org).

find formal training programs (required in some states) at community colleges and vocational schools. Home health aides can work through an agency or on their own. Wages can vary considerably based on the type of care. *Average annual pay:* $21,820. *Key resource:* Virtual Career Network (vcn.org/healthcare). Type "home health aide" into the site's search box.

Physical or occupational therapist—Physical and occupational therapists help people suffering from illnesses or injuries that limit movement. Both professionals focus on strength, flexibility, and coordination, but to different ends. Physical therapists aim to restore movement and mobility, usually involving gross motor skills—walking, playing tennis, and the like. Occupational therapists help people function independently in their day-to-day activities, such as bathing, buttoning clothes, and holding a pen or fork. Both kinds of therapists generally work in clinics, hospitals, and schools. These professions require at least a master's degree in the respective fields to practice. *Average annual pay:* for physical therapists, $79,830; for occupational therapists, $74,970. *Key resources:* American Physical Therapy Association (apta.org), and the American Occupational Therapy Association (aota.org).

Massage therapist—Massage therapists seek to relieve muscle tension and pain and to increase flexibility and mobility. They treat patients who suffer from stress, migraines, back pain, arthritis, and other conditions. Massage therapy often accompanies alternative medicine treatment that complements or takes the place of standard medical treatment. Massage therapists work in private homes, spas, gyms, hospitals, and other health-focused venues. You can work for an employer or yourself—many massage therapists work part time. Training and licensing requirements vary widely, as does pay. You can often find training programs at community colleges and vocational schools. *Average annual pay:* $39,920. *Key resource:* American Massage Therapy Association (amtamassage.org; click "Career Guidance," and note the "Career Path Quiz").

Yoga instructor—Yoga can help people tone and strengthen muscles, increase flexibility, and relax. Although it's possible to make a living as a yoga instructor, teaching yoga is usually a part-time job with pay varying per class. Instructors teach in yoga studios, fitness centers, resort spas, and private homes. For training opportunities, start with your local yoga studios or gyms, which might have their own programs or recommendations for programs. Training usually involves a minimum of 200 hours and can cost $3,000 and up. However, if you plan to teach only in gyms or community centers, you might be able to teach with fewer hours of training. *Average annual pay:* $42,000, according to Indeed.com. *Key resource:* Yoga Alliance (yogaalliance.org).

Patient navigator/advocate—Patient navigators (sometimes called patient advocates or health navigators) guide patients through the health care system. They help patients understand medical advice, work through insurance issues, stick to treatment plans, and stay out of the hospital. This is an emerging position, so while some hospitals, community health centers, and insurance companies employ patient navigators, such jobs are not yet widely available. However, it's a role that can be done independently of these institutions and many community colleges and nonprofit organizations are developing training and certification programs to move more people into this role. A background in social work can be helpful. *Average annual pay:* $44,000, according to SimplyHired.com. *Key resources:* AdvoConnection Blog (advoconnectionblog .com; click "Become a Patient Advocate"), and Society for Healthcare Consumer Advocacy (shca-aha.org/).

> If you have ideas for a role that is particularly relevant to encore seekers, I want to hear from you. Email ECH@encore.org and use the header "Encore Role" in your note. Tell us why it's particularly well suited to encore seekers, and include any helpful resources for those interested in breaking in or learning more about the industry. Thanks for helping others find their way into encore-friendly work.

Community health worker—Community health workers provide health education, guidance, and basic direct services (such as first aid and blood pressure screenings) often to individuals or groups with low incomes. If you want to give back to your community at an intimate level, this is one way to do it. Community health workers typically have a close understanding of the community, often sharing the same cultural background, language, and life experiences as their clients. Government agencies, nonprofit organizations, and health care providers employ community health workers. There is no single training or education requirement for this emerging role, although it helps to have a bachelor's degree in a related field (nursing, social work, nutrition, etc.). Some community colleges offer programs in community health. *Average annual pay:* varies from $29,600–$50,810, or $14–$24 hourly, according to Virtual Career Network. *Key resource:* Virtual Career Network (vcn .org/healthcare; type "community health worker" in the site's search box).

Health or wellness coach—This emerging career path appeals to those who want to help others develop and maintain their mental and physical health. People with professional backgrounds related to well-being—from personal training to social work—are likely candidates. You can coach for an established provider (such as a health plan or hospital) or on your own. One subspecialty is chronic illness coaching—helping people manage diseases such as diabetes and avoid complications and hospital stays. Because there are no national accreditation training standards, certification programs vary in scope, intensity, and cost. *Average annual pay:* $54,000, according to SimplyHired.com. *Key resources:* wellcoachesschool.com, integrativenutrition .com, and healthsciences.org.

Home modification specialist—These specialists in design and construction help aging individuals and people with disabilities live as independently as possible in their own homes. Modifications include ramps, grab bars, adjustable height counters, and wiring for electronic monitoring systems that provide various kinds of data to family members or health care professionals. If you have a background in architecture or construction, this is a chance to put your skills to work for the greater good. *Average annual pay:* $53,000, according to SimplyHired.com. *Key resources:* The National Association of Home Builders certifies specialists to help people age in their homes. (Search nahb.org for "aging-in-place.") Also check out Homemods.org, from the Fall Prevention Center of Excellence (stopfalls.org).

Social Services, Counseling, Coaching

Bereavement/grief counselor—Bereavement counselors help others cope with loss, whether it be the death of a loved one or the end of a relationship or job. Bereavement counselors work for hospices, hospitals, nursing homes, government and nonprofit agencies, or they start their own practices. Community colleges offer programs in bereavement counseling and thanatology, the study of death and dying. Degree programs are available. *Average annual pay* (mental health counselors): $44,850. *Key resources:* The American Academy of Grief Counseling (aihcp.org) and the Association for Death Education and Counseling (adec.org) offer nationally recognized certification in this field.

Child care worker—Taking care of kids as an encore can be tremendously fulfilling (though potentially exhausting). Most states have no education requirements, but many do require child care workers to have some level of training. Much depends on the setting—home, day care center, or school. There are community college and vocational school programs that can teach you the basics. Contact your local child care resource and referral agency for more information, including details on licensing and training opportunities. Find your local contacts at nrckids.org/states/states.htm. *Average annual pay:* $21, 320. *Key resource:* If you think you'd like to open your own day care center, check out Child Care Aware (childcareaware.org).

Pastoral counselor—Many people who go into seminary or theological programs do not end up in front of a congregation. They become counselors. Pastoral counselors are trained in both theology and psychology, using elements of faith and science when providing therapy. You do not have to be ordained. If you are a licensed behavioral health professional and are active in a religious community, you can become certified as a pastoral counselor through the American Association of Pastoral Counselors after meeting a set of requirements, including course work and a supervisory period. For those without a background in theology or psychology, there are two-year master's degree programs in pastoral counseling that cover both subjects. (Note that meeting requirements for state licensure can take an additional couple of years, depending on the state.) Pastoral counselors work in a variety of settings, including counseling centers, hospitals, houses of worship, nursing homes, and private practices. *Average annual pay:* $44,850. *Key resource:* American Association of Pastoral Counselors (aapc.org).

Addiction counselor—Counselors who specialize in treating people with addictions (to drugs, food, gambling, and other potentially harmful substances or behaviors) may work with clients individually or in group sessions. Education, training, certification, and licensing requirements vary by state. In some states, you only need a high school diploma and certification to work as an addiction counselor, although if you want to see clients one-on-one, you may need a master's degree. To find out what your state requires, contact your local state licensing or certification board (addictioncareers.org/find/certinfo/index.asp). *Average annual pay:* $41,030. *Key resource:* Addiction Technology Transfer Center Network (addictioncareers.org).

Career counselor/adviser/coach—In your encore career, why not help others find their own encores? Or at least find jobs that best suit them? Career counselors, advisers, and coaches help clients realize their wants, needs, and desires surrounding work, such as work environment, contact with the public, and salary level. And they cover the practical skills of job hunting, including résumé writing, networking, and interviewing. Depending on the role you choose, you may use standardized tests to measure aptitude, interests, motivations, and personal style. If you have experience in human resources, recruiting, counseling, advising, or related fields, this could be a match for you.

So how are counseling, advising, and coaching different? Navigating the subtleties can be challenging. These roles have more names than the three I mention here, exist in different settings, and require varying levels of education or training. Career counselors generally have master's degrees in counseling, along with state licenses. Career advisers may have graduate-level training in a host of fields, such as adult education or academic advising. There are no requirements to become a career coach, but many coaches opt for voluntary training and certification, available from a host of outlets. Career counselors and advisers may work in colleges, government agencies, and nonprofits. Career coaches work for themselves, as do some counselors. *Average annual pay:* $56,540. *Key resources:* International Coach Federation (coachfederation.org). To find out what licensing your state requires, contact your local regulating board (nbcc.org/directory). Consider the career and education adviser certification from the Council for Adult and Experiential Learning and Indiana University (cael.org/Professional-Development/).

Social worker—Social workers serve as advocates for people dealing with some of the most heart-wrenching issues that affect our society—child abuse, domestic violence, poverty, homelessness, disability, and terminal illness. They connect clients with resources and services, teach them new skills, protect their interests, and provide counseling. Social workers can be placed in various settings, including schools, hospitals, hospices, nonprofits, and government agencies. You will need at least a bachelor's degree to become a social worker. If you want to provide counseling services, you will need a master's degree. *Average annual pay:* $44,410–$54,220. *Key resource:* National Association of Social Workers (beasocialworker.org).

Elder advocacy and gerontology—This is a broad, growing category that encompasses many different kinds of work. Anything that contributes to the well-being of elders can be done in an advocate role. You can be a patient navigator (see page 260) and help the elderly or infirm get the care they need. You can develop or administer programs to engage the elderly in your community. You can do research on the aging process and teach others about the needs of senior citizens. Education and training in gerontology, the study of aging, can help prepare you for such roles. Some certificate programs are only a week long. Check with your local community college, which may also offer an associate's degree in gerontology. *Average annual pay:* Varies based on role. *Key resource:* Association for Gerontology in Higher Education's Careers in Aging (careersinaging.com). Also, try the Association for Gerontology in Higher Education (aghe.org, particularly the "Careers in Aging" tab).

Education

Adjunct professor—Adjunct professors typically have advanced degrees or specialized professional experience and teach one or two courses at a time at universities, community colleges—even online. Unlike traditional full-time faculty, adjuncts work for temporary assignments. They typically do not receive benefits or dedicated office space, and they are not eligible for tenure (a permanent job contract). But those potential drawbacks may not matter to you if you're looking for a part-time encore that will enable you to pass on your knowledge constructively. For this line of work, teaching experience is preferred, but often not required. If you have no teaching experience, check out this resource from Honolulu Community College, which has compiled information on everything from preparing a syllabus to icebreakers you can use with your students: www2.honolulu.hawaii.edu/facdev/guidebk/teachtip/teachtip.htm. *Average annual pay:* Varies greatly, with the national average at roughly $3,000 per course. *Key resource:* Higheredjobs.com.

Teacher—The availability of teaching jobs varies greatly by subject area and location, but it's safe to say most districts will need teachers in science, math, special education, and English as a second language. Alternative, fast-tracked teacher certification programs can have you teaching in one or two years if you have a bachelor's degree. The training may cost anywhere from a few thousand to well over $10,000. *Average annual pay:* Salaries vary by geography, but the national average is around $39,000. *Key resources:* National Center for Education Information online (teach-now.org/map .cfm) and the New Teacher Project–Teaching Fellows (tntp.org/what-we-do/training/teaching-fellows). Also: *Education Week*'s TopSchoolJobs (topschooljobs.org).

Teacher assistant/aide or paraprofessional—Training requirements vary by state, but teacher assistants typically need a high school diploma and often some college education. Those who work with Title I students (from low-income households) must meet federal requirements, which call for an associate's degree or the equivalent. Many teacher assistants work to help support special education students. If you're looking for part-time work, this job could be a good fit; close to 40 percent of assistants work part time. *Average annual pay:* $25,270. *Key resource:* The American Federation of Teachers website (aft.org). Search for "paraprofessionals."

Substitute teacher—If you're thinking about becoming a teacher or just want occasional encore work with kids, consider substitute teaching. Depending on where you live, you might need a bachelor's degree and teaching certificate or just a high school diploma. To find out about opportunities, requirements, and procedures—which can vary from state to state and district to district —call the administrative offices for the school districts near you. (Larger districts will often have this information on their websites.) *Average annual pay:* According to the National Substitute Teachers Alliance, subs earn on average $105 per day.

After-school program support staff—The after-school workforce includes a wide range of people, from credentialed teachers to college students. They serve in various roles, including anything from tutor to activity leader. *Average annual pay:* Varies based on role. *Key resources:* Check with school districts to find out who runs their after-school programs and contact recreation centers and organizations that cater to youths, such as the Boys & Girls Clubs (bgca.org) and the YMCA (ymca.net).

Reading tutor—As a reading tutor, you can help a child achieve the foundation of learning: literacy. Tutors offer private lessons, or work through an established for-profit or nonprofit program. AARP Experience Corps (experiencecorps.org)—in nineteen cities nationwide—trains people fifty-five and older as reading tutors and mentors for kids in kindergarten through third grade. Some tutors who work fifteen hours per week earn a small stipend. OASIS (oasisnet.org) also offers tutoring opportunities in about twenty communities across the country. *Average annual pay:* Some work as volunteers or for a small stipend, but for private tutoring hourly rates vary wildly. If you want to start your own business, connect with professional tutors for advice. *Key resources:* National Tutoring Association (ntatutor.com) and the American Tutoring Association (americantutoringassociation.org).

Nonprofits

Nonprofit fund-raiser/development professional—Raising money is critical to the health of a nonprofit and the community it serves. As a fund-raiser (also called a development professional), you may make direct appeals to individuals or groups and may organize fund-raisers and other special events. You may write proposals for grants (see next entry, grant writer) or direct others in that function. You may work for a nonprofit or for yourself. Fund-raisers need to have the fortitude it takes to ask people for money, and they must be able to strike the right balance of charm, persuasiveness, deference, and gratitude. Many colleges offer certificate programs and noncredit courses in nonprofit fund-raising, and nonprofits and private training firms also offer instruction. *Average annual pay*: $75,595, according to the Association of Fundraising Professionals 2011 report. *Key resources*: Association of Fundraising Professionals (afpnet.org), the Foundation Center (foundation center.org), Chronicle of Philanthropy (philanthropy.com); and Center for Philanthropy at Indiana University (philanthropy.iupui.edu).

Grant writer—If you're a strong researcher and writer, grant writing might be a good fit. Grant writers put together proposals to donors, making a case for why a grant seeker is the best candidate for a particular financial award. (You'll need some powers of persuasion!) You must also be comfortable with numbers, as you'll deal with budgeting and finance in grant applications. Grant writers work on staff or as consultants for nonprofits, universities, religious institutions, and government agencies. They might focus on a specialty with which they are familiar. If you have a science background, for example, you might be well suited to developing proposals related to scientific research. Community colleges, nonprofits, and private training firms offer courses in this high-demand field. *Average annual pay*: $49,000, according to Indeed.com. *Key resources*: American Grant Writers' Association (agwa.us) and the Foundation Center (foundationcenter.org).

Nonprofit social media manager—Nonprofit organizations are recognizing the power of social media for raising awareness. Twitter, Facebook, LinkedIn, and YouTube are some major social media websites, but there are countless others. As a social media manager, you would promote your nonprofit employer's causes and campaigns on various platforms. If you're skilled at building relationships online, this job may be for you. Social media managers are responsible for expanding the organization's following and for getting others to become involved by volunteering, along with writing to elected officials, raising money, and more. They can work directly for a nonprofit, a social media services firm, or as a consultant. Colleges and nonprofit services firms offer programs that can help get you acclimated to social media for nonprofits. *Average annual pay*: Varies greatly. *Key resource*: The Case Foundation (casefoundation.org/topic/social-media). Check out the two gurus in the field, Beth Kantor (bethkantor.org) and Heather Mansfield (diosacommunications.com).

Interim nonprofit executive director—Losing an executive director can be devastating for a nonprofit organization when there's no transition plan in place. An interim executive director can help. If you have nonprofit leadership experience, a short-term interim assignment (which may last several months full or part time) could be a natural fit for you. *Average annual pay:* Pay will be commensurate to the full-time pay of that position. (Check out Guidestar.org to see executive pay at comparable organizations. Simply Hired estimates an average of $60,000 a year.) *Key resources:* Various local nonprofit services firms offer training and placement—for example, the Executive Service Corps of Chicago (esc-chicago.org), the New York Council of Nonprofits (nycon.org), Third Sector New England (tsne.org), and Greenlights for Nonprofit Success in Austin (greenlights.org). To find opportunities near you, search online: "nonprofit interim executive director" and your location.

Green Jobs

Weatherization installer/technician—The boom in weatherization and building retrofitting—methods to protect structures from rain, wind, and other elements—is driving demand for weatherization installers. Such workers, employed by contractors or weatherization agencies, install energy-saving measures (such as energy-efficient windows and insulation) in existing buildings. Community colleges across the country have developed green energy and construction training programs to train new installers and to upgrade the skills of more experienced construction workers. These programs range in length and complexity from one fifteen-hour, noncredit course to multiple-course certificate programs of sixty hours or more. *Average annual pay:* $24,000–$36,000, but varies depending on experience and geography, according to

> For more information about green opportunities, check out *The State of Green Business 2012,* a comprehensive report published by GreenBiz Group, a media company that covers the greening of mainstream businesses. GreenBiz.com.

SimplyHired.com. *Key resource:* Greenforall.org (click on "Green-Collar Jobs Resources").

Solar installation trainers—If you're a skilled builder, you can use your experience to prepare others for green jobs of their own. Solar installation trainers teach both new and experienced construction and electrical system workers how to install solar panels onto the roofs of buildings. Trainers work for community colleges, national training providers, community-based organizations, and solar contractors. As this is a relatively new field, training opportunities are not yet widespread. *Average annual pay:* $25,000, according to Indeed.com. *Key resource:* U.S. Department of Energy Solar Instructor Training Network (www1.eere.energy.gov/solar/instructor_training_network.html).

Energy auditor—Energy auditors help check the efficiency of buildings, chiefly by finding leaks, and offer suggestions for fixing the problems. Auditors work full or part time for contractors, weatherization service providers, utility programs, or independently. This is a great encore if you have experience in building science and residential construction. Keep in mind, you must be able to crawl into tight spaces and spend time on your hands and knees. There are no standard education or training requirements, but some states require course work or certification. A college degree isn't necessary. Various organizations offer training programs; community colleges are establishing such programs on their own or with national training providers, such as CleanEdison. *Average annual pay:* $67,000, according to Indeed.com. *Key resource:* Bureau of Labor Statistics Green Career Information page— (bls.gov/green/greencareers.htm).

Sample Résumés and Bios

B y now you've got the message. Telling your story is a big part of an encore transition, and in order to do that, you're likely to need various tools. These days, it's easy to find good samples and templates for just about any document you need—but I wanted to give you a few ideas for how to address the most common encore situations. Stuff like how to position yourself when your only relevant work experience is through volunteering, or if you're returning to the paid workforce after a long stint as a stay-at-home parent.

In the following pages are a few fictional résumés based on the backgrounds of real people and some sample narrative bios from actual people in their encores.

If you think you've tackled an encore challenge in a particularly smart or creative way, please share your ideas with me (email me at *ECH@encore.org* with the header "résumé," "bio," or "business plan"). I'll be collecting examples to share on my Encore.org blog and for possible future editions of this book. Of course, we would never publish your personal details!

Sample Résumé #1 Ariel Williams started her career as a newspaper journalist and editor and eventually ended up as a communications consultant. Now she wants to move into a communications role for a nonprofit organization or socially minded business. She

---

ARIEL WILLIAMS 5 Langley St. • Park, FL 01111 • 555-123-4567
Twitter: @ArielPRPRO • awil@gmail.com • http://www.linkedin.com/in/arielwilliams

HIGHLIGHTS

- Skilled at handling multiple tasks under deadline with meticulous attention to detail.
- Experienced in creating and delivering strategic and tactical ⋯⋯⋯ messaging for brand positioning.
- Accomplished in guiding team members and counseling leaders on message delivery and public relations.
- Adept at networking and managing relationships with strategic partners and supporters.
- Experienced in enhancing brand awareness through traditional and new media tools.

> Be sure to highlight transferable skills if you've never worked in a particular sector.

> Highlight your facility with new technology if such tools are relevant to the sector you're interested in.

RECENT EXPERIENCE

Marketing and Communications Encore Fellow, *Kid UP! Science Center,* Miami, FL (September 2012–present)

Selected for prestigious Encore Fellowship, a one-year, half-time position; Fellowship program managed by Encore.org matches experienced executives and professionals with high-impact assignments in nonprofit groups.

- Landed museum's first ever television news coverage for exhibit opening in conjunction with Facebook contest. Coverage resulted in over 30,000 comment entries on museum's new Facebook page and led to a 15 percent increase in family memberships.
- Helped secure new $350,000 grant from Hample Foundation to create traveling in-class "field trips" that visit inner-city schools to conduct interactive science experiments.
- Led focus groups and participated in strategic planning to define museum's mission, goals, and brand positioning.

> Whenever possible, describe results achieved, not just responsibilities of a position.

- Advised on website redesign, conducted contest to crowdsource a new logo, and supervised site relaunch. Within one month of launch, site was featured on DoGood.org's list of nonprofit sites to watch.
- Conducted an audit of all social media platforms and worked with four senior staff members to develop strategic goals for enhancing and sustaining the organization's digital presence. Developed social media volunteer program to manage Twitter and Google+ profiles, increasing Web traffic onsite by 25 percent.

Independent Expert, Fort Lauderdale, FL (2009–2011)

- Worked closely with CEOs of several tech start-ups. Oversaw and managed print, broadcast, and digital media pitches and used social media tools, including Facebook and Twitter, to win over sector influencers and land online press.

has recently finished an Encore Fellowship, which has helped her to gain some nonprofit experience and has grown her network in the sector.

> It's fine for your résumé to be on two pages as long as it's well-designed and the second page is worth reading.

- Pitches resulted in media coverage in such outlets as *Forbes, InformationWeek, PC World, CNET News,* and *Popular Mechanics.*
- Secured more than fifty keynote opportunities in the U.S. and overseas for clients' executives at industry conferences.
- Wrote, edited, and managed other writers on the creation of press releases, website content, brochures, reports, proposals, and marketing materials.

Senior Editor, *Oak Consulting,* Bethesda, MD (1995–2009)
- Specialized in business and management and worked with partners in all sectors of this international firm to write, edit, and publish white papers, online content, and print material for Oak Analyst's research for subscription clients.
- Managed global network of more than thirty staff and freelance writers and editors in the production of quarterly newsletter. Responsible for ensuring consistency of quality and voice as well as conformity with editorial and design guidelines.

Reporter & Editor, *The Daily Gazette,* Washington, DC (1983–1995)
- Joined newspaper as junior reporter; promoted to staff writer after two years.
- Developed bimonthly "Domestic Bliss" column, which ran for eight years.
- Promoted to editor in 1990, managing more than twenty-five staff and freelancers and overseeing the development of feature stories for "Washington Life" section.

EDUCATION AND TECHNICAL SKILLS

Master of Arts in Journalism, Lexington University, MI

Bachelor of Arts, *English,* Reade College, Los Angeles, CA

Technical Skills Include: Microsoft Office applications (Word, Excel, Access, and PowerPoint). Web and blog platforms, including Wordpress. Social networking tools including: LinkedIn, Facebook, Twitter, and Google+.

> It's not necessary to include dates if you aren't comfortable sharing them. Experts go both ways.

Sample Résumé #2 Julie Byrn left her job fifteen years ago to raise her kids and is just now reentering the workforce. She is looking for an encore career as a development/ fund-raising coordinator. All of her recent experience is as a volunteer in her community and at her children's school.

> A two-column design can be a good way to save space.

Julie Byrn

1234 Main Street • Oak Park, CO 88823 • 555-123-4567
jbyrn@gmail.com • http://www.linkedin.com/in/juliebyrn

DEVELOPMENT / FUND-RAISING COORDINATOR

Skilled at finding new ways for mission-driven organizations to raise money from community partners and individual donors. Experienced in using research, writing, and strategic planning skills to lead teams in securing new prospects and boosting existing donor contributions.

RECENT EXPERIENCE

Torno Shelter for Women and Children, Oak Park, CO
Fund-Raising Lead (2010–present)

- Chaired committee that organized and ran shelter's first ever "Tour of Homes." Coordinated with business community to gain sponsorships and invited local vendors and partners. Sold tickets locally and offered "Home Away" tickets to people who live out of town. Raised more than $50,000, which was five times what group had ever raised in any one event.

> If your paid job experience is thin, highlight your volunteer work.

- Researched best practice fund-raising events and led team of cold callers on "Be a Hero" promotion, encouraging businesses to partner with non-profit groups. Raised $4,700 in one afternoon.

- Installed PayPal "give now" button on website, which nets $7,500 per year in small gifts attributed to donors who would not otherwise donate.

Bell Elementary PTA, Pueblo, CO
Development Vice President (2008–2010)

> Note when you escalated your involvement and responsibilities in one organization.

- Oversaw and implemented direct-mail campaigns, which resulted in successful rebranding of the school. Check-writing campaign raised nearly $15,000.

- Contacted affiliates and partners to collaborate with school, resulting in 65 percent increase in donated items and time.

Volunteer Coordinator (2002–2008)

- Designed new volunteer recruiting strategy for school in partnership with executive committee and small committee of parents.

- Researched and incorporated new computer system to track volunteer hours, which allows PTA to reward active parent and teacher volunteers.

·········· HIGHLIGHTS ··········

Leadership Skills

- Devising and leading innovative fund-raising campaigns for non-profit organizations.
- Recruiting and mentoring new volunteers.

Communication and Presentation Skills

- Building social media campaigns to persuade donors to enhance their contributions.
- Using PowerPoint and SlideRocket to deliver organized and persuasive presentations to prospective donors.

Strategic Planning and Organizational Skills

- Examining organization's mission, participants' capacity, and monetary needs to identify successful fund-raising techniques.
- Identifying untapped corporate sponsors to expand organizations' reach.

Computer Skills

Word, PowerPoint, SlideRocket, Excel, Outlook. Adobe Creative Suite, Facebook, Twitter.

Education

Bachelor of Arts, Communications, University of the Southeast, Atlanta, GA

> This is where you can highlight your skill sets as opposed to your accomplishments.

Sample Résumé #3 After starting and running his own small business for sixteen years, Herman Chan decided he wanted to become a teacher. He recently returned to college to finish his undergraduate degree and is now seeking a position as a special education teacher.

> Testimonials or endorsements can help frame your story if you are moving into a new field.

HERMAN CHAN
1234 Main Street • Jesper, OH 98745 • 123-456-7890 • Hermanchan@gmail.com
www.linkedin.com/in/Hermanchan • www.Hermanchan.com

SPECIAL EDUCATION TEACHER / SPECIAL EDUCATION SPECIALIST

TEACHING EXPERIENCE

Student Teacher, *Lake View Elementary,* Boston, MA   (Jan–June 2012)
- Collaborated with classroom teacher to improve students' academic performance and growth.
- Created several new lesson plans rated "Excellent" by evaluating teacher team. Modified plans as necessary to address individual students' needs.

> "In my 15 years of teaching, I have never hired someone more suited to working with special needs students. Herman uses his past experiences outside of the classroom to his student's advantage."
> —*Sue Smith, lead special ed teacher, Lake View Elementary*
>
> www.linkedin.com/in/HermanChan

Student Teacher, *Broad Elementary,* Cambridge, MA   (Aug–Dec 2011)
- Worked in a variety of special education classroom settings, including self-contained, support inclusion, and full inclusion programs. Taught students with autism spectrum disorders and developmental challenges.
- Partnered with classroom teachers to prepare student Individualized Education Plans (IEPs).
- Completed training sessions on special educational reform. Conducted research on best practices for serving special needs students, compiled in final paper (available for download: www.HermanChan.com).

VOLUNTEER EXPERIENCE

Board Member, *Tools for Special Needs Schools,* Boston, MA   (2009–present)
- Co-chair of the budget committee. Responsible for lowering yearly expenditures by one-third last year.
- Regularly meet with leaders from several local businesses and encourage them to donate materials and services, including printing, school supplies, and food for programs and events.

> Volunteer work may be more important than an early, unrelated career.

Volunteer, *Tools for Special Needs Schools,* Boston, MA   (2000–2009)
- Joined group as a volunteer business consultant. Advised board regarding business plans and budget.
- Attended public sessions on special needs schools and students. Became well versed in parent, teacher, and student problems and learned how to help provide solutions.
- Met with parents in underserved, low-income communities to advise them about services for their children.

OTHER PROFESSIONAL EXPERIENCE

Founder & Owner, *Herman's Hardware,* Boston, MA   (1995–2011)
For sixteen years, owned and operated local hardware store. Hired and managed two full-time and three part-time employees, maintained accounts, coordinated weekly schedules, and oversaw the purchasing of inventory.

PRESENTATIONS
"ADD and the Public School," Presented at Society of Special Needs Teachers Annual Conference, April 2012

> Recent education can go up top or below.

EDUCATION, CERTIFICATIONS, AFFILIATIONS AND COMPUTER SKILLS
Bachelor of Science, Special Education, Career Switchers Program, Boston of America College, June 2012
Certifications. Special Education Certification (Pending).
Affiliation. *National Association of Special Education Teachers* (2011–present)
Computer Skills. Word, Excel, PowerPoint, and Adobe CS5. Social media tools, including: Twitter and LinkedIn.

Sample Narrative Bio #1

ROSALIND JOFFE

Building on her own experience living with chronic illnesses, including multiple sclerosis and ulcerative colitis, Rosalind Joffe founded the chronic illness career coaching practice, cicoach.com. Dedicated to helping others with chronic illness develop the skills they need to succeed in their careers, Rosalind firmly believes that living with chronic illness does not preclude living a full and successful life.

Rosalind Joffe, coauthor of *Women, Work, and Autoimmune Disease: Keep Working, Girlfriend!* published by Demos Medical, is a recognized national expert on chronic illness in the workplace. As a leading career coach, she has been quoted in *The Wall Street Journal, The New York Times, The Washington Post, The Boston Globe,* msnbc.com, WebMD, and ABC Radio, as well as a variety of regional and national media outlets. Rosalind has published in dozens of disease organization and health journals. She is a sought-after speaker and workshop leader for organizations that include the National Multiple Sclerosis Society, BiogenIdec, State Street Corporation, New Directions, Association of Career Professionals, HealthTalk.com, New England Arthritis Foundation, NENMMS, and the Scleroderma Association.

Rosalind holds a master's in Education, is a certified mediator, and has completed training in focusing practice and the ICF-accredited Corporate Coach University program.

Why I Founded This Company

My personal experience began almost thirty years ago when I was unable to lift myself from bed without help and had lost vision in one eye. I was diagnosed with multiple sclerosis and my life would never be the same. Over the years, the disease was relatively mild and manageable but I continually made decisions, large and small, based on my health. This was particularly true regarding my career.

Then, fifteen years after the initial diagnosis, I was hospitalized with a second autoimmune disease, ulcerative colitis. I had two young children, a husband, and a successful, demanding career.

Getting my health under control was a major challenge. When I was physically able to return to work, however, I confronted an equally daunting challenge. How could I continue to be professionally successful with a disabling disease that got in the way of my ability to perform?

At the same time, this disabling condition meant I faced new concerns:

- How do I talk about this and when?
- How do I manage my tasks when I can barely manage my health?
- How do I plan my career when I can't even plan for tomorrow?

There were few resources to guide me. I resented that most books (and caregivers) advocated that stress is bad, work is stressful, and people with chronic illness should stop working. Many of us don't view that as the only option. I certainly don't.

Through trial and error I reached the point where I could once again thrive in my work. My experience living and working with chronic illness has become my inspiration and forms the core of my work with others.

Here are a few things that I have learned:

- Illness, like any type of adversity, is best dealt with when viewed as a challenge to be met.
- A clear vision of where you are and where you want to be gives you the strength and clarity to move forward.
- Workplace success in the face of illness is transforming. It gives you the power and the confidence to face other challenges large and small.

At the time of my diagnosis, my neurologist predicted that my illness would teach me a valuable life lesson: Illness enables you to see clearly what matters. And to that, I add a lesson of my own: Illness does not preclude professional or personal success.

Sample Narrative Bio #2

STEPHEN RISTAU

Stephen Ristau has dedicated his work to personal and social renewal during thirty-five years as an executive, senior manager, consultant, trainer, and clinician in the service sector. He has worked in nonprofit, government, and corporate environments.

He has served as president and CEO of four nonprofits in the Northeast. His current focus, *PurposeWork*, is expanding the pathways for midlife adults ages fifty and older to nonprofits. He sees great opportunities for nonprofits to engage the talents and passion of experienced professionals to serve and work in their communities, and find greater meaning and purpose in their lives.

Presently residing in the Northwest, he directs the Encore Fellows program for Social Venture Partners Portland, placing retired business leaders in meaningful nonprofit roles.

He is a contributing author of *The Idealist Guide to Careers in the Nonprofit Sector for Sector Switchers* (2008), and has written "People Do Need People: Social Interaction Boosts Brain Health in Older Age" (*Generations, Journal of the American Society on Aging*, 2011, vol. 25, no. 2); "Work and Purpose After 50," a chapter in *Boomers and Beyond: Reconsidering the Roles of Libraries* (American Library Association, 2010); and "Get Involved: Promoting Civic Engagement Through California Public Libraries" (*California State Library Bulletin*, 2010, no. 97).

As part of his own work portfolio, he volunteers weekly at Peninsula Children's Center in North Portland where he reads to toddlers and serves as a "human jungle gym." He also provides interfaith spiritual direction to men and women in metro Portland. He and his wife, Susan, are the proud parents of two adult sons, who live in the Northeast.

Budget Worksheet

F iguring out your finances will make your encore transition much smoother. The worksheets on the following pages will get you started.

Assets/Liabilities Worksheet

Assets	Amount	Notes
Cash		
Checking accounts		
Savings accounts		
IRA or other retirement accounts		
401(k)		
Other investments		
Securities (stocks/bonds)		
Notes receivable (money owed to you)		
Life insurance (surrender value)		
Real estate		
Automobile (present value)		
Other personal property (household goods)		
Other assets		
Total Assets:		

Liabilities

Notes payable		
Bills due		
Credit card debt		
Vehicle loan		
Mortgage		
Unpaid taxes		
Other liabilities		
Total Liabilities:		
Total Assets		
Less Total Liabilites		
= Total Net Worth		

Budget Worksheet

Income (Annually)

For each, indicate the draw you receive annually or you will receive when you start making your transition. For example, if you're forty-eight and plan to start drawing down your 401(k) at 59½, when you can do so penalty-free, the income from that piece now is zero.

	Amount	Notes
Investment interest		
Investment dividends		
Pension (defined benefit or defined contributions: 401(k), 403(b), or 457)		
Annuity		
Rental income from real estate		
IRAs (traditional Roth, rollover)		
Gifts		
Inheritance		
Total income:		

Expenses (Annually)

HOME/HOUSING	Amount	Notes
Mortgage/rent		
Repairs and maintenance		
Homeowners or renters insurance		
Property taxes		
Subtotal		

LIVING EXPENSES		
Utilities (water/sewer/gas/electric)		
Cable		
Telephone/Internet		
Food/groceries		
Clothing and dry cleaning		
Other		
Subtotal		

HEALTH		
Health care premiums (Medicare or private)		
Out-of-pocket expenses (including prescriptions, if not covered)		
Long-term care insurance		
Life insurance		
Subtotal:		

DEBTS		
Home equity loans		
Credit card		
Student loan debt		
Other		
Subtotal:		

TRANSPORTATION		
Car payments		

	Amount	Notes
Car insurance		
Repair		
Parking		
Gas		
Public transport cost		
Other		
Subtotal:		

TAXES

State		
Federal		
Property		
Subtotal:		

DISCRETIONARY/OPTIONAL EXPENSES

Savings		
Entertainment and restaurant meals		
Grooming		
Travel/vacation		
Parental care		
Education (for children or self)		
Sports/hobbies		
Charitable contributions		
Other		
Subtotal:		

FAMILY RESPONSIBILITIES

Parents		
Children		
Other (e.g., pets)		
Subtotal:		
Total expenses:		

Business Plan Builder

Many successful entrepreneurs will tell you that business plans are unnecessary, that they never looked at their plans after putting them together, or that their businesses bear little resemblance to their business plans. That's probably all true—but irrelevant. The main reason to create a business plan is to force yourself to hone your idea, to become an expert in your field, and to become adept at pitching your venture to all kinds of audiences. It's even possible that writing a business plan will lead you to the conclusion that you're not interested in going forward with the venture.

A few key points:

- You may be creating a business plan for potential investors, but it's better to think of it as a document that you'll be sharing with anyone potentially helpful to your venture.

- Business plans tend to go through many iterations as you and your team learn from sharing them with friends, advisers, critics, potential investors, and others interested in getting involved. Treat your business plan as a living document that will change as your vision for your venture evolves.

- Business plans can take many forms—as long as they answer the right questions and persuade readers that a venture is viable, that the team has what it takes for success, and that all the right issues have been considered. There is no right length for a business plan—some are a mere five pages, others run sixty or more.

I've suggested a business plan outline below and some questions to get you thinking about how to flesh it out. The questions in each section are meant to help you think through and write content for each section of your plan. Be prepared to answer these questions in writing and in person, as potential investors or funders, employees, partners, and others you go to for feedback will surely ask them.

Feel free to play around with the format if you find that a different section header or ordering of issues works better for your venture. Nothing here is meant to be rigid. In fact, as you work on this, do some searching online for social venture business plan templates and samples. Looking at many of these will help you figure out how best to structure your own.

And don't worry if you don't have all the answers. Do your research so that your answers are informed but understand that there is a certain amount of guesswork in all of this.

Executive Summary

This may be the most important section of your business plan, but it's best to tackle it after you've finished the other sections. Here's where you get to sell your idea and why you're passionate about it. You'll want to grab your reader from the start and tell a compelling story. Aim to keep this to less than one page.

The summary should answer the following questions:

- What problem is your venture going to solve and why is it necessary? Include any data that supports your case.

- What will success look like? What financial, social, or environmental results are you aiming for over time? (For example, do you plan to save the government $3 million in nursing home costs after the first two years?)

- How much are you seeking from investors? Briefly, how far will that money take you and what will it cover?

Description of the Venture

Here's where you'll describe in more detail the problem your venture will solve. In this section you'll want to show that you know your market well by painting a picture of the customer or market you're serving and describing what characterizes them and differentiates them from others. (Address the issues below as they apply.)

- Who are you trying to reach with this offering? If you are planning a nonprofit, who will benefit from your product or service?

- Why will people be attracted to what you're offering? How is it different than what's already available?

- What is the size of the overall market and what percentage of that larger category will you target? Use relevant data wherever you can.

- How will you reach potential customers in a cost-effective way?

- How will you create significant social impact?

- Why does dealing with this issue or group of people appeal to you? What experience do you have with your potential customers?

Note: You may have several groups of customers—for example, you may be creating a job training program for individuals who need jobs and a separate program designed for coaches, social workers, and job counselors who work with unemployed people. Your plan will need to address both groups.

Sustainability and Social Mission

You may have a separate section outlining the social mission of your venture or it might be woven into the description of your product or service. Here are some of the points you'll want to cover, where relevant.

YOUR PRODUCT OR SERVICE

- What social problem or inequity is your business helping to solve? Is it building community in some way or making life easier for a certain population?

- In what ways is your product or service more environmentally friendly than competing products or services?

YOUR OPERATIONS

- In what ways are your operations, your way of making or delivering your offering, more sustainable or compassionate than the customary way of doing things?

- How does your method of operation encourage socially just and sustainable practices by suppliers and your entire supply chain?

- How will your business treat its employees, suppliers, community, and customers?

YOUR MARKETING

- In what ways will your marketing increase awareness of sustainability, community development, and the desire to find just and sustainable products and solutions?

- In what ways are your distribution and sales methods more socially conscious than the alternatives (for example, more local or less toxic)?

- How will you use the issue of sustainability or social contribution in your marketing?

- How will you ensure that you can deliver on your marketing claims?

Note: Attention to sustainability often means saving money on energy and raw materials. Doing good can translate into more sales (witness the incredible success of Tom's Shoes "buy a pair, give a pair" model). If possible, tie all the claims in this section to the ways they lower business risks and environmental impact and increase profits.

The Venture Team

Here's where you get to tell your encore story and why you are the ideal person to lead this venture.

- What propelled you to start this venture?

- Why have you decided to dedicate your time and talents to these issues?

- How does this venture naturally flow from what you've done before?

- How do you plan to leverage your network and other resources to make this successful?

The Competition

For this section, you'll need to do some research to identify all direct competitors for your venture. You'll want to identify both current competitors and potential ones. For each one you identify, assess its strengths and weaknesses and show how your venture will fill a void or do better than what's already being done. Use the following charts if they are helpful.

CURRENT COMPETITION

Competitor	Strengths	Weaknesses	How you are better

POTENTIAL COMPETITORS

Who might enter your market down the road? Create a second chart for them. How can you make your business strategy robust enough to prevent them from entering the field or to handle competitors if they succeed in opening their doors?

Potential Competitor	Strengths	Weaknesses	How you are better

SUBSTITUTES

If your venture never gets off the ground, how might customers find the service or product they need?

Substitute	Strengths	Weaknesses	How you are better

SUMMARIZE YOUR COMPETITIVE STRATEGY

What is the essence of your overall competitive strategy? How will you win customers? Once you succeed, what will keep others from copying you or doing better? If others enter the market, might that be part of the success you're aiming for? In other words, if the goal of your venture is to change labor practices in factories in China, wouldn't you want others to follow your lead and look to your venture as an example?

Marketing and Sales Plans

Here you'll describe your business model—how you plan to generate revenues or sales, how you plan to spread the word about your venture, and how you plan to grow. You may not need to address all the areas below, but determine which ones apply and build them into your description.

MARKETING COMMUNICATIONS PLAN

- Media: How do you plan to reach your target audience? (Traditional media, social media, trade shows, conferences, web strategy, direct mail, word of mouth, PR, articles, give-aways, memes, etc.)

• Cost: What will your marketing efforts cost in time and dollars?

• Message: What messages do you plan to send? Will you have different messages for different audiences?

BUSINESS MODEL AND PRICING

• What is your business model?

• How will you charge—by the item, the hour, the project, or result? This is another area where you'll want to highlight the double bottom line attributes of your model—how you plan to measure both profits and social impact. (For example, for every unit of healthful snack sold, you plan to contribute 1 percent of gross profits to an organization working on an anti-obsesity campaign.)

• How will your prices relate to your direct costs?

• Include details on your pricing model and what makes you believe customers will pay this price.

• How will your venture sustain itself over time? Will continued investment be needed or will revenues support the growth you're seeking?

• How long will it take for the project to be self-sustaining?

SALES STRATEGY

• Who will do the selling? The founders, a dedicated sales force, distributors, a company sales force, a website, etc.?

• How will you follow up after a successful sale? What will you provide after the transaction?

Operations Plan

In this section, you'll cover the process of making and shipping your product or delivering your service. You'll need to be able to show why this process is cost-effective and efficient. Again, articulate the values behind your venture.

Questions to think about:

- What will you do yourself?

- What will you buy from someone else? What relationship will you have with these suppliers?

- What has to be done to turn your product or service into something you can make and sell in quantity?

- If you're manufacturing something, do you know where the raw materials for your products are coming from? Are you comfortable with the reputations and backgrounds of others you'll be partnering with?

The Team

Investors, funders, and others want to know who is behind the venture and what each of you brings to the table.

Traditionally this section includes a bio highlighting the background and skills of each member of the founding team. If you don't have cofounders, partners, or employees yet, think about other ways you can show who's on board or supporting you. Do you have a team of advisers (lawyers, CPAs, subject matter experts) willing to lend their names and sweat equity to the project? Has anyone invested any money yet?

If the business will require other key employees, advisers, and people that aren't yet on board, list what you are looking for and how you plan to recruit.

While this may not make it into your final business plan, think about how decisions will be made. If you think you'll be questioned about your age, be prepared to talk about your succession plan—how the work would continue if you could no longer be actively involved. This is especially important for social ventures. If you care enough about working on a solution to a social problem, people will want to know how you expect the work to survive you.

Risks and Assumptions

Until now, the business plan has focused largely on the positives, but it's important to be sure you've thought through all the potential risks and challenges you might face and to address them head-on.

Questions to think about and address:

- What are the assumptions on which this business rests? (Ask others who are a bit skeptical for help answering this question.)

- What are the most likely things that could go wrong?

- How will you manage the risks?

Financial Projections

Describe how your business will be financed and how you plan to fund it in the future. Here you'll want to include financial projections over three years. You can decide how sophisticated these documents need to be based on your intended audience. (The SCORE.org website has free templates you can use to create the various financial documents you may need, as well as mentors available to help you use them.)

This business plan builder was created in collaboration with the Bainbridge Graduate Institute, Bainbridge Island, Washington, bgi.edu.

Further Reading and Resources

Local Organizations

(For a clickable map of local organizations, go to Encore.org/connect/local. Descriptions of most of these organizations can be found at *encore.org/connect/all_localresources*.)

AARP EXPERIENCE CORPS
(many cities)
aarp.org/experiencecorps

BOOMERS LEADING CHANGE IN HEALTH
(Denver)
blcih.org

BOOM! THE NEW ECONOMY
(Detroit)
boomtheneweconomy.org

CENTERPOINT INSTITUTE FOR LIFE AND CAREER RENEWAL
(Seattle-based, but also offers online coaching)
centerpointseattle.org

COMING OF AGE
(many cities)
comingofage.org

Features a downloadable e-book, *The Age for Change*

DISCOVERING WHAT'S NEXT
(Boston)
discoveringwhatsnext.org

ENCORE
(Grand Rapids, Michigan)
grfoundation.org/encore

ENCORE LEADERSHIP CORPS
(Maine)
encoreleaders.org

ENGAGED RETIREMENT & ENCORE CAREERS CENTER
(Princeton, New Jersey)
engagedretirement.org

EXPERIENCE MATTERS
(Phoenix)
experiencemattersaz.org

GENERATIONS INCORPORATED
(Boston)
generationsinc.org

LEADERSHIP GREATER HARTFORD THIRD AGE INITIATIVE
(Hartford, Connecticut)
leadershipgh.org/programs/adult-programs/ third-age-initiative.html

LIFE BY DESIGN
(Portland, Oregon)
pcc.edu/climb/life

NEXT CHAPTER KANSAS CITY
(Kansas)
nextchapterkc.org

NEXT CHAPTER PUGET SOUND
(Seattle area)
nextchapterps.ning.com

RE-ENGAGE FOR GOOD
(Broward County, Florida)
cfbroward.org/Our-Leadership-Work/ Re-engage-for-Good.aspx

RESERVE
(New York City; Westchester County, New York; Newark, New Jersey; Miami; and Maryland)
reserveinc.org

SHIFT
(Minneapolis)
shiftonline.org

TECHTOWN
(Detroit)
techtownwsu.org

TEMPE CONNECTIONS
(Tempe, Arizona)
tempeconnections.org

THE TRANSITION NETWORK
(many cities)
thetransitionnetwork.org

VITAL AGING NETWORK
(Minneapolis/St. Paul—with some statewide programs)
vital-aging-network.org

Financial Planning

AARP's WORK AND RETIREMENT TOOLS
aarp.org/work/work_tools
The site has some great tools to calculate Social Security benefits, 401(k) contributions and fees, and various paycheck contribution variations.

FINANCIAL SECURITY PROJECT AT BOSTON COLLEGE
fsp.bc.edu
Comprehensive and impartial research-based financial planning site sponsored by Boston College.

THE SOCIAL SECURITY CLAIMING GUIDE
crr.bc.edu/special-projects/books/ the-social-security-claiming-guide/
A useful and information packed guide created by the Center for Retirement Research at Boston College.

RETIREMENTREVISED.COM
A site focused on retirement investing, benefits, careers, and health care, particularly in hard times.

FURTHER READING
The Hard Times Guide to Retirement Security: Practical Strategies for Money, Work, and Living, by Mark Miller (Bloomberg Press, 2010)

Planning Your Education
Financing Education Options
AMERICAN ASSOCIATION OF COMMUNITY COLLEGES PLUS 50 INITIATIVE
plus50.aacc.nche.edu/Students/tips_student/Pages/FinancialAidResources.aspx
The AACC offers various scholarships, funds, and other financial aid resource links for displaced plus-50 workers.

FEDERAL STUDENT AID, U.S. DEPARTMENT OF EDUCATION
studentaid.ed.gov/PORTALSWebApp/students/english/funding.jsp
Provides essential funding information for adult students.

FINAID GUIDE TO FINANCIAL AID FOR OLDER AND NONTRADITIONAL STUDENTS
finaid.org/otheraid/nontraditional.phtml
Offers information and links to various scholarships and fellowships available for older students.

LEARNINGCOUNTS.ORG
This site from the Council for Adult and Experiential Learning evaluates knowledge learned outside the classroom and assesses whether it can be used for college credit, certification, or advanced standing toward further training—a potential money saver.

Scholarships
FASTWEB
fastweb.com
A free scholarship search engine.

AARP FOUNDATION WOMEN'S SCHOLARSHIP PROGRAM
aarp.org/womensscholarship
Offers scholarships for funding education, training, and skills upgrades for low-income women over fifty.

Finding the Right Program
AMERICAN ASSOCIATION OF COMMUNITY COLLEGES—PLUS50 INITIATIVE
plus50.aacc.nche.edu/Pages/Default.aspx
A database of current community college programs designed for people fifty and older. Includes a community college finder tool.

AMERICAN COUNCIL ON EDUCATION
acenet.edu
Provides a list of programs, services, and other resources for adult learners.

THE EDUPUNKS' GUIDE
edupunksguide.org
A comprehensive guide to learning outside the classroom and creating a personalized and affordable education. Offers a free downloadable e-guide. Founded by Anya Kamenetz, author of *DIY U.*

ENCORE.ORG/COLLEGES

Offers essential information about educational encore pathways across the country at major universities, community colleges, and specialized schools—both online and on campus. Provides lists of programs by sector, practice, state, and alphabetical order.

NATIONAL CENTER FOR EDUCATION STATISTICS COLLEGE NAVIGATOR

nces.ed.gov/collegenavigator
A college search tool from the U.S. Department of Education.

BACK TO SCHOOL FOR GROWNUPS

backtoschoolforgrownups.com
Information and breaking news on adult education.

FURTHER READING

Back to School for Grownups: Your Guide to Making Sound Decisions: (And How Not to Get Run Over by the School Bus), by Laura H. Gilbert, Ph.D. (CreateSpace, 2009)

College Programs with an Encore Focus

BEACON AT STANFORD UNIVERSITY

alumni.gsb.stanford.edu/beacon
A program designed exclusively for Stanford Graduate School of Business alumni who wish to continue their business education to pursue a second career.

EMPOWERED UCLA EXTENSION

encoreci.com
Offers various nine-to-twelve-month online certificate programs via an iPad app in fields like global stability and patient advocacy. A new Apple iPad is shipped to all enrolling students.

HARVARD UNIVERSITY'S ADVANCED LEADERSHIP INSTITUTE

advancedleadership.harvard.edu
A one-year program for experienced professionals interested in solving social problems, in the next phase of their careers. Using the university's resources, fellows learn, teach, mentor, and plan in preparation for their post-fellowship careers.

LEARNINGLIFE AND THE PURPOSE PROJECT (UNIVERSITY OF MINNESOTA)

csh.umn.edu/programs/The_Purpose_Project/home.html
http://cce.umn.edu/learninglife/
The university offers workshops and resources for those considering a career change.

NEXT3 (SUFFOLK UNIVERSITY)

suffolk.edu/49316.html
A university-affiliated program for alumni leaders interested in second careers.

VERMONT LEADERSHIP INSTITUTE (UNIVERSITY OF VERMONT)

snellingcenter.org/leadership/vermont-leadership-institute/vermont-leadership-institute
Sponsored by the Snelling Center for Government at the University of Vermont, this intensive program consists of eight overnight sessions for participants interested in making greater contributions to their organizations, communities, and the state of Vermont.

Fellowships/ Experiential Learning

THE BROAD SUPERINTENDENTS ACADEMY

broadcenter.org/academy/

Trains executives to be placed in underperforming urban school districts. Participants attend weekend sessions for ten months, while continuing to work in their current jobs. Sponsored by the Broad Center for the Management of School Systems.

CALIFORNIA TEACHER CORPS

cateachercorps.org

A statewide organization that places committed candidates in hard-to-staff classrooms while simultaneously earning their teaching credentials.

CITIZEN SCHOOLS

citizenschools.org

The AmeriCorps Teaching Fellowship at Citizen Schools offers two-year teaching and nonprofit experience to fellows while they work in communities and schools around the U.S.

THE ENCORE FELLOWSHIPS NETWORK

encore.org/fellowships

Designed to deliver new sources of talent to organizations solving critical social problems, Encore Fellowships are paid, time-limited fellowships that match skilled, experienced professionals at the end of their midlife careers with social-purpose organizations for a six- to twelve-month period. Fellowships are available in several states and new ones are continuously being added. Check Encore.org/fellowships for current program offerings.

ENCORE HARTFORD

continuingstudies.uconn.edu/professional/ nonprofit/encore/index.html

Connecticut professionals interested in employment in the nonprofit sector are assigned to a two-month, high-level project at a Greater Hartford nonprofit. Part of Encore Connecticut.

ENCORPS TEACHERS

encorpsteachers.com

Helps skilled professionals in the fields of science, technology, engineering, and math make the transition into teaching these subjects in disadvantaged communities in California.

ENCORPS EDUCATOR PATHWAY

certification.inspiredteaching.org/apply. php?p=who

This D.C.-based group recruits and selects teacher candidates interesting in advancing educational reform.

THE NEW TEACHER PROJECT

tntp.org/what-we-do/training/ teaching-fellows

Offers programs for retraining "midcareer" professionals without prior education backgrounds as teachers in challenging school environments. Begins with an intensive pre-service training and culminates in state certification.

REGISTERED APPRENTICESHIP

doleta.gov/oa

A Department of Labor program that connects job seekers with paid employment in various fields and offers hands-on training and college credit.

Resources for Veterans

Veterans may want to consider some opportunities designed specifically for those with a military background, though not necessarily with an encore orientation. The following resources cover everything from fellowships at nonprofits to educational training.

The Mission Continues
missioncontinues.org

Mission Serve
missionserve.org

Paws for Purple Hearts
pawsforpurplehearts.org

Team Rubicon
teamrubiconusa.org

Tempered Steel
temperedsteelinc.org

Troops to Teachers
proudtoserveagain.com

Purple Heart Homes
purplehearthomesusa.org

VERMONT ASSOCIATES
vermontassociates.org
A statewide nonprofit group that provides training and jobs for participants over age fifty-five in high-growth sectors of the economy, as well as community service positions at nonprofits.

Career Exploration/ Reinvention

There are countless valuable resources for job search and reinvention. Those highlighted here are particularly useful to encore seekers.

WORK REIMAGINED
Workreimagined.aarp.org
A project of AARP and LinkedIn, WorkReimagined.org is a social community

and talent exchange for people with twenty-plus years of work experience.

WORKSEARCH INFORMATION NETWORK
aarpworksearch.org
An online employment guide to the job search process from start to finish. Offers assessments and résumé-writing tools. Sponsored by the AARP Foundation.

PIVOTPLANET
pivotplanet.com
A service from the creators of Vocation Vacations that matches people exploring new careers, thinking about starting a business, or seeking to hone skills with expert advisors working in various professions for affordable, one-on-one video or voice-over-IP mentoring sessions.

PRIMECB.COM

A division of CareerBuilder.com that's geared directly to experienced job seekers and retirees. Search job openings, post résumés, find career fairs, and get the latest news on the job market.

RETIREDBRAINS.COM

An independent job and information resource for boomers, retirees, and people planning their retirement who are looking for full-time, part-time, or flex-time employment.

RETIREMENTJOBS.COM

Matches over fifty job searches with employment that matches their lifestyle. Provides both a free and a premium service.

YOURENCORE

yourencore.com

Connects retired scientists and engineers with innovative companies, many of which are in the Fortune 500. Specializes in the life sciences, consumer sciences, food sciences, specialty materials, and aerospace and defense industries.

CAREERONESTOP

careeronestop.org

The U.S. Department of Labor–sponsored site includes information on a wide range of careers including salary, benefits, education, and training, as well as the tools to help get hired.

CITY TOWN INFO CAREER SEARCH

citytowninfo.com/career-stories

Provides realistic and detailed descriptions of various jobs, two hundred in all, with advice and essential tips.

BUREAU OF LABOR STATISTICS OCCUPATIONAL OUTLOOK HANDBOOK

bls.gov/ooh

Features profiles that cover hundreds of occupations with information on how much they pay, what training they require, how to become one, and more. Each profile includes BLS employment projections for 2010 through 2020.

FURTHER READING

One Person/Multiple Careers: A New Model for Work/Life Success, by Marci Alboher (Business Plus, 2007)

100 Conversations for Career Success: Learn to Tweet, Cold Call, and Network Your Way to Career Success, by Miriam Salpeter and Laura M. Labovich (Learning Express, 2012)

Reboot Your Life: Energize Your Career and Life by Taking a Break, by Catherine Allen, Nancy Bearg, Rita Foley, and Jaye Smith (Beaufort Books, 2011)

What Should I Do with the Rest of My Life? True Stories of Finding Success, Passion, and New Meaning in the Second Half of Life, by Bruce Frankel (Avery, 2010)

My So-Called Freelance Life: How to Survive and Thrive as a Creative Professional for Hire, by Michelle Goodman (Seal Press, 2008); *anti9to5guide .com*

AARP Crash Course in Finding the Work You Love: The Essential Guide to Reinventing Your Life, by Samuel Greengard (Sterling, 2008)

Great Jobs for Everyone 50+: Finding Work that Keeps You Happy and Healthy, and Pays the Bills, by Kerry Hannon (Wiley, 2012); *kerryhannon.com*

What's Next? Follow Your Passion and Find Your Dream Job, by Kerry Hannon (Chronicle Books, 2010); *kerryhannon.com*

The Start-up of You: Adapt to the Future, Invest in Yourself, and Transform Your Career, by Reid Hoffman and Ben Casnocha (Crown Business, 2012)

Working Identity: Unconventional Strategies for Reinventing Your Career, by Herminia Ibarra (Harvard Business Review Press, 2004)

Test-Drive Your Dream Job: A Step-by-Step Guide to Finding and Creating the Work You Love, by Brian Kurth with Robin Simons (Business Plus, 2008)

The Pathfinder: How to Choose or Change Your Career for a Lifetime of Satisfaction and Success, by Nicholas Lore (Touchstone, 1998)

What Color Is Your Parachute? for Retirement, Second Edition: Planning a Prosperous, Healthy, and Happy Future, by John E. Nelson (Ten Speed Press, 2010)

Escape from Corporate America: A Practical Guide to Creating the Career of Your Dreams, by Pamela Skillings (Ballantine Books, 2008)

Tweak It: Small Changes, Big Impact: Make What Matters to You Happen Every

Day, by Cali Williams Yost (Center Street/ Hachette, 2013)

Work + Life: Finding the Fit That's Right for You, by Cali Williams Yost (Riverhead, 2004)

Using Social Media

FURTHER READING

Share This! How You Will Change the World with Social Networking, by Deanna Zandt (Berrett-Koehler, 2010)

The Twitter Book, by Tim O'Reilly and Sarah Milstein (O'Reilly Media, 2011)

Social Networking for Career Success: Using Online Tools to Create a Personal Brand, by Miriam Salpeter (LearningExpress, 2011)

The Twitter Job Search Guide: Find a Job and Advance Your Career in Just 15 Minutes a Day, by Susan Britton Whitcomb, Chandlee Bryan, and Deb Dib (Jist Works, 2010)

The Dragonfly Effect: Quick, Effective and Powerful Ways to Use Social Media to Drive Social Change, by Jennifer Aaker and Andy Smith (Jossey-Bass, 2010)

Social Ventures/Encore Entrepreneurship

ACUMEN

acumenfund.org

Provides a one-year global fellowship program for future social sector leaders. Fellows are immersed in world-class leadership training and fieldwork with social enterprises.

ASHOKA

ashoka.org

Offers fellowships to leading social entrepreneurs with innovative solutions to social problems in over sixty countries around the globe in every area of human need.

BAINBRIDGE GRADUATE INSTITUTE

bgi.edu

Through a unique business education that infuses social and environmental responsibility, prepares students in building businesses that are financially successful, socially responsible, and environmentally sustainable.

B LABS

bcorporation.net

A nonprofit organization that certifies B Corporations—corporations that use the power of business to solve social and environmental problems—and offers guides to help companies improve their social and environmental performance.

DOWSER

dowser.org

Reports on social innovation and highlights creative approaches to social change.

ECHOING GREEN

echoinggreen.org

Provides two-year fellowship programs and seed funding to promising social entrepreneurs launching new organizations. Though the fellowships are targeting younger people, the resources here are useful to social entrepreneurs of all ages.

FOUNDATION CENTER

foundationcenter.org

An excellent resource for researching grant-making institutions funding nonprofits. (Also see page 307.)

GIIRS

giirs.org

A B Lab project that rates the social and environmental impact of companies and funds, which in turn can provide companies with enhanced visibility, better fundraising opportunities, and more.

GREEN BUSINESS OWNER.COM

Provides information and inspiration to aspiring green entrepreneurs. Includes webinars, links to resources, and a glossary of green terms.

GLOBAL SOCIAL BENEFIT INCUBATOR

cms.scu.edu/socialbenefit/ entrepreneurship/gsbi

A program of Santa Clara University that helps entrepreneurs focused on lifting people out of poverty. Participants train in an in-residence "boot camp" that includes mentoring and business plan evaluation.

IMPACT REPORTING & INVESTMENT STANDARDS

iris.thegiin.org

IRIS provides streamlined, simplified, and standardized data for organizations to use when reporting their social and environmental impact. IRIS indicators span an array of performance objectives and include specialized metrics for a range of sectors including financial services, agriculture, and energy.

National Business Incubation Association

nbia.org

Assists new, emerging companies and business owners by organizing annual conferences, offering specialized training and education, supplying industry research and statistics, and providing advocacy and networking resources.

Net Impact

netimpact.org

A nonprofit membership group for social entrepreneurs, nonprofit professionals, and "corporate change makers" with volunteer-led chapters all over the world and a network of over 30,000 people. They offer webinars, downloadable tools, a job board, and an annual conference.

The Presidio School

presidioedu.org

Offers graduate degree programs in sustainable management, including MBA, MPA, a dual MBA/MPA, and a three-month executive certificate in sustainable leadership. Located in San Francisco.

Sansori

sansori.org

Offers part-time or yearlong "Jam Sessions," collaborative educational programs for aspiring social entrepreneurs to develop and launch their projects.

Senior Entrepreneurship Works

seniorentrepreneurshipworks.org

A nonprofit organization designed to help entrepreneurs fifty-five and older build sustainable businesses by providing training courses, support, news, and research.

Skoll Foundation

skollfoundation.org

Awards grants to social entrepreneurs and organizations, funds a $20 million-plus portfolio of program-related and mission-aligned investments. Partnered with various organizations including the Saïd Business School at the University of Oxford and the Sundance Institute.

Small Business Administration

sba.gov

In addition to offering counseling and training, provides government support through loans, grants, and other financial assistance to small businesses across the nation.

SoCap

socialcapitalmarkets.net

An annual event series that connects leading global investors, foundations, institutions, and social entrepreneurs.

Social Venture Network

svn.org

A membership community for social entrepreneurs to share collective knowledge, resources, trends, advice, and support, and connect investors. Holds multiple events and conferences.

Social Venture Partners

socialventurepartners.org

A global network of nonprofit investors and philanthropists.

Springboard Innovation

springboardinnovation.org

Offers programs and resources for emerging

entrepreneurs interested in designing and launching sustainable solutions for local or global challenges.

**STANFORD CENTER FOR
SOCIAL INNOVATION**
csi.gsb.stanford.edu
Releases a useful newsletter with the latest research from the field of social innovation.

FURTHER READING
How to Change the World: Social Entrepreneurs and the Power of New Ideas, by David Bornstein (Oxford University Press, 2007)

Social Entrepreneurship: What Everyone Needs to Know, by David Bornstein and Susan Davis (Oxford University Press, 2010)

Forces for Good, Revised and Updated: The Six Practices of High-Impact Nonprofits, by Leslie R. Crutchfield and Heather McLeod Grant (Jossey-Bass, 2012)

The Power of Unreasonable People: How Social Entrepreneurs Create Markets That Change the World, by John Elkington and Pamela Hartigan (Harvard Business Review Press, 2008)

Be Bold, by Cheryl L. Dorsey, Lara Galinsky (Echoing Green, 2006)

Work on Purpose, by Lara Galinsky with Kelly Nuxoll (Echoing Green, 2011)

Where Good Ideas Come From: The Natural History of Innovation, by Steven Johnson (Riverhead Trade, 2011)

Enchantment: The Art of Changing Hearts, Minds, and Actions, by Guy Kawasaki (Portfolio Hardcover, 2011)

Start Something That Matters, by Blake Mycoskie (Spiegel & Grau, 2012)

The Blue Sweater: Bridging the Gap between Rich and Poor in an Interconnected World, by Jacqueline Novogratz (Rodale Books, 2010)

Intrapreneuring in Action: A Handbook for Business Innovation, by Gifford Pinchot and Ron Pellman (Berrett-Koehler Publishers, 2000)

Social Entrepreneurship in Education: Private Ventures for the Public Good, by Michael R. Sandler (R&L Education 2010)

Little Bets: How Breakthrough Ideas Emerge from Small Discoveries, by Peter Sims (Free Press, 2011)

Rippling: How Social Entrepreneurs Spread Innovation Throughout the World, by Beverly Schwartz (Jossey-Bass, 2012)

Tactics of Hope: How Social Entrepreneurs Are Changing Our World, by Wilford Welch (Earth Aware Editions, 2008)

Leaving Microsoft to Change the World: An Entrepreneur's Odyssey to Educate the World's Children, by John Wood (HarperBusiness, 2007)

Creating a World Without Poverty: Social Business and the Future of Capitalism, by Muhammad Yunus (PublicAffairs, 2009)

Volunteering
Directories
ALL FOR GOOD
allforgood.org

Inspired by President Obama's 2008 call to service, this search engine is a huge database of volunteer opportunities on the web. Opportunities range from prominent nonprofit partners to grassroots-based organizations.

CREATE THE GOOD
createthegood.org

AARP's site for volunteering is loaded with lists of short- and long-term opportunities and events as well as simple how-to guides for things like how to hold a winter coat drive or help members of your community prepare for a natural disaster.

HANDSON NETWORK
handsonnetwork.org

A worldwide network of 250 volunteer actions centers that connect people with volunteer opportunities in their local communities, with a particular focus on using individual and corporate time and talent to solve social problems.

IDEALIST.ORG

Search for volunteer opportunities and events, connect with organizations, and tap into their useful resource centers. You can even create your own project and find supporters through the site. (Also see page 307.)

INTERNATIONAL ASSOCIATION OF JEWISH VOCATIONAL SERVICES
iajvs.org

A nonprofit network of thirty-two national and international human service agencies in major metropolitan areas in the United States, Canada, and Israel. The member agencies provide an array of services including career management and skills training.

OASIS
oasisnet.org/GetInvolved/Volunteer.aspx

A nationwide nonprofit that promotes successful aging programs through lifelong learning, healthy living, and social engagement. Centers offer continuing education classes and volunteer opportunities for older adults.

SPARKED
sparked.com

Sparked offers opportunities for "microvolunteering"—giving back with tasks that can be done online, often in a matter of minutes or hours. Suitably bite-sized activities include: product brainstorming, social media, IT, and design.

VOLUNTEERMATCH
volunteermatch.org

One of the largest online databases for volunteer opportunities. Creates volunteer programs for corporations wanting to make volunteering easier for their employees.

International
AMERICAN JEWISH WORLD SERVICE
ajws.org

A human rights organization dedicated to aiding hundreds of grassroots organizations working to promote health, education, economic development, disaster relief, and social and political change in the developing world. Provides travel, work, and learning opportunities for both individuals and groups.

CHF International

chfinternational.org

The Cooperative Housing Foundation—known simply as CHF International—serves more than 20 million people each year in more than 25 countries around the world, helping improve the social, economic, and environmental conditions of at-risk communities. Offers full-time, volunteer, and consultant jobs.

Cross-Cultural Solutions

crossculturalsolutions.org

Offers year-round, one to twelve-week volunteer programs for 50-plus volunteers in dozens of countries. Volunteers can travel alone or with friends and family. Opportunities are available for those with mobility challenges.

Encore Service Corps

encoreservicecorps.org/whatwedo.cfm

A nonprofit volunteer service organization for skilled professionals with previous overseas development experience. Projects range from setting up training programs for teachers to creating legal aid services for refugees.

Fly for Good

flyforgood.com

Negotiates airfare discounts for volunteers and provides essential facts about different types of volunteer activities and destinations. Also includes a trip finder and quiz.

Global Volunteers

globalvolunteers.org

Affiliated with the United Nations and UNICEF, this organization pairs short-term volunteers with ongoing community development projects directed by local leaders and targeted at serving at-risk children.

GreenFORCE

www.greenforce.org

Global volunteering with a green orientation, from marine conservation to panda protection in China.

Road Scholar

roadscholar.org

Provides thousands of service learning trips in both the U.S. and abroad. Trips are assigned an Activity Level rating from Easy to Challenging for participants to select the appropriate programs for their physical ability.

United Nations Educational, Scientific and Cultural Organization

unesco.org

The world aid organization offers various fellowships and programs, as well as full-time employment for people at every professional life stage.

International Labour Organization

ilo.org

The U.N. agency, which deals mostly with labor standards and policies, offers both full-time and short-term employment in many countries around the world for skilled professionals.

U.S. Agency for International Development

usaid.gov

A background in development is not required for all positions at the Foreign

Service agency, which offers both career and limited-term appointments around the world and in Washington, D.C.

VOLUNTOURISM.ORG
Offers international volunteer opportunities for individuals interested in both the traditional elements of tourism and social service.

WORKING ABROAD
workingabroad.com
An international networking service that matches volunteers with grassroots organizations around the world. The organization offers opportunities for all skill levels in both short- and long-term programs. Main areas of focus are wildlife and habitat conservation, environmental education and management, teaching, social work, and organic agriculture and cultural development.

Board Service

See page 171 for resources on board service.

National and Community Service

See page 171 for National and Community Service resources.

Field-Specific
Nonprofit/Social Good

These sites are useful for either familiarizing yourself with nonprofit roles or for job search (some do both). Also see page 36 on job boards.

BRIDGESTAR'S TRANSITION TO A NONPROFIT LEARNING CENTER
bridgestar.org/LearningCenters/Transition.aspx

Features advice on getting started and finding opportunities in the nonprofit sector, in addition to articles, sample résumés, job listings, and success stories.

CHANGE.ORG
An online platform that lets anyone create their own grassroots campaign for change. The site provides free training, advice, tools for online and offline campaigning, as well as strategic support, connections to potential partners, and media outreach.

CHARITYCHANNEL— CAREER SEARCH ONLINE
charitychannel.com/professional-growth/ career-search-online
A useful career database for nonprofit professionals.

THE CHRONICLE OF PHILANTHROPY'S CAREERS PAGE
philanthropy.com/section/Jobs/224
One of the most popular news sources for nonprofit leaders also provides career ideas and advice, employer profiles, median salaries, and a useful career database.

GUIDESTAR
guidestar.org
Guidestar gathers and publicizes information about nonprofit organizations. Their free database includes up-to-date information on the mission, programs, leaders, goals, accomplishments, and needs of hundreds of nonprofits.

COMMONGOOD CAREERS
cgcareers.org
A recruiting firm that deals exclusively

with filling positions at the nation's leading nonprofits and social innovators.

ExecSearches.com

A job board dedicated exclusively to filling executive, midlevel, and fund-raising positions in the nonprofit, government, education, and health sectors.

Idealist.org

Idealist is a hub for all kinds of nonprofit activity, not just job listings. It has extensive listings for nonprofit jobs and internships, including postings for opportunities outside the U.S. Also offers customized emails to help you track opportunities that match your search criteria.

Opportunity Knocks.org

Search jobs, post your résumé, and browse the nonprofit jobs resource page on this useful site.

The Foundation Center

foundationcenter.org
With a massive database of foundations and public charities, the Foundation Center provides useful information on philanthropy fundraising and grant programs, along with excellent resources for researching nonprofits. It also operates research, education, and training programs along with five regional library/learning centers and hundreds of information centers located nationwide and around the world. Updated daily.

The NonProfit Times Career Center

nonprofitjobseeker.com/career-resources.html
Search jobs by state or title and read articles on résumé advice, job-hunting guidance,

and career planning tips. Check out the free e-newsletter here: *nonprofitjobseeker.com/signup/index.html*

Further Reading

The Nonprofit Career Guide: How to Land a Job That Makes a Difference, by Shelly Cryer (Fieldstone Alliance, 2008)

The Idealist.org Handbook to Building a Better World: How to Turn Your Good Intentions into Actions that Make a Difference, by Idealist.org and Stephanie Land (Perigee Trade, 2009)

The Idealist Guide to Nonprofit Careers for Sector Switchers, by Steven Joiner and Meg Busse (Hundreds of Heads Books, 2010)

Jobs That Matter: Find a Stable, Fulfilling Career in Public Service, by Heather Krasna (Jist Works, 2010) *heatherkrasna.com.*

Change Your Career: Transitioning to the Nonprofit Sector, by Laura Gassner Otting (Kaplan Publishing, 2007) *nonprofitprofessionals.com.*

Education

Adjunct Professor Online

adjunctprofessoronline.com
A job site for adjunct and visiting professors, online education instructors, and other part-time higher education employment.

The Chronicle of Higher Education Job Board

chronicle.com/section/Jobs/61
Offers faculty, research, administrative, and executive job listings for the education sector.

EDUCATION WEEK TOPSCHOOLJOBS
topschooljobs.org
Browse jobs and find career advice.

HIGHEREDJOBS
higheredjobs.com
View job listings by category (faculty, administrative, or executive), location, or institution type.

NATIONAL ASSOCIATION OF INDEPENDENT SCHOOLS
nais.org
AIS represents approximately 1,400 independent schools and associations in the U.S. Their site provides a teacher directory, news, trends, and other useful information.

NATIONAL CENTER FOR ALTERNATIVE CERTIFICATION
teach-now.org
A go-to site for information on acquiring alternative teaching certification. The center provides advice for prospective educators, policymakers, legislators, and researchers.

THE PUBLIC CHARTER SCHOOLS JOB BOARD
jobs.publiccharters.org
A job board from the National Alliance for Public Charter Schools.

Health Care Jobs/Training

AMERICAN HOSPITAL ASSOCIATION
AHACareerCenter.org
Part of the National Healthcare Career Network.

AMERICAN ASSOCIATION OF COLLEGES OF NURSING
aacn.nche.edu

Representing more than 690 nursing schools, AACN is a useful source for assessing and identifying nursing programs nationwide.

AMERICAN MEDICAL ASSOCIATION'S CAREERS IN HEALTH CARE DIRECTORY
ama-assn.org/go/alliedhealth
The AMA's directory lists information for more than eighty health care careers, as well as 8,400 accredited educational programs. Their e-Letter covers education trends and career-related issues.

CARE AND COMPLIANCE GROUP
careandcompliance.com
A training resource for administrators, caregivers, and health care professionals interested in acquiring their licensing and certification for careers in assisted living facilities and residential communities.

DISCOVERNURSING.COM
Sponsored by Johnson & Johnson, this website helps prospective nurses discover degree programs and specializations, look up scholarships and financial aid, and view stories from current nurses.

EXPLOREHEALTHCAREERS.ORG
A joint initiative involving national foundations, professional associations, health career advisors, educational institutions, and college students, this free website provides up-to-date information about the health professions and links to health-related education and training programs, financial aid resources, specialized learning opportunities, and current issues in health care.

EXPLORING CAREERS IN AGING

businessandaging.blogs.com

A guide to the explosion of entrepreneurial and job opportunities in gerontology.

HEALTHCAREERCENTER.ORG

Provides reliable and up-to-date job search, career development, and employment information.

AMERICAN HEALTH CARE ASSOCIATION— LONG TERM CARE CAREER CENTER

careers.ahcancal.org/jobs

A free database for job seekers interested in working in nursing facilities, assisted living, and other long-term care programs.

NURSINGLINK

nursinglink.monster.com

A career site for nursing jobs from Monster.com

VIRTUAL CAREER NETWORK: HEALTHCARE

vcn.org/healthcare/

Sponsored by the U.S. Department of Labor, Employment and Training Administration and under the leadership of the American Association of Community Colleges, this site provides information on health care jobs, education and training programs, and offers online courses.

FURTHER READING

Career Opportunities in Health Care, by Shelly Field (Ferguson Publishing Company, 2007)

Health Care: Field Guides to Finding a New Career, by S. J. Stratford (Ferguson Publishing Company, 2009)

Government Jobs

GOVLOOP

govloop.com

A social networking site with job postings, community blogs, resources, and directories connecting over 50,000 federal, state, and local government innovators.

PARTNERSHIP FOR PUBLIC SERVICE

ourpublicservice.org

A nonprofit, nonpartisan organization that works directly with federal agencies to recruit talent.

PUBLICSERVICECAREERS.ORG

A source of information, advice, and postings for public sector jobs. Cosponsored by the Association for Public Policy Analysis and Management, the American Society for Public Administration, and the National Association of Schools of Public Affairs and Administration.

STATE AND LOCAL GOVERNMENT ON THE NET

statelocalgov.net/50states-jobs.cfm

A directory of official state, county, and city government websites and a great resource for employment listings.

USAJOBS

usajobs.gov

The federal government's official one-stop source for federal jobs and employment information.

Green Jobs

GRAY IS GREEN

grayisgreen.org

An environmental education, advocacy, and action organization for older adults interested in learning about sustainability, advocating for sound climate change policy, and serving as resources for younger people involved in sustainability.

GREEN CAREER CENTRAL

greencareercentral.com
Offers coaching programs and workshops to assist experienced professionals in transitioning to greener, more sustainable careers. Be sure to check out the Green Economy Map: *greencentral.com/map.*

GREEN DREAM JOBS

sustainablebusiness.com
A service of Sustainable Inc. aimed at employers and job seekers. Its job board lists green jobs at all levels with a diverse mix of employers.

GREEN ECONOMY POST

greeneconomypost.com
Check out the green jobs and careers resources tab and search for green jobs in your state.

GREENJOBS

greenjobs.com
Provides services to employers and job seekers interested in renewable energy employment worldwide.

GREEN JOB SPIDER

greenjobspider.com
Search thousands of green jobs by location and sector.

GREEN JOBS NETWORK

greenjobs.net
A site for job seekers focused on environmental and social responsibility.

Check out their Green Collar Blog, which includes listings of educational opportunities.

SUSTAINLANE.COM'S GREEN COLLAR JOBS BOARD

sustainlane.com/green-jobs
Besides green job postings, this site offers articles, information, advice, and resources, including "writing a green résumé" and "writing a green cover letter."

U.S. DEPARTMENT OF AGRICULTURE'S AGRICULTURE CONSERVATION EXPERIENCED SERVICES PROGRAM

acesprogram.org
Offers full- and part-time jobs for experienced individuals fifty-five and older that want to support conservation and environmental protection efforts. A partnership between the National Older Worker Career Center and the Natural Resources Conservation Service.

U.S. GREEN BUILDING COUNCIL CAREER CENTER

careercenter.usgbc.org
The nonprofit council promotes environmentally friendly building design and construction and the LEED organization is essential for anyone interested in understanding the field.

FURTHER READING

Green Careers: Choosing Work for a Sustainable Future, by Jim Cassio and Alice Rush (New Society Publishers, 2009)

Green Careers for Dummies, by Carol L. McClelland (For Dummies, 2010)

Other Recommended Reading

65 Things to Do When You Retire, 65 Notable Achievers on How to Make the Most of the Rest of Your Life, by Mark Evan Chimsky (Sellers Publishing Inc, 2012)

All the Money in the World: What the Happiest People Know About Getting and Spending, by Laura Vanderkam (Portfolio Hardcover, 2012)

The American Way to Change: How National Service and Volunteers Are Transforming America, by Shirley Sagawa (Jossey-Bass, 2010)

The Big Shift: Navigating the New Stage Beyond Midlife, by Marc Freedman (PublicAffairs 2011)

Boundless Potential: Transform Your Brain, Unleash Your Talents, Reinvent Your Work in Midlife and Beyond, by Mark S. Walton (McGraw-Hill, 2012); has a chapter called "The Encore Manifesto."

Composing a Further Life: The Age of Active Wisdom, by Mary Catherine Bateson (Knopf, 2010)

The Couple's Retirement Puzzle: 10 Must-Have Conversations for Transitioning to the Second Half of Life, by Roberta K. Taylor and Dorian Mintzer (Lincoln Street Press, 2011)

Doing Sixty and Seventy, by Gloria Steinem (Elders Academy Press, 2006)

Don't Retire, Rewire!, by Jeri Sedlar and Rick Miners (Alpha, 2002)

Drive: The Surprising Truth About What Motivates Us, by Daniel H. Pink (Riverhead Trade, 2011)

Encore: Finding Work that Matters in the Second Half of Life, by Marc Freedman (PublicAffairs, 2008)

Fifty Is the New Fifty: Ten Life Lessons for Women in Second Adulthood, by Suzanne Braun Levine (Viking, 2009)

Good to Great and the Social Sectors, by Jim Collins (HarperBusiness, 2005)

Halftime: Moving from Success to Significance, by Bob Buford (Zondervan, 2008)

The Happiness Project: Or, Why I Spent a Year Trying to Sing in the Morning, Clean My Closets, Fight Right, Read Aristotle, and Generally Have More Fun, by Gretchen Rubin (Harper Perennial, 2011)

Happiness: Unlocking the Mysteries of Psychological Wealth, by Ed Diener and Robert Biswas-Diener (Wiley-Blackwell, 2008)

The Number: What Do You Need for the Rest of Your Life and What Will It Cost?, by Lee Eisenberg (Free Press, 2006)

A Long Bright Future, by Laura Carstensen (PublicAffairs, 2011)

The New Frugality: How to Consume Less, Save More, and Live Better, by Chris Farrell (Bloomsbury Press, 2010)

New Passages, by Gail Sheehy (Ballantine, 1996)

The Power of Half: One Family's Decision to Stop Taking and Start Giving Back, by Hannah Salwen and Kevin Salwen (Mariner Books, 2011)

Project Renewment: The First Retirement Model for Career Women, by Bernice Bratter (Scribner, 2008); *projectrenewment .com*

Reset: How This Crisis Can Restore Our Values and Renew America, by Kurt Andersen (Random House, 2009)

Ripe: Rich, Rewarding Work After 50, by Julia Moulden (Julia Moulden, 2011)

Self-Renewal: The Individual and the Innovative Society, by John W. Gardner (W. W. Norton & Company, 1995)

Smart Women Don't Retire—They Break Free: From Working Full-Time to Living Full-Time, by The Transition Network and Gail Rentsch (Springboard Press, 2008)

Something to Live For: Finding Your Way in the Second Half of Life, by Richard J. Leider (Berrett-Koehler Publishers, 2008)

Switch: How to Change Things When Change Is Hard, by Chip Heath and Dan Heath (Crown Business, 2010)

The Secret Life of the Grown-up Brain: The Surprising Talents of the Middle-Aged Brain, by Barbara Strauch (Penguin, 2011)

The Third Chapter: Passion, Risk, and Adventure in the 25 Years After 50, by Sara Lawrence-Lightfoot (Sarah Crichton Books, 2009)

Transitions: Making Sense of Life's Changes, by William Bridges (Da Capo Press, 1980)

The Wall Street Journal Complete Retirement Guidebook: How to Plan It, Live It and Enjoy It, by Glenn Ruffenach and Kelly Greene (Three Rivers Press, 2007)

Where Good Ideas Come From: The Natural History of Innovation, by Steven Johnson (Riverhead Trade, 2011)

Acknowledgments

I ran into a nagging problem while writing this book. So many people were hesitant to be interviewed because they didn't want to put the spotlight on themselves. In some cases, they only agreed to do an interview if I would promise to focus on the social problem they championed. The children learning to read, the ex-offenders trying to make a fresh start, the dearth of fresh food for schoolkids, the victims of terror, and on and on. Only after I convinced them that talking about themselves would help others on the verge of their own encores did people open up. Sometimes I got in and out with one interview. But often I was a relentless nudge, asking my prying questions through repeated calls and emails. First and foremost, I want to thank every person who agreed to share a story.

This book represents the work of thousands of pioneers embarking on encore careers, hundreds of organizations working to make them a common occurrence, and one group that's both leading and anchoring their efforts, Encore.org (formerly known as Civic Ventures).

The founder and CEO of Encore.org, Marc Freedman, my colleague and friend, put a name to the encore phenomenon and his vision guides us all. Without him, this book and all of the work it represents would not exist.

My other Encore.org colleagues were all partners in this effort, but none more so than Stefanie Weiss, who was with me every step of the way, helping shape, word-smith, and fine-tune nearly every page. Every writer should have a Stef in her life. Michele Melendez did a heroic job of putting together the Encore Hot List. David Bank, Doug Braley, Cal Halvorsen, Lyle Hurst, Michelle Hynes, Jim Emerman, Judy Goggin, John Gomperts, Alexandra Kent, Antoinette La Belle, Leslye Louie, Lyle Hurst, Nancy Peterson, Phyllis Siegel, and Ruth Wooden shared their expertise, read numerous passages, and provided feedback—on short notice, often more than once. David Cohen, Sarah Maple, David Morse, Terry Nagel, Aireen Navarro, Laura

Robbins, Carol Rudisill, Richard Smith, and the entire Encore.org board of directors also contributed mightily to the work on which this book is based. Dana Blecher joined the team as the book edits came to an end and she brought new energy and ideas just as we moved from writing to marketing. And Aaron Pfannebecker created a master spreadsheet to keep track of encore stories that we are now sharing as a model for others to use in projects like this.

Several funders have supported the work of Encore.org: the Atlantic Philanthropies, the David and Lucile Packard Foundation, the Deerbrook Charitable Trust, the John Templeton Foundation, the MetLife Foundation, S.D. Bechtel Jr. Foundation, the Skoll Foundation, and the Virginia G. Piper Charitable Trust.

Many experts gave their time and knowledge as I filled in gaps in my understanding of the encore landscape. If you see your name in the pages of this book, know that I'm grateful for it. Special shout-outs go to Carol McClelland, for her vision on the exercises in Chapter 3, and to Miriam Salpeter, for her guidance on the résumés in Appendix B. Virginia Cruickshank, Lisa DiMona, Lisa Futterman, Andy Goodman, Marty Nemko, Ellen Schall, Peter Scherer, Phyllis Snyder and the team at CAEL, and Mary Sue Vickers all advised on aspects of this book.

I don't often mention my experience at Workman Publishing to other authors because it would inspire too much jealousy, but now is my chance. Maisie Tivnan was a writer's dream—an editor who dug deeply into the subject, made every draft sing more beautifully, yet always honored my words and voice. It helped that she was also so much damned fun to be around. So many others—Suzie Bolotin, David Schiller, Page Edmunds, Bob Miller, Jessica Weiner, Selina Meere, Courtney Greenhalgh, John Jenkinson, Jenny Mandel, and Justin Krasner—confirmed that this book was in the deft hands of professionals who see publishing as a service to the world as much as a business. Thanks also to Jessica Rozler, Jarrod Dyer, Raquel Jaramillo, and Janet Vicario, who contributed behind the scenes. I'm heartened to know that I'll continue to run into many of you on the streets of our neighborhood and at Prodigy Coffee.

A marvelous community of fellow writers, editors, and others influenced my writing life and my thinking on work and careers in the years leading up to this book: Barry Adler, Christine Bader, Brent Bowers, Ben Casnocha, Kathy Chetkovich, Helen Coster, Susan Sandler Brennan, Jennine Cohen, Elena Deutsch, Dory Devlin, Peggy Doyle, Jennifer Edwards, Misa Fujimura-Fanselow, Micki Goldberg, Ellen Goodman, Dominique Hawkins, Deborah Epstein Henry, Christine Kenneally, Kibum Kim, Jennifer Kohler, Phyllis Korkki, Jennifer Dinn Korman, Adelaide Lancaster, Carrie Lane, Katherine Lanpher, Heidi Levin, Suzanne Braun Levine, Ellen Maguire, Courtney Martin, Phyllis Messenger, Nancy Miller, Sarah Milstein, Sarah McKinney, Michael Melcher, Katie Orenstein, Dan Pink, Belinda Plutz, Barbara Raab, Scott Rambardan, Renee Reso, Jennifer Rosenzweig, Gretchen Rubin, Charles Salzberg, Kevin Salwen, Hannah Seligson, Ramit Sethi, Susan Shapiro, Deborah Siegel, Jolie Solomon, Penelope Trunk, Amy Whitaker, Larry Vranka, Kamy Wicoff, Lauren Weisenfeld, and Cali Williams Yost.

Close at hand are the people who have supported me in the most intimate ways as I worked on this project. My mother, proof that age is only a number, fills me with optimism for my own future. My brother offers a daily glimpse of what it takes to be a social entrepreneur. My nana, now ninety-seven, reminds me of how important it is to cherish—and understand—our elders. Jay, my partner in love and life, is a model of continual reinvention. He also ensures that wherever I go in my travels, I am always eager to come home. You all remind me that what we do close to home matters as much as what we do out in the world.

Index

Marcia Ciriello

Marci Alboher is a vice president of Encore.org, the nonprofit organization leading the way for millions of people to pursue second acts for the greater good. She is also the author of *One Person/Multiple Careers*, and created the "Shifting Careers" column and blog for *The New York Times*. Her work and commentary have been featured in countless national media outlets including *USA Today* and NBC's *Today* show. Ms. Alboher lives with her husband in New York City. Follow Marci (@heymarci) and Encore.org (@encorecareers) on Twitter.

Marci Alboher is available for select speaking engagements. Please contact speakersbureau@workman.com.

Visit encorecareerhandbook.com for additional resources and free downloads.